S0-BRI-110

WITHDRAWN

SCSU

JAN 23 2004

H.C. BULEY LIBRARY

Second Edition

Testing Students With Disabilities

Martha L. Thurlow
Judy L. Elliott
James E. Ysseldyke

Second Edition

Testing Students With Disabilities

Practical Strategies for Complying
With District and State Requirements

CORWIN PRESS, INC.
A Sage Publications Company
Thousand Oaks, California

b. 26069623
34.95

Copyright © 2003 by Corwin Press

All rights reserved. When forms and sample documents are included, their use is authorized only by educators, local school sites, and/or noncommercial entities who have purchased the book. Except for that usage, no part of this book may be reproduced or utilized in any form or by any means, electronic or mechanical, including photocopying, recording, or by any information storage and retrieval system, without permission in writing from the publisher.

For information:

Corwin Press, Inc.
A Sage Publications Company
2455 Teller Road
Thousand Oaks, California 91320
www.corwinpress.com

Sage Publications Ltd.
6 Bonhill Street
London EC2A 4PU
United Kingdom

Sage Publications India Pvt. Ltd.
B-42 Panchsheel Enclave
Post Box 4109
New Delhi 110 017 India

Printed in the United States of America

Library of Congress Cataloging-in-Publication Data

Thurlow, Martha L.
   Testing students with disabilities : practical strategies for complying with district and state requirements/Martha L. Thurlow, Judy L. Elliott, James E. Ysseldyke.— 2nd ed.
       p. cm.
   Includes bibliographical references (p.) and index.
   ISBN 0-7619-3808-7 (cloth) -- ISBN 0-7619-3809-5 (paper)
   1. Educational tests and measurements—United States. 2. Children with disabilities—Educaton—Ability testing—United States. 3. Educational accountability—United States. I. Elliott, Judy L. II. Ysseldyke, James E. III. Title.
   LB3051 .T526 2002
   371.9′04—dc21

                                    2002034792

This book is printed on acid-free paper.

02 03 04 05 06 10 9 8 7 6 5 4 3 2 1

Acquisitions Editor:	Robert D. Clouse
Editorial Assistant:	Erin Clow
Typesetter:	C&M Digitals (P) Ltd
Production Editor:	Astrid Virding
Cover Designer:	Tracy E. Miller
Production Designer:	Michelle Lee

0
LB
3051
.T526
2003

Contents

Preface

So much has happened since we wrote the first edition of this book. The reauthorization of the Individuals with Disabilities Education Act (IDEA) had just taken place (in 1997), and educators and others were just beginning to realize that this law required that students with disabilities be included in district and state assessments. In addition, special education funding depended on public reporting of the participation and performance of students with disabilities in these assessments.

District and states are now recognizing that these requirements are not going away. With the signing of the Elementary and Secondary Education Act (ESEA) in 2002, requirements for state testing increased. As a result, every state will soon have (if they do not already) statewide tests administered to *all students* in grades 3-8. And, both ESEA and IDEA require that students with disabilities be included in these assessment systems.

Since we wrote the first edition of this book, we have learned a lot about how to facilitate the meaningful assessment of students with disabilities in district and state assessments. We know now how very important the people in the schools are to making sure that the requirements of both IDEA and ESEA are met. Questions will continue to arise. For example: How should good decisions be made about whether a student with a disability should take the regular assessment or the alternate assessment? How do you decide which students need which accommodations, and whether a needed accommodation will result in a score that is comparable to one from a test administered without accommodations? Where does the Individualized Education Program (IEP) fit into all of this, and how does it all relate to instruction? Are students with disabilities who are not native English-language speakers exempt from all these requirements? If not, how can these students be included in district and state assessments in a meaningful way? What do parents need to know to make the testing of students with disabilities in district and state assessments a valued experience? How can we use the scores that come back from district or state assessments? These are just some of the questions this book answers.

This book has been improved, with much new information included on the critical topics of participation in assessments, assessment accommodations, and alternate assessments. We have expanded our treatment of parent involvement, IEPs and testing and making it work in the school building—collaboration among educators and support from administrators. New topics in this edition include (1) access to the general curriculum, (2) assessment and accountability requirements of both IDEA and ESEA, (3) research findings on the effects of testing accommodations, (4) meeting assessment requirements for students with disabilities who are English Language Learners, (5) electronic and online testing, and (6) how to use assessment results to improve programs and instruction. In addition, while we had a chapter on alternate assessments in our first edition, the information there was based primarily on our thoughts about what could be. Now that states have developed their assessments and we have seen them being implemented, we know a lot more about alternate assessments—and we summarize it in this second edition.

Audience

This book is an essential resource for all district and school professionals, especially with the increased importance of district and state assessments, and their integration into educational accountability systems. We believe that the book is also relevant for state-level personnel, who must stay in touch with the ways in which their requirements (like federal and local requirements) are implemented—and the potential impact that they may have. It is important for administrators at all levels to be aware that practice can influence policy, just as it is assumed that policy will influence practice.

Overview

This book is intended to provide you with helpful information about including students with disabilities in district and state assessment systems. We provide practical strategies for ensuring that this inclusion is meaningful for the system and for the student. We include in this book a variety of forms and checklists you can use. Each of these appears in the chapter in which it is introduced and also in the Resource section at the end of the book, in reproducible form for making copies to use.

To facilitate the implementation of the ideas in this book, we provide another resource at the end of the book—a section titled, "Conducting Staff Development." This is designed to help in the delivery and dissemination of information about the what, why, how, and what-ifs of assessment programs and accommodations decisions for students with disabilities. This resource includes information on some of the most important points that need to be made about assessment and accountability, as well as some specific activities in which people can engage. Reproducible handouts and overheads are provided in this section as well.

In this edition, we again include a list of technical assistance and dissemination networks that can provide information relevant to the topics covered in this book. Some of them are national resources; others are regional. Web sites offer a wealth of information on topics related to those addressed in this book, and we urge those who have not yet "surfed" on the topics covered in this book to do so. And, as readers implemented the ideas in this book and elsewhere, and are ready to focus on improving the test performance of students with disabilities, we also have written another book—*Improving Test Performance of Students With Disabilities,* published by Corwin Press.

We have attempted to make this book usable to the extreme, with both information and strategies, and with materials to support both. We hope that as you use this book, you will provide us with feedback on its usefulness in meeting your needs.

Acknowledgments

We have written and revised this book based on our years of accumulated experience as practitioners, administrators, researchers, and staff developers. Of course, we could not have completed the book without the influence of many people and events. It was the initial work of the National Center on Educational Outcomes that pushed us to face the fact that practitioners, not just policymakers, need information on how best to test students with disabilities in district and state assessments. Numerous individuals from state departments of education and districts also urged us to continue to make information available to those most likely to bring about the changes toward which policymakers are striving.

We owe a large debt of gratitude to our colleague, Dorene Scott, who has been our "information specialist" as we revised this book. She donated her free time at night and on weekends as we tried to recall where we had seen this or that article, or as we tried to remember a specific resource that we needed.

We also want to thank those individuals who took the time to review this revision of the book. We hope that their approval of it reflects how you will react as you start your journey toward good assessment practices for students with disabilities in district and state assessments.

Martha L. Thurlow
Judy L. Elliott
James E. Ysseldyke

Corwin Press would like to acknowledge the following reviewers:

Lynne Winters
Assistant Superintendent
Research, Planning, and Evaluation
Long Beach Unified School District (CA)

Steven Kukic
Utah State Director of Special Education

Edward Roeber
Director
Student Assessment Program
Council of Chief State School Officers (CCSSO)

Edward R. Wilkens
Director
Northeast Regional Resources Center
Burlington (VT)

Tes Mehring
Dean, Teacher's College
Emporia State University
Emporia (KS)

Elizabeth Werre
Professor, Special Education
Pensacola Junior College
Pensacola (FL)

Denise Meister
Assistant Professor, Education
Pennsylvania State University
Middletown (PA)

Kathleen Pierce
Assistant Professor, Graduate Education
Rider University
Lawrenceville (NJ)

Beverly Petch-Hogan
Professor
Department of Elementary, Early, and Special Education
Southwest Missouri State University
Cape Girardeau (MO)

About the Authors

Judy L. Elliott is currently the Assistant Superintendent of Special Education in the Long Beach Unified School District (LBUSD), Long Beach, California. LBUSD is the third largest urban school system in the state. Formerly a Senior Researcher at the National Center on Educational Outcomes, she worked and continues to assist districts and state departments of education in their efforts to update and realign curriculum frameworks, instruction, and assessments to include all students. Her research interests focus on effective instruction, IEP development and its alignment with standards and assessments, decisions making for accountability, accommodation, and assessment as well as translating information on standards and assessments for various audiences, including parents, teachers, school boards, and other community groups. Dr. Elliott continues to serve as a national consultant and staff development professional to school districts and organizations. Judy has trained hundreds of thousands of staff, teachers, and administrators, both in the South Pacific and United States, in areas to include linking assessment to instruction and intervention, strategies and tactics for effective instruction, curricular modification for students with mild to significant disabilities, intervention and teacher assistance teams, authentic and curriculum-based evaluation, instructional environment evaluation, collaborative teaching, strategies for difficult-to-manage students, accountability and assessment practices. Some of her most recent co-published books are *Improving Test Performance of Students with Disabilities; Strategies and Tactics for Effective Instruction;* and *Timesavers for Educators.*

Martha L. Thurlow is Director of the National Center on Educational Outcomes. In this position, she addresses the implications of contemporary U.S. policy and practice for students with disabilities and English Language Learners, including national and statewide assessment policies and practices, standards-setting efforts, and graduation requirements. Dr. Thurlow has conducted research for the past 30 years in a variety of areas, including assessment and decision making, learning disabilities, early childhood education, dropout prevention, effective classroom instruction, and integration of students with disabilities in general education settings. Dr. Thurlow has published extensively on all of these topics, and has among her publications several collaborative works with other organizations (such as the National Governors' Association, the Council of Chief State School Officers, the Federation for Children with Special Needs, and the National Education Association—NEA). She also is a co-author with Judy Elliott of *Improving Test Performance of Students with Disabilities*, and co-Editor with Bob Algozzine of *Exceptional Children*, the research jourunal of the Council for Exceptional Children.

 **James E. Ysseldyke's** research and writing have focused on issues in assessing and making instructional decisions about students with disabilities. He has authored over 23 books. His most recent are *Special Education: A Practical Approach for Teachers; Assessment; Critical Issues in Special Education* and *The Challenge of Complex School Problems*. He has published over 30 book chapters, more than 200 articles in professional journals, 300 technical reports, an instructional environment system (TIES-2) and a teacher evaluation scale. Dr. Ysseldyke has served as editor of 8 professional journals and on editorial boards of over 50 others. He has been an invited speaker and presenter at more than 125 international, national and state conferences. Dr. Ysseldyke has sat on more that 17 advisory boards. His most recent advisory services include the Early Childhood Longitudinal Study (ECLS) and OERI's National Institute on Student Achievement, Curriculum, and Assessment (NISACA). Over the years Dr. Ysseldyke has received more than 20 awards for his scholarly accomplishments. Honors include being the first recipient of the Lightner Witmer Award presented by the School Psychology Division of the American Psychological Association, the distinguished teaching award presented by the University of Minnesota, and the Guest of Honor of the American Educational Research Association. He is the 1995 recipient of the Council for Exceptional Children Research Award.

Why Students With Disabilities Should Be in District and Statewide Accountability Systems

---

Topics

- ☐ Defining Accountability, Assessment, and Testing
- ☐ Reasons for Wanting Students With Disabilities in the Accountability System
- ☐ Assessment and Accountability Requirements of Federal Education Laws
- ☐ Overview of This Book

In this chapter, you will . . .

- – review the definitions of accountability, assessment, and testing, and recognize the differences among them.
- – learn some of the reasons for promoting an inclusive accountability system.
- – examine the specific assessment and accountability requirements of federal education laws.
- – gain a general overview of the content of the book.

We developed this book to help you comply with district and statewide testing requirements and at the same time meet the challenge of accountability for the diversity of students in our schools today. In this chapter, we summarize many of the reasons why it is important for students with disabilities to take district and state tests. For these reasons to make

---

BOX 1.1

Myth or Truth? Do You Know?

Read each statement below and decide whether it is a myth or the truth about current practice.

- Assessment information on student performance is just one piece of evidence that might go into an accountability system.
- Assessment is a narrower term than testing.
- Standards-based reform emphasizes the results of education rather than the process.
- One reason for including students with disabilities in the accountability system, along with other special needs students, is that it gives us a more accurate picture of the status of education.
- There is amazing consistency from one place to the next in the high rates at which students with disabilities are excluded from assessments.
- Several education laws emphasize the need to include all students in educational accountability systems.
- An unintended but documented consequence of exclusion of some students from accountability systems is increased rates of referral to special education.

---

sense, you need to understand the distinctions between accountability, assessment, and testing. Thus, we start by defining these terms.

Early in each chapter, we list topic-specific myths and truths that you will be able to identify when you finish the chapter. Those for Chapter 1 are presented in Box 1.1.

Along with providing the background information that you will need to answer questions about why students with disabilities should participate in district and statewide tests, this chapter outlines the framework for the rest of the book.

Defining Accountability, Assessment, and Testing

Accountability and assessment are not the same thing, and testing is just one type of assessment. It is important to keep the distinctions among these terms in mind as we talk about compliance with district and statewide testing. It is also important to realize that classroom assessments, with which we are most familiar, are related to district and state tests and the notion of accountability (Commission on Instructionally Supportive Assessment, 2001; Education Commission of the States, 1998).

Accountability has been defined in many different ways. In relation to education, a respected definition is that "accountability refers to the systematic collection, analysis and use of information to hold schools, educators and others responsible for the performance of students and the education system" (Education Commission of the States, 1998, p. 3).

BOX 1.2

**Desired Evidence for Accountability Has Shifted
From the Process and Context of Education to the Results of Education:
Examples of Each Type of Evidence**

Educational Process and Context	Educational Results
Student-teacher ratio	Student performance on district tests
Number of teachers with master's degrees and above	Student performance on statewide assessment
Adequacy of school buildings	Graduation rate
Per pupil expenditures	Drop-out rate
Length of school day	Postschool status of graduates
Number of days in school year	SAT/ACT scores
Number of students in special education	GED completion rates
Number of students in compensatory education	
Parent involvement in schools	
Percentage of students taking advanced placement classes	

Although this definition is a bit academic, it simply means that accountability is evidence that schools are doing what they are supposed to be doing. We believe that

> a system is accountable for **all** students when it makes sure that all students **count** in the **evaluation program** of the education system.

The evidence that people want to see has changed over time (see Box 1.2). In the past, people accepted evidence about the educational process and the context of education. Examples of this type of evidence were student-teacher ratios, numbers of teachers with advanced degrees, and so on. Today, in part as a result of standards-based reform, the evidence that people demand is focused on the results of education. Have students achieved the skills that the public thinks are important for them to achieve? Can they read? Can they solve mathematical problems? For the most part, although not entirely, the evidence that people collect on the results of education is obtained from assessments.

Assessment refers to the collection of data (Salvia &Ysseldyke, 2001). Data can be collected in many different ways, one of which is testing. Most people think of testing when they think of assessment, but assessment also includes collections of student work, such as portfolios, interviews, and observations, to name a few. *Testing* typically refers just to multiple-choice, forced-choice (e.g., true, false), and open response (e.g., essay) types of assessments. All of these can contribute to accountability.

Testing is a narrower term than *assessment*, and *assessment* is a narrower term than *accountability*. As you read this book, you will learn why it is essential that all students be included in educational accountability systems. You also will find out why it is important to include more students with disabilities in current district and statewide testing.

Standards-based reform promotes the setting of high standards, identifying indicators of successfully meeting those standards, and ways to measure student progress toward the indicators. Associated with these are analyzing data and reporting the results. We have already alluded to one of the changes that has emerged as a result of standards-based reform—the shift from a focus on the process and context of education to a focus on the results of education. There has also been a narrowing of focus to academic kinds of results. Although not all policy-level people agree with these shifts, preferring instead to continue to collect process information, it remains true that the emphasis of standards-based reform is on students achieving high academic standards and that this achievement is documented by having students take tests to demonstrate what they know and can do.

Reasons for Wanting Students With Disabilities in the Accountability System

There are many good reasons why students with disabilities should be included in educational accountability systems. Some of these reasons are presented here.

Reason 1: For an Accurate Picture of Education

We do not obtain a fully representative, accurate picture of education, particularly of student performance in education, if we do not have all students in the accountability system. In most places, 10% or more of the population of students is not incorporated if the accountability system excludes students with disabilities. In some places, we are talking about a much greater percentage.

Nationwide, the number of students with disabilities is equivalent to the total populations of Idaho, Montana, Nevada, North Dakota, South Dakota, and Wyoming. The number of students with disabilities exceeds the population of 32 states. Those with disabilities are a significant portion of the student population and need to be included in that population if we are to obtain an accurate picture of education.

Reason 2: For Students With Disabilities to Benefit From Reforms

Today, more than in the past, educational reforms are being driven by the results obtained from accountability systems. When students with disabilities are not included in the district and statewide accountability systems on which reforms are based, it is likely that the reforms may not

BOX 1.3

Students Tested in Selected School Districts
During 1992–1993 School Year

District	Number of Students Tested	Number of Students Enrolled in Grades Tested	Percentage of Students Tested
Baltimore	51,602	57,517	90
Indianapolis	13,355	15,732	85
Detroit	139,941	169,439	83
Pittsburgh	30,182	36,960	82
Oklahoma City	8,599	12,534	69
Boston	32,866	49,948	66

SOURCE: From "Don't Test, Don't Tell," by Bill Zlatos, 1994, *American School Board Journal*, November, p. 26. Copyright 1994 by National School Boards Association. Reprinted with permission. All rights reserved.

meet their needs. In essence, the saying "out of sight, out of mind" could be applied to what happens when policy and education reform decisions are made on the basis of accountability results that do not include all students.

Reason 3: To Make Accurate Comparisons

Increasingly, accountability information is used to make comparisons among states or among districts within a state. In the past, the participation rates of students with disabilities varied from one place to the next. For example, in the 1990 trial state administration of the National Assessment of Educational Progress (NAEP), also known as the nation's report card, the variation in the rates of exclusion of students with disabilities ranged from 33% to 87%. In other words, in one state 33% of all students with disabilities had been excluded from the assessment, and in another state 87% had been excluded. Another study (Zlatos, 1994) demonstrated similar variability among school districts across the United States in their rates of exclusion of students overall (see Box 1.3 for a sample of the Zlatos data). With these kinds of variability, comparisons become questionable. The only solution to unfair comparisons is for all students to be included in all accountability systems—always.

Reason 4: To Avoid Unintended Consequences of Exclusion

There are two very powerful unintended consequences of the exclusion of students from accountability systems. These usually occur when there are significant consequences associated with the test results (e.g., a school is accredited if students receive a certain score on an assessment that is administered at a specific grade level). First, it has been demonstrated that students are retained in the grades preceding the one in which the assessment is administered. As evidence of this, Allington and McGill-Franzen (1992) found that when a school accreditation assessment was administered in Grade 3, many of those students who should have been in Grade 3 had been retained in Grades 1 and 2, thus delaying their entry into the grade at which they would be tested and affect scores.

A second unintended consequence is increased referral to special education. This outcome was found by Allington and McGill-Franzen and has been confirmed in states that have high school graduation exams coupled with policies that allow students with disabilities (on IEPs) to obtain a diploma without having to pass the test but by meeting their IEP goals. Dramatic increases have been noted in referral rates in the high school years in these places, an occurrence that is completely inconsistent with normal referral trends.

Reason 5: To Meet Legal Requirements

Legal requirements related to participation in assessment and assessment accommodations have existed for some time now through Section 504 of the Rehabilitation Act (1973) and continued through the Americans With Disabilities Act (ADA). Education legislation also recognizes the importance of having all students in the educational accountability system. Title I of the Elementary and Secondary Education Act (ESEA) requires that program accountability be based on student performance on statewide assessment systems and that students with limited English proficiency and students with disabilities be included in these systems. The 1997 reauthorization of the Individuals With Disabilities Education Act (IDEA), which funds special education programs, also requires that states report on the participation of students with disabilities in their state assessment programs and that an alternate assessment be used for those students who cannot be included in the statewide assessment program. These laws are examined in more detail in the next section of this chapter.

Reason 6: To Promote High Expectations

When students are excluded from testing, it reflects an opinion that they are not able to meet the expectations represented in the test. For the majority of students with disabilities, parents and teachers tell us that they want these students to meet the same high standards that the rest are supposed to meet. Students with disabilities tell us that they want to be taught and tested on the same things as other students are. We are lowering the standards that students with disabilities must meet if we do not have them in the same accountability system as other students. For the majority of students with disabilities, this is a gross injustice. Only by holding high expectations can we expect students to meet them. And, when accountability is one part of our educational system's high expectations, then students must be in the accountability system.

Reason 7: To Promote Access to the General Curriculum for Students With Disabilities

A phrase that emerged when IDEA was reauthorized in 1997 was "access to the general curriculum." The concept here was different from the notions of integration, mainstreaming, and inclusion – it was referring to the need for the education of students with disabilities to be anchored in the general education curriculum and standards. Time after time, we have heard that the requirement that students with disabilities be included in the state assessment has led to the realization that students were not being exposed to the general curriculum in the ways that they should be to have true access to the curriculum. Albeit unintended, perhaps, a consequence of participation in assessments and accountability systems has been improved access to the general curriculum.

Assessment and Accountability Requirements of Federal Education Laws

The two laws that have had the most impact on the inclusion of students with disabilities in assessment and accountability systems have been the 1997 reauthorization of the Individuals with Disabilities Education Act, and the 1994 reauthorization of Title I of the Elementary and Secondary Education Act (which was reauthorized with expanded requirements in 2001). Each of these laws has the common requirement that students with disabilities be included in assessment systems. Some of the specific language of the laws that reinforces these concepts is included in Box 1.4.

Overview of This Book

To help you do what you need to do to comply with district and state requirements and, at the same time, do what is best for the student, we have organized this book to first address what you need to know and then to address what you need to do. Thus, Chapters 2 through 7 address what you need to know about the participation of students with disabilities in assessments, what accommodations are, how to decide which accommodations are appropriate for use in assessments, the characteristics of alternate assessments, and how to use data from them.

Chapters 7 through 10 address how you can move toward a fully inclusive accountability system. Included in these chapters are discussions on how the IEP can promote greater participation in the accountability system, what teachers and parents can do to foster this participation and make it productive for all involved, and ideas for professional development in local districts and school buildings.

Box 1.4

Language on Students With Disabilities and State or District Assessments From IDEA 1997 and ESEA 2001

Topic	IDEA 97	ESEA 01
Participation	(A) IN GENERAL – Children with disabilities are included in general State and district-wide assessment programs, with appropriate accommodations, where necessary. . . . the State or local educational agency – (i) develops guidelines for the participation of children with disabilities in alternate assessment for those children who cannot participate in State and district-wide assessment programs; and (ii) develops and, beginning not later than July 1, 2000, conducts those alternate assessments. **612(a)(17)(A)**	(I)(ii) Not less than 95 percent of each group of students described in subparagraph (C)(v) who are enrolled in the school are required to take the assessments, consistent with paragraph (3)(C)(xi) and with accommodations, guidelines, and alternative assessments provided in the same manner as those provided under section 612(a)(17)(A) of the Individuals with Disabilities Act. . . . **1111(b)(2)(I)** (v)(II) The achievement of – (aa) economically disadvantaged students; (bb) students from major racial and ethnic groups; (cc) students with disabilities; and (dd) students with limited English proficiency. **1111(b)(2)(C)**
Reporting	(B) REPORTS – The State educational agency makes available to the public, and reports to the public with the same frequency and in the same detail as it reports on the assessment of nondisabled children, the following: (i) The number of children with disabilities participating in regular assessments. (ii) The number of those children participating in alternate assessments.	(C) REQUIREMENTS – Such assessments shall – (xiii) enable results to be disaggregated within each State, local educational agency, and school by gender, by each major racial and ethnic group, by English proficiency status, by migrant status, by students with disabilities as compared to nondisabled students . . . . **1111(b)(3)(C)**

(Continued)

Box 1.4

Language on Students With Disabilities (Continued)

Topic	IDEA 97	ESEA 01
	(iii) (I) The performance of those children on regular assessments (beginning not later that July 1, 1998) and on alternate assessment (not later than July 1, 2000), if doing so would be statistically sound and would not result in the disclosure of performance results identifiable to individual children. . . . **612(a)(17)(B)**	
Accountability	The IDEA Amendments of 1997 made a number of significant changes to the law. . . . the amendments strengthened the focus of the law on improving results for children with disabilities. . . . changes that promote . . . higher expectations for children with disabilities and accountability for their educational results. . . . **Executive Order 12866**	(G) MEASURABLE OBJECTIVES – Each State . . . (iii) shall identify a single minimum percentage of students who are required to meet or exceed the proficient level on the academic assessments that applies separately to each group of students described in subparagraph (C)(v) . . . **1111(b)(2)(G)** Each group of students described in subparagraph (C)(v) must meet or exceed the objectives set by the State under subparagraph (G). . . . **1111(b)(2)(I)**

Summary

In this chapter, we introduced you briefly to the notion of accountability for *all* students. We distinguished between *testing* (a vary narrow term), *assessment,* and *accountability.* While we are striving for accountability for all students, we also are striving to include almost all students with disabilities in the regular assessment, taking the same tests (with and without accommodations) as given to other students. We also pointed out seven reasons to avidly pursue including all students in the accountability system.

Now, check your knowledge about the myth/truth statements presented at the beginning of this chapter (see Box 1.5 for answers). Try to give an explanation for why each statement is correctly identified either as a myth or as the truth.

BOX 1.5

Myth or Truth Answers

TRUTH   Assessment information on student performance is just one piece of evidence that might go into an accountability system.
Explanation: In addition to student performance, an accountability system might include information on other educational results (e.g., graduation rate) and process data (e.g., student-teacher ratio, extent of parent involvement). [See page 3]

MYTH   Assessment is a narrower term than testing.
Explanation: Testing is narrower than assessment (assessment includes other methods, such as interviews and observations, in addition to testing), and assessment is narrower than accountability. [See page 4]

TRUTH   Standards-based reform emphasizes the results of education rather than the process.
Explanation: The emphasis of standards-based reform has corresponded to a shift away from process and toward educational results. Another trend has been a narrowing of focus to academics. [See page 4]

TRUTH   One reason for including students with disabilities in the accountability system, along with other special needs students, is that it gives us a more accurate picture of the status of education.
Explanation: The picture that we have of education is not fully representative and accurate if we do not include all students. [See page 4]

MYTH   There is amazing consistency from one place to the next in the high rates at which students with disabilities are excluded form assessments.
Explanation: There is tremendous variability in inclusion rates from one place to another. [See page 5]

TRUTH   Several education laws emphasize the need to include all students in educational accountability systems.
Explanation: Besides Section 504 and the ADA, several laws require that students with disabilities be afforded the opportunity to participate in educational accountability systems. [See page 6]

TRUTH   An unintended but documented consequence of exclusion of some students from accountability system is increased rates of referral to special education.
Explanation: Evidence from research by Allington and McGill-Franzen (1992), as well as anecdotal information, indicates that referral to special education has been a common consequence of exclusion of students on IEPs from the accountability system. [See page 6]

Resources For Further Information

Allington, R., & McGill-Franzen, A. (1992). Unintended effects of reform in New York. *Educational Policy, 6*(4), 397-414.

Commission on Instructionally Supportive Assessment. (2001). *Building tests to support instruction and accountability: A guide for policymakers*. Washington, DC: National Education Association.

Education Commission of the States. (1998). *Designing and implementing standards-based accountability systems*. Denver, CO: Author.

Education Commission of the States. (1999). *Education accountability systems in 50 states*. Denver, CO: Author.

Goertz, M. E., & Duffy, M. C. (2001). *Assessment and accountability systems in the 50 states: 1999-2000*. Philadelphia: Consortium for Policy Research in Education.

Krentz, J., Thurlow, M., & Callender, S. (2000). *Accountability systems and counting students with disabilities* (Technical Report 29). Minneapolis: University of Minnesota, National Center on Educational Outcomes.

McGrew, K. S., Thurlow, M. L., Shriner, J. G., & Spiegel, A. (1992). *Inclusion of students with disabilities in national and state data collection systems* (Tech. Rep. 2). Minneapolis: University of Minnesota, National Center on Educational Outcomes.

National Research Council. (1999). *Testing, teaching, and learning: A guide for states and school districts*. Washington, DC: National Academy Press.

Nolet, V., & McLaughlin, M. J. (2000). *Accessing the general curriculum: Including students with disabilities in standards-based reform*. Thousand Oaks, CA: Corwin.

Salvia, J., & Ysseldyke, J. E. (2001) *Assessment* (8th ed.). Boston: Houghton Mifflin.

Zlatos, B. (1994). Don't test, don't tell: Is "academic red-shirting" skewing the way we rank our schools? *American School Board Journal, 181* (11), 24-28.

2

Deciding How Students Participate in District and State Tests

---

Topics

- ☐ Recognizing the Need for Accountability
- ☐ Involving Others in Decision Making
- ☐ Thinking About the Goals of instruction
- ☐ Criteria for Good Participation Decisions

In this chapter, you will . . .

- learn some myths and truths about accountability systems and students with disabilities.
- review the purpose of and need for assessment.
- think carefully about the goals of instruction for individual students.
- examine criteria for making decisions about a student's participation in assessment.

In Chapter 1, we summarized many of the reasons why it is important to have students with disabilities be part of the accountability system. Accountability for student learning, of course, is the primary reason, one that must be kept in mind when making participation decisions. But because educators are directly concerned with the welfare of students as well as the practical considerations of actually administering the test, other considerations necessarily come into play. The purpose of this chapter is to address these considerations.

When you finish this chapter, you will be able to identify which of the statements in Box 2.1 are myths and which are the truth.

Box 2.1

Myth or Truth? Do You Know?

Read each statement below and decide whether it is a myth or the truth about current practice.

- Most states have accountability systems for the school performance of students with disabilities.
- Inclusion in educational accountability systems is particularly important for students with disabilities.
- It is unfair to students with disabilities to require them to participate in district and state assessments.
- IEP teams are responsible for deciding how a student will participate in state and district assessments.
- The student's instructional goals are the primary factor in determining whether a student with disabilities should participate in a regular large-scale assessment.

How do you decide about the way in which a student takes part in the accountability system? Should the student take the district or state test, or be part of the alternate assessment? Answering these questions involves asking and answering other questions. The kinds of questions that need to be answered are these:

- How do you balance the need for accountability with the goals of the student's instruction?
- Who needs to be involved in making decisions about whether students participate in tests, and what do they need to know?
- What criteria should guide decisions about the participation of students with disabilities in a district or state test?

In this chapter, we begin to answer each of these questions. This provides you with the guidelines and rationale that you need to make the best decisions for educational accountability, on the one hand, and for the student, on the other.

Recognizing the Need for Accountability

Although we have already covered many of the reasons for wanting students in the educational accountability system, it is important to keep them in mind when thinking about individual students. It is important also to realize that education has been woefully negligent in promoting accountability for *all* students. Most states have not had accountability systems for the school performance of students with disabilities. This is changing with the requirement for students with disabilities to be in the Title I accountability system.

Historically, most states included almost none of their students with disabilities in their regular accountability systems. In part, this was due to the low participation of students with disabilities in state assessments.

Because educational accountability is important for all students, particularly students with disabilities, educators need to take responsibility for finding ways to ensure the participation of students with disabilities in these accountability systems. Steps must be taken to recognize the need for accountability and to dispel myths about the negative effects of testing.

Documenting the Reasons Why Students With Disabilities Should Participate in the Accountability System and Why Most Should Be in the Regular Assessment

It is helpful to keep available a list of the reasons for wanting students with disabilities in the accountability system, regardless of whether they are in the regular assessment or the alternate assessment. The list should also address why most students should be in the regular assessment. This list can be shared with those who may raise question about the need for all students to be in the accountability system and for those who question their participation in existing tests. It also can help dispel myths about the negative effects of testing. Keeping a list of reasons, to which you might add over time, is especially helpful for IEP teams whose membership changes. In Box 2.2, we list the major reasons why students should participate in the accountability system and in existing assessments. Add your own reasons, especially ones that are directly relevant to your own district or state.

Dispelling Myths About the Negative Effects of Testing and Confirming the Reality of Positive Effects

You should always have available a number of anecdotes to dispel myths about the negative effects of testing (e.g., extreme emotional stress for students with disabilities). Build a notebook of these anecdotes in your own district or state. Here are some that we have heard during visits to numerous states and districts:

- Students are being taught test-taking strategies to reduce the stress associated with testing. Both students with disabilities and students without disabilities are affected in varying degrees by the effects of stress at the time of testing. Students who experience stress can benefit from a variety of stress-reduction techniques. These strategies are being directed to all students who need them, not just students with disabilities, because all benefit from strategy instruction.
- In Kentucky, a state with an accountability system that provides funds to buildings for meeting targeted levels of improvement, all

---

BOX 2.2

Reasons Why Students With Disabilities Should Participate in the Accountability System and in Existing Assessments

---

- Students are more likely to benefit from instructional changes and educational reforms when they are included in the accountability system.
- Participation in assessments and inclusion in accountability is a first step toward increased access to the general curriculum.
- Both IDEA and Title I require their participation.
- Students need to gain skills involved in taking tests.
- The possibility of corruption in accountability systems is reduced when all students are included in the accountability system.
- Participation in the accountability system provides an avenue for program monitoring and evaluation.
- Most students with disabilities have mild disabilities and should be pursuing the same educational goals as other students; these students should be taking the same assessments either with or without accommodations.
- Full participation in the accountability system facilitates making policy decisions that are applicable to all students.

---

personnel in the building (including custodians and cooks as well as regular and special education teachers) assume responsibility for helping all children learn. This shared responsibility is a direct result of the fact that all students are included in the accountability system and count toward decisions about rewards.

- Complaints that testing narrows the curriculum so that it focuses almost completely on the content of the tests are countered with the view that finally students are being taught what are considered the essential elements for them to learn.
- Parents of students with disabilities, and the students themselves, are asking for more opportunities for the experience of testing, so that work-related and postsecondary education assessments will not be a shock.
- When students with disabilities are exempted from tests that their peers are taking, they often feel "different" even though they usually see themselves as being like their peers. When these students are included in the tests, they feel part of the group.
- In New York, where all students are required to pass rigorous Regents Exams, more students with disabilities are now passing the exams than took them in previous years.
- Many students in the alternate assessment are being instructed on more than just self-care skills.
- Teachers who work with alternate assessment students are finding a new professionalism in their work because they no longer feel like they are babysitting their students.

It is also helpful to have strategies in mind for how you can turn an unsuccessful testing experience into a positive one. The most common concern about having students with disabilities participate in an assessment is that it will be too stressful for them. This is handled well in states that have a history of administering accountability assessments and including students with disabilities in them. First, it is recognized that all students experience some distress when faced with a test, particularly if the importance of it is emphasized by the teacher. Furthermore, there are some students whose past experiences have produced a lack of confidence and learned helplessness about taking tests.

Second, there is the realization that any additional distress experienced by students with disabilities is most often due to their lack of test-taking experiences. These students can be prepared to take tests by telling them what the test will be like, educating them in an array of test-taking skills, and making them aware of how to prepare physically for a test. This will decrease their feelings of stress about taking tests. More information on this is presented in Chapter 9 and in our book, *Improving Test Performance of Students with Disabilities*.

These are just a few examples of strategies for dealing with potentially negative experiences when students with disabilities participate in accountability assessments. A good exercise is to have IEP team members (or other groups of personnel) identify common concerns about the participation of students with disabilities and then generate strategies for addressing them.

Involving Others in Decision Making

The IEP team makes the decision about how students with disabilities participate in district and state assessments. Parents, teachers, other school personnel, and students should be informed partners in this decision-making process. To become informed, they need to know the following:

- Purposes of assessments
- Need for accountability assessments
- Nature of the district or state assessment being administered

This information is usually not common knowledge. Therefore, an effort must be made to ensure that this information is available to all parties who should contribute to decisions. Staff information sheets sometimes are adequate to convey information to school personnel. For parents, an option is to set up parent information teams, in which a knowledgeable parent of a student with disabilities conveys relevant information to other parents of students with disabilities.

It is also important to ensure that staff and students not directly involved in decision making understand the purposes for taking assessments and why some students may need accommodations in order to participate in district and state assessments. These topics are addressed in Chapter 8.

BOX 2.3

Information on the Purposes of Assessments Used in Schools

Purpose	Explanation
Eligibility or Reevaluation	Assessment information is used along with other information to determine whether a student is eligible to receive or to continue to receive special education services.
Instructional	Assessment information is used to determine what to teach and how to teach it. Linked to this is information on the progress of students given what is being taught and how it is being taught. For example, if all students perform poorly on a classroom test, the decision might be to review the material or to teach it in a different way.
Accountability	Assessment information is used to provide a picture of the status of education. It can document how well an individual student is doing (student accountability), or how all students in a system are doing (system accountability). Consequences may be applied to either type of accountability (e.g., rewards for schools; earning a high school diploma for students).

Purposes of Assessment

Most parents and teachers of students with disabilities think about assessments used for making eligibility or reevaluation decisions when they hear the term *assessment* or *testing*. Thus, it is critical to distinguish among assessments used for the following purposes:

- Eligibility and reevaluation decisions
- Classroom instructional decisions
- Accountability (either system-level or student-level)

Box 2.3 contains information that can be used to communicate the differences in purposes. This information communicates the basics of what parents, teachers, other school personnel, and students need to know. Additional information on the first two purposes of assessment presented in Box 2.3 can be found in most introductory textbooks on special education.

Conveying the Need for Accountability Assessments

Many parents and school personnel will not know about district or state assessments, much less about the roles of these as accountability tools. The information presented in Chapter 1 is relevant for everyone. These are the major points to make:

- We need to know how students are performing in school, not just whether they are in school.
- Schools are held accountable in different ways—through public reporting of scores of students in the schools, by presenting awards and rewards to schools whose students perform well, and by imposing sanctions on schools whose students do not perform well.
- Educational reforms and instructional changes are driven by assessments when the performance on those assessments counts in some way (they are reported, or they are the basis for consequences).
- Students who do not participate in the assessments tend to be left out of the educational reforms and changes in instruction that accompany assessments used for accountability.

Other information on accountability that is directly relevant to your state or district should be discussed as well.

Describing the Current District or State Assessment

It is important for all individuals involved in making decisions about the participation of students with disabilities in an assessment to know more about the assessment. What kind of information do they need in addition to information on the purpose of the assessment? The more concrete and understandable the assessment can be made, the better. It is best to examine a copy of the assessment (or, if it is a secured test, a previous version of it or copies of practice tests). If this is not possible, the information that you need to know about the assessment, and that needs to be shared with others, includes the following:

- Name of the test
- Content areas covered by the test
- Grades tested
- How the test is administered (e.g., in classroom or other room, how many days, how long testing sessions are)
- Nature of the items (e.g., multiple-choice, extended response, writing sample, performance)
- What is done with student scores (e.g., individual reports, school reports, state report)

Information on the test should be available from your district assessment and evaluation division (if one exists) or from the person responsible for setting up testing. It always helps decision making when people know as much as possible about what they are discussing.

Thinking About the Goals of Instruction

Tests are developed with different purposes in mind. These purposes may or may not be consistent with the desire for educational accountability. Thus, in making the decision about how a student participates, first make sure that you know why the test is being given. Then think about the goals of the student's instruction in relationship to this purpose.

Taking a Broad Perspective When Thinking About Instructional Goals

A broad perspective is one that involves thinking about where instruction is supposed to lead the student. For an individual student with disabilities, think about whether the student is working toward (a) the *same* instructional goals as students without disabilities, (b) *modified* goals, or (c) *alternate* goals:

- *Same:* Goals that reflect preparation for participation in typical life experiences in the areas of education, employment, and social networks
- *Modified:* Goals that reflect preparation for participation in typical life experiences, with some modifications introduced to support the realization of these goals
- *Alternate:* Goals that reflect preparation for self-care and life skills, with support for engaging in training, employment, and social network building

Thinking about instructional goals is not the same as thinking about content standards (what you want students to know and be able to do). While all students can work toward the same general content standards, some may be working toward those standards with different instructional goals. Whenever thinking about the three types of goals as applied to an individual student, it is important to start with the first set and then change as circumstances require. The younger the student, the more important it is to think about that student as working on the same instructional goals as other students. Identifying instructional goals is illustrated for three students in Box 2.4. Note how the instructional goals may change over time, as they do for Carolyn. Note also that while we have presented three illustrations here, the population of students with disabilities does not break down equally across these three types of goals. Rather, it is more likely that the greatest percentage of students with disabilities (probably 85% or more) fall within the first two kinds of instructional goals that we have described (same and modified), whereas only 15% or less of students with disabilities need to be working toward the third kind of instructional goals (alternate). All of these students can be working toward the same standards.

Thinking More Carefully About Those Students With Alternate Instructional Goals

Low expectations for students with disabilities is a serious concern. The concern is justified. There is a significant amount of evidence that low expectations are held for many students with disabilities. Therefore, whenever

BOX 2.4

Instructional Goals for Three Students at Three Points in Time

Alice	Barbara	Carolyn
Alice is a student with a learning disability.	Barbara is a student with moderate mental retardation.	Carolyn is a student with a significant cognitive disability.
Grade 3: Alice's goals for instruction focus on reading, mathematics, and writing, the same as most students in the classroom. Her goals also focus on content area learning in social studies and science.	**Grade 3:** The goals of Barbara's instruction are the same as those of most students in the classroom—reading, mathematics, and writing are the primary focus.	**Grade 3:** Carolyn's instructional goals are focused on establishing relationships with her peers, developing beginning communication skills, and moving about the school building independently.
Grade 8: The goals of Alice's instruction continue to be the same as they are for the majority of students in the classroom.	**Grade 8:** Barbara's goals are basically the same as other students in the classroom, although she spends more time in instruction on employment-related skills.	**Grade 8:** The goals of Carolyn's instruction are focused on maintaining peer relationships and expanding communication skills. In addition, Carolyn's program is beginning to focus on developing community-based skills such as recreational activities, shopping, and getting about in the neighborhood.
Grade 11: Alice's instructional goals are like those of other students in the classroom, focusing on the coursework needed to meet diploma credit requirements.	**Grade 11:** Barbara's instructional goals now focus on transition and employment skills, with support on basic academic instruction in reading, mathematics, and writing.	**Grade 11:** Carolyn's goals now focus on community-based living and employment skills. She spends little time in the high school setting.

you identify a student for whom you have set alternate instructional goals, it is important to rethink those goals and to make sure they do not reflect low expectations for the student. In a similar vein, of course, it is important to make sure that unrealistically low expectations are not the reason why a student is pursuing modified goals.

School personnel may work with a student, and parents may attend IEP meetings and visit their child's school regularly, yet they may not be able to verbalize the goals of the child's instruction and educational experiences. Thus, it is always important to revisit this topic, especially when the conversation is about participation in assessments.

Determining the Intent of the Test

There are many reasons why students take tests. Whenever the intent of a test is to inform the public and policymakers and whenever it is used to determine consequences for others than the student, there should be no question about the participation of all students in the assessment system (either the regular assessment or the alternate assessment).

When the purpose of a test is to assign consequences to the student (as in tests used to determine whether a student is promoted from one grade to the next or will receive a high school diploma), it is extremely critical that the decision-making process begin when the student first starts school, or when the student is first identified as having a disability. Again, this decision should be directed in almost all cases toward including the student in the regular assessment, perhaps with accommodations. Very careful plans must be implemented and monitored throughout the transition through school to ensure that the student remains on target to participate successfully in and pass the test administered. Parents must be involved in these decisions from the beginning.

Comparing the Intent of the Test With Students' Instructional Goals

The next step in making a decision about how the student with disabilities will participate in the assessment system is to compare the intent of the test with the students' instructional goals. As this is done, however, it should be kept in mind that almost all students with disabilities should be participating in regular assessments; only in a few cases should the decision be that a student will participate in the alternate assessment (see Box 2.5). Considerations for IEP teams making the decision are provided in Chapter 8.

Every effort should be made to have each student with a disability participate in the regular assessment. This approach, extended to some relatively rare cases (see Box 2.6), means that a student might participate in the regular mathematics assessment, even though most of that student's instructional goals lead to participation in an alternate assessment.

BOX 2.5

Comparing Test Intent and Student Instructional Goals

Test Intent	Instructional Goals	Participation Decision
System accountability (e.g., for public reports or to determine staff, school, or district rewards)	Same	Participate in regular assessment with accommodation where needed
	Modified	Participate in regular assessment with accommodation where needed
	Alternate	Participate in alternate assessment
Student accountability (e.g., for grades, promotion, or diploma)	Same	Participate in regular assessment with accommodation where needed
	Modified	Participate in regular assessment in early grades with accommodation, where needed, but reconsider as student approaches graduation
	Alternate	Participate in alternate assessment

Participation in an alternate assessment and some parts of the regular assessment (sometimes referred to as partial participation) should be relatively rare. Students should never be pushed into the alternate assessment because they are not expected to do well on the regular assessment. However, they may be pushed into participation in the regular assessment because of unique abilities or skills in certain areas.

Meeting Test Preparation Needs

A student may not be prepared to take an assessment even though the appropriate decision is that the student participate in the assessment. When

---

BOX 2.6

Billy's Participation in Both the Regular and the Alternate Assessment

---

Billy is a high school student who has mental retardation. He receives all of his content area instruction, except math, in a self-contained setting. Despite his mental retardation, Billy has good skills in the area of math and for this reason is enrolled in general education math class. Billy is learning the same curriculum as other students in the class, takes the same tests (passing them), and is an active participant in class. He is earning a regular high school credit in math.

In the past, Billy would not have been in an accountability system at all. Billy would have been assigned to the state's alternate assessment because of his mental retardation and his focus on educational goals different from those of most students in the high school.

But Billy is one of a very few special students who could participate in both the regular assessment and the alternate assessment. His educational focus in mathematics qualifies him to participate in the regular math assessment even through he also participates in the alternate assessment.

---

there is a history of excluding students with disabilities from assessments, it is likely that not enough thought has been given to preparing these students to participate in testing.

Many terms related to test preparation have been used, such as *test-wiseness* and *test-taking skills*. We have organized these into three areas:

- *Test approach skills* (e.g., good nutrition, adequate sleep, relaxation techniques): what students learn to do that will help in many situations other than test taking
- *Test-taking skills* (e.g., reading all options, knowing the meaning of phrases like "find the one that is different" and "which one comes next in the following sequence"): what general test strategy training programs teach students; they incorporate the skills most often referred to as "test-wiseness"
- *Test preparedness* (e.g., understanding the purpose of the test, knowing what kinds of items appear on the test, understanding directions and scoring procedures specific to the test): what students learn through direct instruction, with examples and practice tests linked directly to the test to be taken

Of course, these aspects of test preparation are relevant to all students, but those with disabilities may be more likely to need direct instruction on

---

BOX 2.7

Participation Decision-Making Form

---

1. Is the student working on the same instructional goals as other   [ ] YES   [ ] NO
   students in the classroom?

   (If answer to 1 is YES, student should participate in the regular assessment)

2. If NO, is the student working on instructional goals modified   [ ] YES   [ ] NO
   (many are the same, but some are modified slightly)?

   (If answer to 2 is YES, student should participate in the regular assessment)

3. If NO, is the student working on alternate instructional goals?   [ ] YES   [ ] NO

   (If answer to 3 is YES, student should participate in an alternate assessment)

4. If the student is working on alternate instructional goals, are   [ ] YES   [ ] NO
   there any areas of unique skills that could be assessed through
   the regular assessment?

   (If answer to 4 is YES, student should participate in both the regular and an
   alternate assessment)

---

these skills than those without disabilities. Further information on these is
provided in Chapter 9.

Documenting Reasons for the Decision

The reasons for the decision that is made about a student's participation in an assessment should be documented on the student's IEP. The
reasons that are documented should be monitored (see Chapter 8). Very
few students should be excluded from the regular assessment.

Criteria for Good Participation Decisions

It is helpful to use a decision-making form to guide participation decisions. An example of a decision-making form is shown in Box 2.7. This
form should be adjusted for the specifics of your district or state assessment. Take into consideration the purpose of the assessment as well as the
student's instructional goals. Also, note the time at which the decision is
being made, in relation to the time that the test is administered. There may
be a need to reconsider the participation decision closer to the time that the
test is administered. If so, note the need to reconsider the decision at
another time.

BOX 2.8

Myth or Truth Answer

MYTH   Most states have accountability systems for the school performance of students with disabilities.

Explanation: Most states do not have accountability systems for the school performance of students with disabilities. [See page 13]

TRUTH   Inclusion in educational accountability systems is particularly important for students with disabilities.

Explanation: Educational accountability is important for all students, but especially for students with disabilities who otherwise tend to be left out of educational reforms and access to the curriculum. [See pages 14 and 15]

MYTH   It is unfair to students with disabilities to require them to participate in district and state assessments.

Explanation: There are many reasons to want students with disabilities to participate in district and state assessments, among them are access to the benefits of educational reforms, developing test-taking skills, and influencing policy decisions. The negative effects of assessment have been exaggerated. [See page 14 and Box 2.2]

TRUTH   IEP teams are responsible for deciding how a student will participate in state and district assessments.

Explanation: IDEA requires that IEP teams document whether the student will take the regular state assessment or participate in an alternate assessment. Parents, teachers, other school personnel, and students are all integral informed partners in this decision-making process. [See page 16]

TRUTH   The student's instructional goals comprise the primary factor in determining whether a student with disabilities should participate in a regular large-scale assessment.

Explanation: When considering participation decisions, it is most important to think about the goals of a student's instruction in relation to the purpose of the assessment. [See page 19]

The National Center on Educational Outcomes has developed a general set of criteria that districts and states can use to evaluate their guidelines on the participation of students with disabilities in assessments. These guidelines are easily translated into criteria that local decision makers can use to guide individual decisions about the participation of students in district and state assessments. The translated criteria are as follows:

- Decision makers start from the premise that all students, including all students with disabilities, are to participate in the accountability system and, to the extent possible, in the regular assessment.

- Decisions are made by people who know the student, including the student's strengths and weaknesses.
- Decision makers take into account the student's instructional goals, current level of functioning, and learning characteristics.
- The student's program setting, category of disability, or percentage of time in the classroom does *not* influence the decision.
- The student is included in any part of the test for which the student receives *any* instruction, regardless of where the instruction occurs.
- Before a decision is made to have a student participate in an alternate assessment, decision makers reconfirm that only 1% to 2% of all students in their district or state are in the alternate assessment.
- Parents are informed of participation options and about the implications of their child *not* being included in a particular test or in the accountability system. They are encouraged to contribute to the decision-making process.
- The decision is written on the student's IEP, and possibly on additional forms, and the reason for the decision is documented.

Additional information on these criteria and their application is presented in Chapter 8.

Summary

In this chapter, we described the process of deciding how a student with disabilities should participate in a district or state test. Because the topic of accountability assessments is new to most school personnel and parents, particularly in relation to students with disabilities, it is important to start by recognizing the need for accountability and then involving others in the decision-making process. We need to think about the goals of a student's instruction and follow some criteria for good participation decisions to round out the process described in this chapter.

Now, check your knowledge about the myth/truth statements presented at the beginning of this chapter (see Box 2.8 for answers). Try to give an explanation for why each statement is correctly identified either as a myth or as the truth.

Resources for Further Information

Elliott J., Thurlow, M., & Ysseldyke, J. (1996). *Assessment guidelines that maximize the participation of students with disabilities in large-scale assessments: Characteristics and considerations* (Synthesis Rep. 25). Minneapolis: University of Minnesota, National Center on Educational Outcomes.

Elliott, J. L., & Thurlow, M. L. (2000). *Improving test performance of students with disabilities.* Thousand Oaks, CA: Corwin Press.

Heubert, J. P., & Hauser, R. M. (1999). *High stakes testing for tracking, promotion, and graduation.* Washington, DC: National Academy Press.

Nolet, V., & McLaughlin, M. J. (2000). *Accessing the general curriculum: Including students with disabilities in standards-based reform.* Thousand Oaks, CA: Corwin Press.

Thurlow, M., Olsen, K., Elliott, J., Ysseldyke, J., Erickson, R., & Ahearn, E. (1996). *Alternate assessments for students with disabilities* (NCEO Policy Directions 5). Minneapolis: University of Minnesota, National Center on Educational Outcomes.

Thurlow, M., Ysseldyke, J., Erickson, R., & Elliott, J. (1997). *Increasing the participation of students with disabilities in state and district assessments.* (NCEO Policy Directions 6). Minneapolis: University of Minnesota, National Center on Educational Outcomes.

Ysseldyke, J., Thurlow, M., & Olsen, K. (1996). *Self-study guide for the development of statewide assessments that include students with disabilities.* Minneapolis: University of Minnesota, National Center on Educational Outcomes.

3

Assessment Accommodations: Who Is Eligible? For What?

Topics

- ☐ Accommodations: What Are They?
- ☐ Accommodations: What is the Controversy?
- ☐ What Happens During Instruction?
- ☐ Analyzing the Test's Requirements
- ☐ Knowing Your District or State Accommodations Policies
- ☐ Involving Others in Making Accommodations Decisions
- ☐ Criteria for Good Accommodations Decisions

In this chapter, you will . . .

- – learn what accommodations are, their purpose, and the controversy that surrounds them.
- – review the link and flow between instructional accommodations and assessment accommodations.
- – examine considerations in providing assessment accommodations in relationship to what a test is attempting to measure.
- – inspect criteria for making assessment accommodation decisions.

In Chapter 2, we suggested some of the many ways in which assessment accommodations are important for students with disabilities. Accommodations are changes in testing materials or procedures that enable the student with disabilities to participate in an assessment in a way that allows abilities to be assessed rather than disabilities.

BOX 3.1

Myth or Truth? Do You Know?

Read each statement below and decide whether it is a myth or the truth about current practice.

- The most commonly used accommodations in state assessments are Braille and large-print editions of tests.
- One purpose of accommodations is to avoid measuring the student's disability.
- Norm-referenced assessments generally allow more accommodations than do criterion-referenced assessments.
- Most instructional accommodations should not be used during assessments.
- IEP teams always determine what accommodations students with disabilities will use during assessments.

In the past, Braille and large-print editions of exams, sign language presentation of oral directions, and individualized administrations were commonly accepted accommodations but not necessarily the ones used most often. Today, accommodations are viewed from a much broader perspective. This often makes it more difficult to decide whether a student should receive accommodations during assessment and, if so, what they should be. The purpose of this chapter is to address considerations in making these decisions.

When you finish this chapter, you will be able to identify which of the statements in Box 3.1 are myths and which are the truth.

How do you decide whether a student needs an accommodation in assessment? And, if a student needs an accommodation, how do you decide what it (or they) should be? These questions are intertwined with each other and lead to other questions. Here are the kinds of questions that this chapter will help you answer:

- What kinds of accommodations can be used during assessment?
- What do testing accommodations have to do with classroom instruction?
- Who should be involved in making decisions about assessment accommodations?
- What criteria should guide decisions about the use of testing accommodations in district and state assessments?

Specific accommodations that might be used and the ways in which they relate to student needs are addressed in Chapter 4. The purpose of this chapter is to provide you with the guidelines and rationale that you will need to make the best decisions about the use of testing accommodations for students with disabilities. The first step in moving forward is to know a little about what accommodations are and the controversy that surrounds them.

Accommodations: What Are They?

Most people think of Braille, large print, individualized testing, and extra time as accommodations, but there are many more accommodations that can be used for testing. One way to think about accommodations is in terms of what is changed—the *setting* in which the assessment is administered, the *timing* of the assessment, the *scheduling* of administration, the *presentation* of the assessment, or the *response* that the student makes to the assessment. There are also *other* kinds of changes. Box 3.2 lists examples of each of these types of accommodations. Many more examples are provided in Chapter 4.

In this book we use the term "accommodation" to refer to any change in materials or procedures used for testing. In states and districts across the country, however, many other terms are also used. Most often, pairs of terms are used to distinguish between changes in materials or procedures that are considered to be acceptable and not acceptable (e.g., accommodation versus modification, allowed versus not allowed, standard versus nonstandard, permissible versus nonpermissible, reportable versus nonreportable). Only 11 states do not make distinctions in their terminology. Because terms are used in different ways in different places, it is important always to clarify exactly what is meant by any terms used: Is the change considered appropriate? Does it have implications for reporting? Will a score count when the change is implemented? These questions, in fact, reflect the considerable controversy that surrounds accommodations in testing.

Accommodations: What Is the Controversy?

Accommodations are provided to students with disabilities to "level the playing field" when they take an assessment. Without accommodations for their disabilities, an assessment may inaccurately measure what these students know and are able to do. The measure will reflect the disability rather than the student's knowledge and skills.

This premise about the purpose of accommodations in assessments is relatively easy to understand when thinking about common accommodations, ones that are used by most of society today. Take eyeglasses, for example. Glasses are an accommodation for a visual disability. Without glasses, many of us would not be able to read the words in assessments, and many of us would not be able to demonstrate our skills during the most common of all performance assessments—the driver's license test. Glasses help "level the playing field" for those of us who need them so that the test can measure our *ability* rather than our *disability*.

Box 3.2

Examples of Six Types of Assessment Accommodations

Setting	Timing
• Individual • Small group • Study carrel • Separate location • Room with special lighting • Adaptive or special furniture • Room with special acoustics • Minimal distractions environment	• Extended time • Flexible schedule • Frequent breaks during testing • Frequent breaks on one subtest but not another

Presentation	Response
• Audio tape • Braille edition • Large print • Audio amplification devices, hearing aids • Noise buffers • Prompts on tape • Increased space between items • Fewer items per page • Simplify language in directions • Highlight verbs in instructions by underlining • One complete sentence per line in reading passages • Key words or phrases in directions highlighted • Sign directions to student • Read directions to student • Re-read directions for each page of questions • Multiple choice questions followed by answer down side with bubbles to right • Clarify directions • Cues (arrows, stop signs) on answer form • Provide additional examples • Visual magnification devices • Templates to reduce visible print	• Mark in response booklet • Use brailler • Tape-record for later verbatim translation • Use of scribe • Word processor • Communication device • Copying assistance between drafts • Adaptive or special furniture • Dark or heavy raised lines • Pencil grips • Large diameter pencil • Calculator • Abacus • Arithmetic tables • Spelling dictionary • Spell checker • Paper secured to work area with tape/magnets

Scheduling	Other
• Specific time of day • Subtests in different order • Across multiple days	• Special test preparation • On-task/focusing prompts • Others that do not fit into other categories

Another reason that accommodations may be used is to ensure that the student can participate in an assessment. For example, a student with a significant motoric disability that prevents the grasping of writing utensils may be unable to take a writing test unless allowed to have a scribe. Even though this accommodation may not be considered appropriate for a writing test, it is necessary for this student to be able to participate at all.

Little controversy surrounds accommodations for sensory and physical disabilities. In part, this is due to the visibility of these disabilities. The public can easily see that these disabilities exist and that without some adjustments, those with sensory and physical disabilities will not be able to participate in the assessment at all, or if they can participate, it is likely to be less meaningful without accommodations than with them.

The controversy generally arises for those accommodations that are used with less visible disabilities, such as learning disabilities and emotional disabilities. Because these disabilities may be directly related to the content or procedures of assessments, their use becomes controversial. For example, a reading disability is directly related to the content of reading tests and tests that rely on reading skills to test other content areas. Making accommodations for needs that arise related to the reading disability may seem to give the student an advantage when reading is a part of the assessment.

It is often argued that accommodations allowed only for students with disabilities are ones that all students could use to their benefit. This may be true, but in most cases it is not. Many of our assumptions about what accommodations might be beneficial to students are incorrect.

Several states have taken a broader perspective on accommodations by allowing them (or subsets of them) for all students—not just students with disabilities or students with limited English proficiency. For example, policies in both Kansas and Wyoming indicate that any student who regularly receives an accommodation during classroom instruction or testing may use the accommodation during statewide testing. Policies in other states indicate that certain accommodations may be used with all students (e.g., Minnesota—scheduling and setting accommodations are available to any student; Oregon—any student may have extra time or work in a test environment conducive to effective work; Washington—all students are permitted to have extended time, frequent breaks, testing during a time of day beneficial to the student's performance, carrels, preferred seating, special lighting, furniture, acoustics, calming music, reread directions, point to item, physical assistance, tape-read directions, and dictionaries).

Legally, accommodations must be provided to students with disabilities, but the law does not say which accommodations are acceptable and which ones are not. All states now have written guidelines to indicate which accommodations are acceptable for use during specific assessments. Some districts also have produced guidelines. Unfortunately, most of these guidelines are not easily applied when making decisions about an individual student and that student's accommodations needs.

To make good decisions, you need to think about what happens during instruction and combine that information with other information (e.g., from the student). Then, you need to compare these decisions with existing state or district guidelines to make a final recommendation on the accommodations the student will use when participating in a specific assessment.

What Happens During Instruction?

There should be a direct link between what happens during instruction and what happens during assessment. Accommodations should not be introduced for the first time during an assessment. Also, consideration of what the district or state assessment requires must be linked with what happens during instruction. Finally, it is important to know what accommodations your district or state allows.

Classroom Accommodations

There should be a link between accommodations a student uses during instruction (to help learning take place) and during classroom tests (to accurately reflect what the student has learned) and the accommodations recommended for the student when taking a district or state assessment. But how do you know what kinds of accommodations should be used during classroom instruction?

There are going to be some accommodations used during instruction that may not be appropriate for use during assessment. For example, a student who requires multiple prompts to complete a task might not be provided this during a test, or a student who uses a calculator to complete mathematical problem-solving tasks might not be allowed to use it on an assessment that measures the ability to calculate math facts. It is important to delineate and clarify these exceptions.

Virtually no preservice or inservice training is provided on instructional accommodations, although some training is provided on accommodations for classroom testing. Surveys of teachers have revealed that there are many possible accommodations that might be used. For example, a national sample of general education teachers perceived the most helpful testing accommodations to be "(a) giving individual help with directions during tests, (b) reading test questions to students, and (c) simplifying wording of test questions" (Jayanthi, Epstein, Polloway, & Bursuck 1996, p. 99).

Several possible instructional accommodations are listed in Box 3.3. The multitude of accommodations that could be used should not be applied haphazardly to individual students. The underlying theme to remember is that instructional accommodations must be related to the student's unique learning needs.

Box 3.3

Possible Instructional Accommodations

Organizational Strategies	Curriculum & Instruction Strategies	
Vary Arrangement • Room arrangement • Seating arrangement • Grouping of students • Scheduling of instruction • Lesson rules/routine • Other	**Vary Content** • Amount to be learned • Time allotted to learn • Number of objectives • Difficulty level • Alternative methods • Other	**Vary Response** • Oral • Written • Gestural • Individual/group • Frequency • Complexity • Other
Vary Human Resources • Co-teachers • Peer tutors • Cooperative learning • Volunteers • Other	**Vary Presentation** • Lecture/group discussion • Kinds of demonstration • Controlled seatwork • Guided independent practice • Pace of instruction • AV/mediated instruction • Other	**Vary Reinforcement** • Grading • Verbal • Activities • Tangible • Contract • Group contingencies • Natural contingencies • Other

SOURCE: This table is adapted from Table 1, "Accommodations for Instructing Students with Special Needs" by N.L. Arllen, R.A. Gable, and J.M. Hendrickson (1996).

Reprinted with permission of the Helen Dwight Educational Foundation. Published by Heldref Publications, 1319 18th Street, NW, Washington, DC 20036-1802. Copyright © 1996.

It is important also to remember that just because a student needs an accommodation does not mean that the student will be able to use it. Students may need both training and practice to appropriately use accommodations they need during instruction. For example, there is evidence that students with spelling disabilities do not perform better, and may even perform more poorly, when allowed to use a spell checker during a writing assignment. This may be because they have not been taught how to use the spell checker, so it provides them no help at all, or because they have not had enough practice using it, so it actually interferes with their performance.

Thus, accommodations are not something that should be considered for the first time just before the assessment is to occur. Nor should they be considered for the first time during the school year in which the student will be assessed. There is a need for systematic consideration of accommodations from the beginning of the student's educational career (best), or from the onset of IEP services.

Another approach that has great potential is to incorporate more accommodating test procedures during the development of test times. For example, Delaware developed a grid to help its test developers view items in terms of students' strengths and weaknesses so that they could develop items that would enhance strengths and reduce the barriers created by areas of weakness. Thus, for students with strengths in the areas of speaking, reciting, and debating, task administration procedures would allow the use of recorded directions, and students could respond via spoken avenues, including the use of voice recognition technology. For students with challenges in the areas of visual and spatial relationships, task administration might provide step-by-step directions, perhaps tape-recorded, and allow extra time, or on the response end, the students could respond in their first language (if other than English), point to the answer, or respond in the test booklet rather than on a separate answer sheet.

Much additional thought needs to be given to how to develop assessments that reduce the need for external accommodations. Moving toward "universally designed assessments"—assessments that are developed for a broader range of students than in the past—has been recommended by the National Center on Educational Outcomes. This will involve adjustments to test conceptualization, test construction, test tryout, item analysis, and test revision.

It is important to be systematic in making decisions about classroom accommodations because they will affect assessment accommodations. Box 3.4 illustrates in a worksheet format the types of questions that can help guide decisions about instructional and classroom test accommodations.

Analyzing the Test's Requirements

Preparation is a key element in the successful and meaningful participation of a student with disabilities in assessments. Preparation depends on a good analysis of the test's requirements and matching these requirements to the student. Making good decisions about needed accommodations is a fundamental part of this analysis.

School personnel and parents need to be vigilant in carrying out these analyses during the early and middle school years, but by the time students are in high school, they need to be learning these analysis skills as well. Why? So that when these students enter a postsecondary education or employment situation they are able to advocate for themselves about the need for accommodations and the kinds of accommodations needed.

In Box 3.5 we provide some ideas of questions that might be used when analyzing a test's requirements. The questions are designed to ask about **what the test requires the students to be able to do** to take the test. Answers to these questions should help determine the kinds of accommodations the student might need to participate in the assessment. Consideration of the kinds of accommodations used for classroom instruction should come into

BOX 3.4

Classroom Accommodations Worksheet

Follow these steps to identify accommodations that are needed for classroom instruction and for classroom tests for a specific student. Be sure to consider the specific characteristics, strengths, and weaknesses of the student for whom this worksheet is being completed. For each step, be sure to separately consider instruction and tests, and use the questions to spark ideas about useful accommodations. You will find it helpful to complete this worksheet with other individuals who know the student.

	Reflections on Each Question	Possible Instructional Accommodations	Possible Classroom Test Accommodations
1. What helps the student learn better or perform better? What gets in the way of the student showing what he or she really knows and can do?			
2. What have the student's parents or guardian told you about things that they do to help the student complete household tasks or school homework?			
3. What are the student's strengths and weakness? What skills or behaviors often get in the way of learning or performance?			
4. What accommodations has the student been taught to use? Are there other accommodations on which the student needs training?			
5. For which accommodations have effects been observed? What accommodations is the student willing to use?			

(Continued)

BOX 3.4

Classroom Accommodations Worksheet (Continued)

	Reflections on Each Question	Possible Instructional Accommodations	Possible Classroom Test Accommodations
6. Have any quantitative data (e.g., from one-minute tests) been collected on the effects of accommodations?			
7. Is there any other relevant information that might affect the provision of accommodations, either during classroom instruction or during tests?			

SOURCE: Reprinted by permission of the publisher, from J.L. Elliott and M.L. Thurlow, *Improving Test Performances of Students With Disabilities on State and District Assessments* (2000), pp. 84–85.

play here because if it looks as though a student will need an accommodation to perform on the assessment, the accommodation should be one that the student is getting for classroom instruction and testing.

Add your own questions to those in Box 3.5; the ones provided serve only as a guide to the types of questions that might be asked. This decision-making tool will be most useful if it is generated by you and your colleagues, based on what you know about what the test requires of students. It would also be beneficial to have parents participate in the process of generating questions that should be asked when considering accommodations. As students get older, they are also an excellent source of information on needed accommodations.

Most district and state tests are criterion-referenced tests. They measure the student's performance against a specific criterion. In many ways, these types of tests create the fewest challenges for accommodations. On the other hand, both norm-referenced assessments and graduation exams (even though they are typically criterion-referenced tests) create special challenges for providing accommodations to students who need them.

BOX 3.5

Analyzing the Test: Questions to Ask

Requirement	Sampling of Questions to Ask
Setting	• Can the student focus on his or her own work with 25 to 30 other students in a quiet setting? • Does the student display behaviors that are distracting to other students? • Can the student take the test in the same way as it is administered to other students?
Timing	• Can the student work continuously for the entire length of a typically administered portion of the test (e.g., 20 to 30 minutes)? • Does the student use accommodations that require more time to complete individual test items?
Scheduling	• Does the student take a medication that dissipates over time, so that optimal performance might occur at a certain time of day? • Does the student's anxiety level increase dramatically when working in certain content areas, so that these should be administered after all other content areas are assessed?
Presentation	• Can the student listen to and follow oral directions given by an adult or an audiotape? • Can the student see and hear? • Can the student read?
Response	• Can the student track from a test booklet to a test response form? • Is the student able to manipulate a pencil or other writing instrument?
Other	• Is this the first time that the student will be taking a district or state assessment?

Norm-Referenced Tests

Norm-referenced tests create special challenges for thinking about accommodations because in the past most of these tests were developed without consideration of students with disabilities, and usually only a few students with disabilities were included in the normative sample. Those who are included typically did not use accommodations (even if they needed them).

Frequently, a key aspect of norm-referenced testing is that individuals in the normative sample all take the test under the same "standard" conditions. Anything that deviates from the standard conditions is not included when calculating normative scores. This means that if a student does use an accommodation, that student's scores cannot be compared with scores of the normative sample. Essentially, the result is that the student's score does not count.

Some tests do allow for certain accommodations (usually Braille and large-print editions of the test). Sometimes when they do so, special norming studies are conducted so that the scores can be used. Often, this is not the case, however, so that even when students take the Braille version of the test, for example, their scores are not aggregated with those of other students. Examples of accommodations allowed by some of the more commonly used norm-referenced assessments are provided in Box 3.6. It is evident from this table that many issues must be addressed if students with disabilities are to be assessed appropriately in norm-referenced tests. Comparing this table to what it would have looked like just 5 years ago also reveals that testing companies are beginning to recognize the need to include accommodated test takers in their standardization samples. Some companies have developed innovative ways to think about the selection of accommodations in terms of the extent to which they deviate from standardization conditions; implications for different kinds of interpretations (individual versus group) have been addressed as well.

What should you do if your district is using a norm-referenced test that does not allow the accommodations a student needs? There are several principles to follow:

- Take the position that the student needs to be included in the assessment. Remember, the criteria for participation should be linked to the goals of the student's instruction.
- Determine what accommodations the student needs and whether any of them might be eliminated without causing significant changes in the student's performance.
- Identify minimal accommodations that others will agree do not significantly change the nature of a standard administration (e.g., taking the assessment individually, marking in the test booklet rather than on an answer sheet).
- If there are accommodations that the student needs but that do not meet standard conditions, allow the student to take the assessment using those accommodations.
- Insist that the scores of students who take the assessment using non-approved accommodations be reported separately, at a minimum by reporting the number (or percentage) doing so and, more ideally, by reporting aggregate scores for these students (see Chapter 7 for considerations in reporting scores).

These, of course, are interim steps until test developers include students with disabilities in normative samples, using the accommodations that are needed to participate in assessments.

Promotion/Graduation Tests

Tests with high stakes for students, such as determining whether they move from one grade to the next or whether they earn a diploma, create special difficulties for students with disabilities because states have differing guidelines about the use of accommodations during these assessments. Although most states do allow accommodations to be used, these are not always the ones that individual students need.

Because of the high stakes for students, there is generally some procedure for making special accommodations requests. This should be done for individual students when it is evident that the use of an accommodation is essential to the accurate measurement of a student's skills. If approval is not possible, and if passing the test is the only way to be promoted or to graduate, it is essential that the student's instruction be focused on ways to compensate for the unavailable accommodation.

Knowing Your District or State Accommodations Policies

Districts and states have written policies about the use of accommodations during district or state assessments. Sometimes, these policies are quite general (e.g., allowing whatever the student uses during instruction) and other times quite specific (e.g., extended time may be used during one assessment but not during another, and if used, the student's score will not be included in summaries of performance). Often, they are in between.

Selected state-level assessment accommodation policies for graduation exams in those states that had them in 2001 are shown in Box 3.7. It is obvious from this table that policies often vary tremendously. When other kinds of assessments are entered into the mix (e.g., those used for school accountability purposes), policies vary even more. Thus, it is important to be familiar with the policies that guide your own district or state assessment.

The information in Box 3.7 very likely is already out of date. That is because policies are changing all the time. For this reason, it is critical to be alert for changes in policies in your district and state. It is also important to be looking for hidden consequences of using accommodations. Districts and states may allow certain accommodations to be used but not allow the scores from assessments in which these accommodations were used to be included with the scores of others. This has important negative consequences, which were highlighted in Chapter 2.

How do you make a decision about an accommodation if it is one the student needs but whose use invalidates the score, resulting in that assessment not being counted? This is a difficult question for which there is no precise answer. It requires that the individual situation and

Box 3.6

Selected Norm-Referenced Tests and Accommodations Allowed

Norm-Referenced Test	Accommodations Allowed
Iowa Test of Basic Skills (ITBS) Iowa Test of Educational Development (ITED) [Riverside Publishing]	Individually or in small group; quiet environment; distraction free environment, special lighting; magnifying equipment; adaptive or special furniture; typewriter; communication device; pointing to answer; dictating answer; large-print edition; reduced number of items on page; signing of directions; markers to maintain place; papers secured with tape; directions reread as needed (except for Listening Test).

Metropolitan Achievement
  Test/8 (MAT/8)
[Harcourt Educational
  Measurement]
	Breaks between subtests; more frequent breaks; multiple test sessions over several days; extended time (up to twice the time); time of day; small group; individual setting; learning/study cards; special lighting; adaptive or special furniture; location with minimal distractions; noise buffers; preferential seating; hospital/home administered; large print; repeating directions; interpreting directions (via signing, cued speech); secure papers to work area with tape/magnets; provide cues (arrows and stop signs) on answer forms; visual aids (templates, masks or markers); amplification equipment (hearing aid, auditory trainer); large diameter pencil, pencil grip, special pencil or pen.

Stanford Achievement Test/9
  (SAT 9)
[Harcourt Educational
  Measurement]
	Separate room; small group; large-print booklet; magnifying device; translations of words or phrases; windows or markers to frame text used by child; highlighter used by child.

Terra Nova 2 Terra Nova California Achievement Tests/6 Terra Nova California Test of Basic Skills/5 (CTBS/5) [CTB McGraw-Hill]	Use visual magnifying equipment; use large-print edition; use audio amplification equipment; use markers to maintain place; mark responses in test booklet; mark responses on large-print answer document; indicate responses to scribe (for selected-response items); record responses on audio tape (except for constructed-response writing items); use sign language to indicate response (for selected-response items); use computer, typewriter, Braille writer or other machine (e.g., communication board) to respond; use template to maintain place for

(Continued)

Box 3.6

Selected Norm-Referenced Tests (Continued)

Norm-Referenced Test	Accommodations Allowed
	responding; indicate response with other communication devices; take test alone or in a study carrel; take the test with small group or different class; take the test at home or in care facility (e.g., hospital) with supervision; use adaptive furniture; use special lighting or acoustics; take more breaks that do not result in extra time or opportunity to study information in a test already begun; have flexible scheduling (e.g., time of day, days between sessions) that does not result in extra time or opportunity to study information in a test already begun.

consequences be examined. For example, if it means that a student's score on a graduation exam is judged invalid, a special appeal will have to be lodged, or the student might participate in the assessment without the accommodation. Another choice is participating in the exam with the accommodation but realizing that the student is ineligible to receive a diploma. Different types of assessments very likely will lead to different decisions. Such decisions are difficult to make and should be documented, with parents and students (when appropriate) signing off on them.

Involving Others in Making Accommodations Decisions

Involving others in making decisions about accommodations is the first step in making good decisions about the use of accommodations in assessments. All states and districts require that the IEP team make decisions about accommodations—instructional and assessment accommodations. This is consistent with IDEA requirements. It is critical to be sure that accommodation decisions reflect input from several team members, not just signing off on the recommendation made by an individual member of the team (see Chapter 8).

Those who make decisions about accommodations need to know about the following:

- Nature and purpose of the assessment
- Instructional accommodations the student uses

Box 3.7

Selected Accommodations Policies for High School Graduation Exams

State	Setting		Timing		Scheduling		Presentation		Response	
	Individually	Separate Room	Extended Time	With Breaks	Special Time	Multiple Days	Braille Edition	Read Aloud	Proctor/ Scribe	Answer on Test
Alabama	X			X	X		X	*	X	X
Florida	X	X	X	X	X		X	*	X	X
Georgia	X	X	X	X	X		X	X		X
Indiana	X		*	X	X		X	*	*	X
Louisiana	X	X	X	X	X	X	*	*	*	X
Maryland	X	X	X	X	X	X	X	*	X	X
Massachusetts	X	X		X	X		X	X	X	X
Minnesota	X	X	X	X	X		X	*	X	X
Mississippi	X	X	X	*	X	X	*	*	X	X
Nevada	X	X	X	X	X	X	X	*	*	X
New Jersey	X	X	X	X			X	*	X	X
New Mexico	X	X	X	X	X	X	X	*	X	X
New York	X	X	X	X	X	X	X	X	X	X
North Carolina	X		X	X		X	X	*	X	X
Ohio	X		X				X		X	
South Carolina	X	X	X	X	X	*	X	X	X	X
Tennessee	X		*		X		X	*	X	X
Texas	X			X			X	*	X	X
Virginia	X		*	*	X	X	*	*	*	X
Washington	X	X	X	X	X	X	X	*	X	X

X = acceptable; * = not acceptable in some cases or score may not be aggregated or reported. Information in this table was adapted from Thurlow, Lazarus, Thompson, and Robey (2002), "State Policies on Assessment Participation and Accommodations," with permission from the National Center on Educational Outcomes.

- State or district accommodations guidelines
- Needed preparation for optimal use of accommodations
- How accommodations might change over time

Each of these topics plays a role in making final decisions about accommodations that a student might use during district and state assessments.

Nature and Purpose of the Assessment

To some extent, the way an assessment is designed can have an influence on the need for accommodations. This is consistent with the concept of universally designed assessments. For example, presenting items both graphically and in plain text can reduce the need for reading accommodations. This is why Delaware is attempting to develop assessments from the beginning, taking these considerations into account and thereby reducing the need for external accommodations.

The purpose of the assessment (graduation exam, accountability measure) and whether it is a norm-referenced or criterion-referenced one also will have an impact on the need for accommodations. Typically, norm-referenced tests are less amenable to the use of accommodations because for many tests the norms are based only on standard administrations of the assessment.

People familiar with the assessment for which accommodations decisions are being made should provide information to decision makers, even if they are not going to be involved in the decision. If you are asked to be involved in decision making without knowing about the nature and purpose of the assessment, it is critical that you obtain this information. It should be available from your local assessment coordinator or the state assessment division.

Instructional Accommodations the Student Uses

Teachers are generally the ones who know best the kinds of accommodations a student needs during instruction. It is very important that all teachers who work with a student provide input to the IEP team on the accommodations that they use with the student during instruction. Despite the IDEA requirement that a general educator must attend IEP meetings, it is often not the student's teachers who are there, but rather a representative of the curriculum and instruction department. Setting up a procedure for each and every teacher who works with a student to provide input to the IEP team will dramatically improve the information that the team considers in making its accommodation decisions.

Teachers are not the only ones who have information for the IEP team decision. Many parents observe their children making accommodations for themselves as they carry out household tasks, interact with others, and do their homework. This information can be valuable in determining accommodations that the child needs, even though the accommodations may not have been implemented at school. Of course, the time to have this discussion with parents is during initial IEP meetings so that the accommodations can be used during instruction and then implemented for the district or state assessment.

When making decisions about accommodations, IEP team members need to have not only information on the reasons why students should be provided with them during assessments but also a copy of the questions to help determine needed accommodations for individual students. Again, the questions in Box 3.5 are a good start; your own version is apt to be even better.

A list of possible accommodations is also helpful for the IEP team to have when making accommodations decisions. The lists provided in

Chapter 4 are useful for this purpose. It is important, however, that these lists serve as mind ticklers rather than constraints on possible accommodations that the IEP team might consider.

Students themselves can offer valuable insights about needed accommodations. Heightening their awareness of needed accommodations, in fact, should be a goal of their instruction, so that by the time they are into high school and approaching postsecondary education or the work world, they will know which accommodations they need to request.

State or District Accommodations Guidelines

All states now have written guidelines about the use of accommodations, usually detailed for each test that is administered. When districts have their own tests, they also may have written guidelines about the kinds of accommodations that are allowed. After identifying the accommodations that a student needs, compare these with what the written guidelines say. It is especially important to note the following:

- Whether the needed accommodation is considered to invalidate the score a student obtains
- What happens to the student's score if the accommodation is used (is it treated the same as other scores, or is it separated in some way?)
- If the accommodation is considered invalid or is not allowed, whether there are alternative avenues for gaining approval for its use (e.g., Department of Education approval)

All these factors contribute to the ultimate decision about recommended accommodations.

Preparation for Optimal Use of Accommodations

Use of accommodations during instruction is a key element in preparing students for the optimal use of accommodations during assessment. However, consideration must also be given to whether there are ways to assist the student in using accommodations during assessment. The example of students who do not use extended time as an accommodation is a case in point. Students who have directions read to them in class but who must listen to a tape cassette for the assessment (usually for security purposes) will need to have some experience with managing the tape player before the test.

In many cases, it will also be necessary to spend time with the student discussing accommodations. Without a thorough understanding of the appropriateness of accommodations, students who need them may reject them at test time—not wanting to look different from their peers. As students get older, they will begin to make choices about their use of accommodations. Ensuring that their choices are informed choices is the responsibility of all educators.

How Accommodations Might Change Over Time

Accommodations that a student uses many change over time. Two kinds of changes in accommodations are likely to occur. First, different kinds of accommodations might be needed as the child gets older. For example, a young child with disabilities may need directions read, but as the child matures and gains reading skills, this accommodation may no longer be necessary.

Second, the way in which decisions are made about accommodations should change over time, with the student taking more responsibility for knowing what kinds of accommodations are needed. This helps the student make the transition through high school into postsecondary settings, be they additional training or work.

Criteria for Good Accommodations Decisions

Just as criteria were developed for states to use to evaluate their guidelines on the participation of students with disabilities in assessments, criteria also have been developed for states to use to evaluate their guidelines on accommodations that are allowed during assessments (Elliott, Thurlow, & Ysseldyke, 1996). These accommodations guidelines are easily translated into criteria that local decision makers can use to guide individual decisions about accommodations that students need when they participate in district and state assessments. The translated criteria are as follows:

- Decisions are made by people who know the student, including the student's strengths and weaknesses.
- Decision makers consider the student's learning characteristics and the accommodations currently used during classroom instruction and classroom testing.
- The student's category of disability or program setting does *not* influence the decision.
- The goal is to ensure that accommodations have been used by the student prior to their use in an assessment—generally, in the classroom during instruction and in classroom testing situations. New accommodations should not be introduced for the district or statewide assessment.
- The decision is made systematically, using a form that lists questions to answer or variables to consider in making the accommodation decision. Ideally, classroom data on the effects of accommodations

---

BOX 3.8

Myth or Truth Answers

MYTH   The most commonly used accommodations in state assessments are Braille and large-print editions of tests.
Explanation: Braille and large print are among the most frequently allowed accommodations, but there are many others that are used more frequently. [See page 29]

TRUTH   One purpose of accommodations is to avoid measuring the student's disability.
Explanation: The purpose of accommodations is to level the playing field, which means assessing a student's abilities rather than the student's disabilities. Another purpose is to enable students to take a test that they might not be able to otherwise. [See page 30]

MYTH   Norm-referenced assessments generally allow more accommodations than do criterion-referenced assessments.
Explanation: Since most norm-referenced tests have been developed without consideration of students with disabilities, and without including them in the standardization sample, these types of assessments generally allow fewer accommodations than criterion-referenced assessments. [See page 37]

MYTH   Most instructional accommodations should not be used during assessments.
Explanation: There should be a link between accommodations used during instruction and during classroom tests and the accommodations recommended for the student when taking a district or statewide assessment. [See page 44]

TRUTH   IEP teams always determine what accommodations students with disabilities will use during assessments.
Explanation: All states and districts require that IEP teams be involved in decisions about accommodations a student will use during assessments. This is consistent with IDEA requirements. [See page 42]

---

are part of the information entered into decisions. Decisions and the reasons for them may be noted on the form.

- Parents (or students at an appropriate age) are involved in the decision by either participating in the decision-making process or at least being given the analysis of the need for accommodations and by signing the form that indicates accommodations that are to be used.

- The decision is documented on the student's IEP and elsewhere as needed (e.g., test coordinator's forms).

Additional information about these criteria and their application is included in Chapter 7.

Summary

In this chapter, we discussed some of the general considerations in making decisions about the use of accommodations during assessments. Decision makers should be individuals who know the student, and they need to take into consideration the purpose and characteristics of the test, the accommodations that are allowed in state or district policies, needed preparation for using the accommodations, and what the consequences are of deciding to use an accommodation.

Check your knowledge now about the myth/truth statements presented at the beginning of this chapter (see Box 3.8 for answers). Give an explanation for why each statement is correctly identified either as a myth or as the truth.

Resources for Further Information

Arllen, N.L., Gable, R.A., & Hendrickson, J.M. (1996). Accommodating students with special needs in general education classrooms. *Preventing School Failure, 41*(1), 7-13.

CTB McGraw-Hill. (2001). *Guidelines for inclusive test administration.* Monterey, CA: Author.

Elliott, J., & Roeber, E. (1996). *Assessment accommodations for students with disabilities* (videotape recording). Alexandria, VA: National Association of State Directors of Special Education.

Elliott, J., Thurlow, M., & Ysseldyke, J. (1996). *Assessment guidelines that maximize the participation of students with disabilities in large-scale assessments: Characteristics and considerations* (Synthesis Rep. 25). Minneapolis: University of Minnesota, National Center on Educational Outcomes.

Elliott, J., Ysseldyke, J., Thurlow, M., & Erickson, R. (1997). *Providing accommodations for students with disabilities in state and district assessments* (NCEO Policy Directions 7). Minneapolis: University of Minnesota, National Center on Educational Outcomes.

Elliott, S.N., Braden, J.P., & White, J.L. (2001). *Assessing one and all: Educational accountability for students with disabilities.* Arlington, VA: Council for Exceptional Children.

Fuchs, L.S., & Fuchs, D. (2001). Helping teachers formulate sound test accommodation decisions for students with learning disabilities. *Learning Disabilities Research & Practice, 16*(3), 174-181.

Jayanthi, M., Epstein, M.M., Polloway, E.A., & Bursuck, W.D. (1996). A national survey of general education teachers' perceptions of testing adaptations. *Journal of Special Education, 30* (1) 99-115.

King, W.L., Baker, J., & Jarrow, J.E. (n.d.). *Testing accommodations for students with disabilities.* Colombus, OH: Association on Higher Education and Disability.

Rogan, J., & Havir, C.L. (1993). Using accommodations with students with learning disabilities. *Preventing School Failure, 38*(1), 12-15.

Thompson, S.J., Johnstone, C.J., & Thurlow, M.L. (2002). *Universal design applied to large scale assessments* (Synthesis Report 44). Minneapolis: University of Minnesota, National Center on Educational Outcomes.

Thompson, S., & Thurlow, M. (2002). *Universally designed assessments: Better tests for everyone!* (NCEO Policy Directions 14). Minneapolis: University of Minnesota, National Center on Educational Outcomes.

Thurlow, M.L., Lazarus, S., Thompson, S., & Robey, J. (2002). *2001 state policies on assessment participation and accommodations* (Synthesis Report 46). Minneapolis: University of Minnesota, National Center on Educational Outcomes.

Thurlow, M.L., & Wiener, D.J. (2001). Considerations in the use of nonapproved accommodations. *Assessment for Effective Intervention, 26*(2), 29-37.

Ysseldyke, J., Thurlow, M., Bielinski, J., House, A., Moody, M., & Haigh, J. (2001). The relationship between instructional and assessment accommodations in an inclusive state accountability system. *Journal of Learning Disabilities, 34*(3), 212-220.

Accommodations to Consider

In this chapter, you will . . .

- – examine six categories of assessment accommodations.
- – review the do's and don'ts in testing accommodations.
- – become familiar with the issue of upholding assessment integrity.
- – learn what research says about the effects of assessment accommodations.

In Chapter 3, we discussed the philosophy behind assessment accommodations for students with disabilities and identified general guidelines for making good accommodations decisions. In this chapter, we provide information on possible accommodations for a student to use during assessments. We also give you just a hint of some of the technical issues that require consideration and what the research tells us.

When you finish this chapter, you will be able to identify which of the statements in Box 4.1 are myths and which are the truth.

BOX 4.1

Myth or Truth? Do You Know?

Read each statement below and decide whether it is a myth or the truth about current practice.

• Most states allow setting accommodations and presentation accommodations in their statewide testing programs.
• The most controversial accommodations fall within the areas of presentation and response accommodations.
• Most national college admissions exams allow a variety of accommodations with no penalty to the student.
• Out-of-level testing is an appropriate accommodation for students with mental retardation in accountability assessments.
• Electronic testing has tremendous potential for making assessments more accessible and meaningful for the full range of students in today's schools.
• Research findings are now available that define which accommodations invalidate test scores.

What are the kinds of accommodations that might be considered for district and state assessments? Should accommodations be used one at a time, or will students need more than one accommodation? Here are the kinds of questions this chapter will help you answer:

• What are the major kinds of accommodations, and specific examples, that can be used during assessment?
• What are the do's and don'ts that should be considered when making decisions about recommending accommodations for specific students?
• How can one determine which accommodations invalidate test scores?

As noted in Chapter 3, there are several types of accommodations and many different accommodations within each type. Different types of accommodations have different levels of acceptance. In the past, timing and scheduling accommodations were often considered controversial; they still are when the test is timed. Since most state tests now are not strictly timed tests, presentation and response accommodations generally are most controversial. This is because they raise the issues of whether the accommodations (a) provide an unfair advantage and (b) change what is being measured.

Setting Accommodations

Setting accommodations are changes in the place in which an assessment is given. They can include changes in the conditions of the assessment setting as well as changes in the location of the assessment (see Box 4.2).

BOX 4.2

Examples of Setting Accommodations

Conditions of setting	Location
Minimal distractive elements (e.g., books, artwork, window views)	Study carrel
Special lighting	Separate room (including special education classroom)
Special acoustics	Seat closest to test administrator (teacher, proctor, etc.)
Adaptive or special furniture	Home
Individual student or small group of students rather than large group	Hospital
	Correctional institution

The most common reason why students may need setting accommodations is that they have difficulty focusing attention when in a group setting. This may be exhibited either by a student who engages in behaviors other than attending to the test (e.g., tapping pencil and watching other students) or by a student disturbing other students in a group setting. Setting accommodations may be needed in conjunction with others. For example, when a student needs extended time for an assessment or needs frequent breaks during an assessment, it often is useful also to have the student take the assessment in a separate setting or in a small group, where the special timing requirements will not complicate the assessment of those students who will take the assessment under regular timing conditions. The need for setting adjustments also may arise when a student uses special equipment that may take extra time to use (such as a Brailler to produce a response, or a tape recorder to give oral directions that can be repeated according to student needs).

States differ in the types of setting accommodations allowed in statewide assessments (see Box 4.3, which is a summary of information from Thurlow, Lazarus, Thompson, & Robey, 2002). Sometimes, states allow different setting accommodations depending on the specific assessment being administered. Although the information in Box 4.3 gives a general picture, it is important to be aware of your own state's guidelines. Realize also that they do change, and states are not always able to get the information out to those who really need to be familiar with it.

National exams (e.g., ACT, GED, and SAT) also have specific setting accommodations that are allowed. These are summarized in Box 4.4.

As students progress through school, begin to familiarize them with the kinds of accommodations allowed in different assessments. Increasingly, they should be helped to consider what accommodations they need during assessments, so that when they enter postsecondary

BOX 4.3

Examples of Setting Accommodations Allowed by States

| State | Condition | | | | Location | | | | |
	Small Group	Individually	Adaptive Furniture	Acoustics	Study Carrel	Separate Room	Seat Location	Hospital	Student Home
Alabama	X	X	*	X	X		X		*
Alaska	X	X	X	X	X	X			
Arkansas	X	X			X		X		
Arizona	X	X	X	X		X			
California	X	X				X			
Colorado	X	X	X	X	X	X	X	X	X
Connecticut	*	*							
Delaware	X	X	X	X			X		
Florida	X	X	X	X	X	X			
Georgia	X	X	X	X	X	X			
Hawaii	X	X					X		
Idaho	X	X	X	X	X	X	X		
Illinois	X	X		X	X	X			
Indiana	X	X	X	X			X		
Iowa	X	X	X	X	X	X	X		X
Kansas	X	X		X	X	X			
Kentucky						X			
Louisiana	X	X			X	X	X		
Maine	X	X			X	X	X		X
Maryland	X	X			X	X	X	X	X
Massachusetts	X	X			X	X	X		
Michigan	X	X	X	X				X	X
Minnesota	X	X	X	X	X	X	X		
Mississippi	X	X	X	X	X	X	X		*
Missouri	X	X							
Montana	X	X				X			
Nebraska	X	X	X	X	X	X	X		X
Nevada	X	X	X	X	X	X			*
New Hampshire	X	X			X	X	X		*
New Jersey	X	X	X	X	X	X	X	X	X
New Mexico	X	X	X	X	X	X	X	X	X
New York	X	X	X	X	X	X	X		
North Carolina	X	X					X	X	X
North Dakota	X	X	X	X		X	X		
Ohio	X	X							

(Continued)

BOX 4.3

Examples of Setting Accommodations Allowed by States (Continued)

State	Condition				Location				
	Small Group	Individually	Adaptive Furniture	Acoustics	Study Carrel	Separate Room	Seat Location	Hospital	Student Home
Oklahoma	X	X	X	X	X	X			
Oregon	X	X			X	X			*
Pennsylvania	X	X	X	X	X	X	X		
Rhode Island	X	X	X	X		X	X		
South Carolina	X	X	X	X		X			
South Dakota	X	X	X	X		X	X	X	X
Tennessee	X	X			X		X		*
Texas	*	X							
Utah	X		X	X	X		X		
Vermont					X	X	X		
Virginia	X	X	X	X	X		X	X	X
Washington	X	X	X	X	X	X	X		X
West Virginia	X	X	X	X		X	X		
Wisconsin	X	X	X	X	X	X	X		
Wyoming	X	X	X	X	X	X			

X = acceptable; * = not acceptable in some cases or score may not be aggregated or reported. Information in this table is adapted from Thurlow, Lazarus, Thompson, and Robey (2002), "State Policies on Assessment Participation and Accommodations," with permission from the National Center on Educational Outcomes.

settings or employment they can identify and request accommodations they might need in assessment situations.

Timing Accommodations

Timing accommodations are changes in the duration or organization of time during testing. They can include changes in how much time is allowed as well as how the time is organized see (Box 4.5).

Accommodations in the timing of a test are among the most frequently requested. There are many valid reasons for timing accommodations, but there are also cautions that must be observed in selecting them.

As mentioned previously, there are a wide variety of accommodations used that may require the addition of timing accommodations. For example, certain equipment takes more time to use, thus requiring extended time. There are some accommodations that create fatigue, such as the use of magnification equipment or tape recorders and earphones, thus requiring additional breaks during assessment.

BOX 4.4

Examples of Setting Accommodations Allowed in National Tests

ACT	GED	SAT

Seating near front of room
Separate room (for extra time)
Wheelchair accessible room
	One-on-one testing at health
	   facility or home
	Private room
		Nonidentified
		   on Web site

Processing disabilities are often cited as a reason for needing timing accommodations. Students who have difficulty processing written text may need extended time to read and comprehend directions and item text. Students with dysgraphia (difficulty writing) or motor disabilities may need more time to write their responses.

Timing accommodations should be used with caution because there is some evidence that they tend to be overly requested and actually may work to the detriment of some students. Overrequesting an accommodation suggests that it is being recommended even though the student does not use it. Nonuse by a student could be due to not needing the accommodation (e.g., it doesn't help to have more time) or embarrassment about it. Being allowed more time than other students may not be viewed positively by the student, especially as the student gets older (middle school and high school). There is an important need for instruction (both for those using accommodations and for other students) about the need for accommodations and the concept of "leveling the playing field" rather than providing "unfair advantages."

There are several reasons why timing accommodations may work to the detriment of a student, and these should be considered and balanced against the extent to which the accommodations might "level the playing field." For example, providing a student with additional breaks opens up the possibility of breaking concentration or interrupting a sequence of items or section of the test. Extending the time allowed to finish an assessment may encourage nonproductive guessing or changing answers when they should not be changed. It is important to try to balance the potential positive and negative effects of all timing accommodations under consideration. If the student is old enough, the student should be encouraged to signal when a break is needed.

States differ in the extent to which they allow timing accommodations and the nature of those allowed (see Box 4.6, which is based on Thurlow et al., 2002). Again, be aware that the information in Box 4.6 is a static representation of information that changes frequently as states revise their guidelines. Check your own district and state guidelines.

National exams also allow some timing accommodations. These are summarized in Box 4.7. In the past, when timing accommodations were

---

BOX 4.5

Examples of Timing Accommodations

Duration	Organization
Changes in duration can be applied to selected subtests of an assessment or to the assessment overall	Frequent breaks, even during parts of the assessment (e.g., during subtests)
Extended time (i.e., extra time)	Extended breaks between parts of the assessment (e.g., between subtests) so that assessment is actually administered in several sessions
Student determined	

---

used in the ACT and the SAT they were reported as "special" (ACT) or considered to produce a nonstandard administration. In other words, these assessments were "flagged," which means that institutions receiving the students' scores also were given something like the following "caution":

> One or more of the tests administered on this date were taken under nonstandard testing conditions. . . . The degree of comparability of the resulting scores with those achieved under standard conditions is not known. Final responsibility for interpreting the examinees' scores rests with the score recipients.

This is no longer true. As for other national tests, such as the Graduate Record Examinations (GRE), the Graduate Management Admission Test (GMAT), the Test of English as a Foreign Language (TOEFL), and Praxis, "flagging" is no longer practiced. When these tests are taken with approved accommodations, they are treated like all other tests.

Scheduling Accommodations

Scheduling accommodations are changes in when testing occurs. They can include changes in the time of administration as well as changes in how the administration of the assessment is organized (see Box 4.8). The list of scheduling accommodations again makes it evident how accommodations often are intertwined. For example, when an assessment is given at a specific time of the day that is different from the time when other students take the test, setting accommodations necessarily are being used also as the test probably will be administered to the student individually in a separate setting.

BOX 4.6

Examples of Timing Accommodations Allowed by States

State	Duration		Organization	
	Extended Time	Student Determined	Breaks During Testing	Multiple Sessions
Alabama	*	X	*	
Alaska			X	X
Arkansas			*	
Arizona			X	X
California	*		*	*
Colorado	X	X	X	X
Connecticut	X		X	X
Delaware	*	X	X	X
Florida	*		X	X
Georgia	*		*	
Hawaii			*	
Idaho	*		X	X
Illinois	X		X	X
Indiana	X	X	X	X
Iowa	X		X	X
Kansas			X	
Kentucky	X			
Louisiana	*		X	X
Maine	X	X	X	X
Maryland	*		*	X
Massachusetts			X	X
Michigan	X			X
Minnesota	X		X	X
Mississippi	*	*	*	X
Missouri	*			X
Montana	X			
Nebraska	*		*	X
Nevada	*		*	
New Hampshire	X		X	
New Jersey	X	X	X	
New Mexico	X		X	X
New York	X		X	X

(Continued)

BOX 4.6

Examples of Timing Accommodations Allowed by States (Continued)

State	Duration		Organization	
	Extended Time	Student Determined	Breaks During Testing	Multiple Sessions
North Carolina	X		X	X
North Dakota	X		X	X
Ohio	X			X
Oklahoma	*		X	
Oregon	X		X	X
Pennsylvania	X		X	
Rhode Island	X		X	
South Carolina	X		X	X
South Dakota	*		X	X
Tennessee	*			
Texas			X	
Utah			X	
Vermont	X			
Virginia	X		X	X
Washington	X	X	X	
West Virginia	*		*	X
Wisconsin	X		X	X
Wyoming	X		X	X

X = acceptable; * = not acceptable in some cases or score may not be aggregated or reported.
Information in this table is adapted from Thurlow, Lazarus, Thompson, and Robey (2002), "State Policies on Assessment Participation and Accommodations," with permission from the National Center on Educational Outcomes.

There are many reasons for the use of scheduling accommodations for students with disabilities. Some reasons reflect the need to coordinate assessment with the effects of medication; others relate to using an optimal order to reduce frustration effects. Again, an interaction with another accommodation might be reflected in the need for scheduling accommodations.

As with other types of accommodations, states differ in their policies about the use of scheduling accommodations (see Box 4.9, which is based on Thurlow et al., 2002). Scheduling accommodations are less common than other types of accommodations. Again, be alert to your own district and state guidelines.

BOX 4.7

Examples of Timing Accommodations Allowed in National Tests

ACT	GED	SAT
Extended testing time (up to 1½ standard time)	Extended time Frequent breaks (supervised)	Extended time

---

National exams typically do not recognize scheduling accommodations. They do generally provide different days to take the assessment, but this is provided as a convenience for the test administrators, not as an accommodation for the test taker.

Presentation Accommodations

Presentation accommodations are changes in how an assessment is given to a student. The main types of presentation accommodations are format alterations, procedure changes, and use of assistive devices (see Box 4.10). These may overlap when accommodations are actually administered, but for our purposes here, it helps to think about them as three distinct types.

Clearly, there are many more presentation accommodations than those we have listed here, and those presented in Box 4.10 are not all that might be provided. Furthermore, it is within the presentation accommodations that most controversy arises. Questions are raised about the comparability of scores from an assessment in which the directions are clarified for the student or in which the assessment is read to the student. These issues and ways to address them in decision making are discussed later in this chapter.

The variability in student need for presentation accommodations is great, as is evident in the list of possible accommodations provided here. Students with sensory disabilities (hearing and visual impairments) may need a large-print or Braille version (format alterations), an interpreter to sign directions or a reader to read directions (procedure changes), or magnification or amplification devices (assistive devices). Students with learning or emotional disabilities also may need presentation accommodations. Perhaps the most typically requested presentation accommodations for these students are procedure changes, particularly reading the test, rereading directions, and answering questions about directions and items. Like timing accommodations, some of the presentation accommodations are considered controversial. These are discussed later in this chapter.

Presentation accommodations allowed by states are highly variable (see Box 4.11, based on Thurlow et al., 2002). This variability reflects the

BOX 4.8

Examples of Scheduling Accommodations

Time	Organization
Specific time of day (e.g., morning midday, afternoon, after ingestion of medication) Specific day of week Over several days	In a different order from that used for most students (e.g., longer subtest first, shorter later; math first, English later) Omit questions that cannot be adjusted for an accommodation (e.g., graph reading for student using Braille) and adjust for missing scores

differing perspectives on their appropriateness. On the other hand, several of the presentation accommodations are widely accepted, such as Braille and large-print editions of assessments.

The policies of national assessments (e.g., ACT, GED, and SAT) related to presentation accommodations are similar to those for timing accommodations (see Box 4.12)—many accommodations that previously were considered "non-national" (ACT—audiocassette, Braille, reader) or were considered nonstandard administrations (SAT—audiocassette, Braille, test reader) are no longer "flagged."

Response Accommodations

Response accommodations are changes in how a student responds to an assessment. The main types of response accommodations are format alterations, procedure changes, and use of assistive devices (see Box 4.13). As with presentation accommodations, these types may overlap when accommodations are actually administered, but for our purposes here it helps to think about them as three distinct types.

Even though response accommodations are relatively few in number, there is much controversy about some of them. Generally, it is questions about the "fairness" of some of these accommodations that are raised. These issues and ways to address them are presented later in this chapter.

BOX 4.9

Examples of Scheduling Accommodations Allowed by States

State	Timing		Organization	
	Over Several Days	Specific Time of Day or Week	Best Time for Student	Subparts in Different Order
Alabama			X	
Alaska	*			
Arkansas	X		X	
Arizona			X	
California	X			X
Colorado	X	X	X	
Connecticut	*			
Delaware				
Florida	*		X	
Georgia			X	X
Hawaii				
Idaho	X		X	
Illinois	X		X	X
Indiana			X	
Iowa			X	
Kansas				
Kentucky				
Louisiana	X		X	
Maine		X	X	
Maryland	X		X	
Massachusetts			X	
Michigan			X	X
Minnesota			X	
Mississippi	X		X	
Missouri				
Montana			X	X
Nebraska	X		X	
Nevada	*		X	
New Hampshire			X	
New Jersey				
New Mexico	X		X	
New York	X		X	

(Continued)

BOX 4.9

Examples of Scheduling Accommodations Allowed by States (Continued)

State	Timing		Organization	
	Over Several Days	Specific Time of Day or Week	Best Time for Student	Subparts in Different Order
North Carolina	X			
North Dakota	X			X
Ohio				
Oklahoma	X		X	
Oregon			X	
Pennsylvania				
Rhode Island	X	X	X	*
South Carolina	*	*	X	
South Dakota	X		X	
Tennessee			X	
Texas				
Utah	X		X	
Vermont				
Virginia	X		X	
Washington	*		X	
West Virginia			X	X
Wisconsin			X	
Wyoming	X		X	

X = acceptable; * = not acceptable in some cases or score may not be aggregated or reported.
Information in this table is adapted from Thurlow, Lazarus, Thompson, and Robey (2002), "State Policies on Assessment Participation and Accommodations," with permission from the National Center on Educational Outcomes.

The primary reason for providing response accommodations is to meet needs related to physical and sensory disabilities that limit the student's ability to respond. However, processing difficulties that limit the ability to get to a response also may be a reason for requesting such accommodations as using a calculator or spell checker when the target skill is math problem solving (not calculation) or written composition (excluding mechanics).

As with other types of accommodations, states vary in the response accommodations that are allowed (see Box 4.14, which is based on Thurlow et al., 2002). Like presentation accommodations, some response accommodations are widely accepted, such as marking in the test booklet rather than on an answer sheet with bubbles, whereas others are highly controversial, such as use of a spell checker.

BOX 4.10

Examples of Presentation Accommodations

Format Alterations	Procedure Changes	Assistive Devices
Braille edition	Use sign language to give directions to student	Audiotape of directions
Large-print version		Computer reads directions and/or items
Larger bubbles on answer sheet	Reread directions	Magnification device
One complete sentence per line in reading passages	Write helpful verbs in directions on board or on separate piece of paper	Amplification device (e.g., hearing aid)
Bubbles to side of choices in multiple-choice exams	Simplify language, clarify or explain directions	Noise buffer
		Templates to reduce visible print
Key words or phrases highlighted	Provide extra examples	Markers or masks to maintain place
Increased spacing between lines	Prompt student to stay focused on test, move ahead, read entire item	Dark or raised lines
		Pencil grips
Fewer number of items per page	Explain directions to student anytime during test	Magnets or tape to secure papers to work area
Cues on answer form (e.g., arrows, stop signs)	Answer questions about items anytime during test without giving answers	

National exams do allow some response accommodations (see Box 4.15). As with other accommodations, the use of these no longer raises the "flagging" issue.

Other Accommodations

There are a few accommodations that do not fit within the five types of accommodations described above. Some of these are appropriate, and others are not.

Out-of-Level Testing

Out-of-level testing is an "other" accommodation considered inappropriate for accountability assessments. In out-of-level testing, the third-grade version of the test might be administered to a fifth-grade student.

BOX 4.11

Examples of Presentation Accommodations Allowed by States

State	Format			Procedure		Assistive Device			
	Braille Edition	Large Print	Read Test	Sign Directions	Read/Clarify Direction	Magnification	Amplification	Noise Buffer	Templates
Alabama	*	X	*	X		X	X	X	X
Alaska	X	X	*	*	X	X	X	X	X
Arkansas	X	X	*	X		X		X	
Arizona	*	*			*	X	X		X
California	*	X	*	X	X	X	X		X
Colorado	X	X	*	*	X	X	X	X	
Connecticut	X	X	*	X	X	X			
Delaware	X	X	*	X	X	X	X	X	X
Florida	X	X	*	X	X	X			X
Georgia	*	X	*	*	X	X	X		
Hawaii	X	*			*				
Idaho	X	X	*	X	X	X	X	X	X
Illinois	X	X	*						
Indiana	*	X	*	*	*	X	X	X	
Iowa	X	X	*	X	X	X			
Kansas	X	X	*	X		X			X
Kentucky			X	X	X	X	X	X	X
Louisiana	*	X	*	X	X	X			
Maine	X	X	*	*	X	X	X	X	X
Maryland	*	X	*	X	X		X		
Massachusetts	X	X	X	X	X	X	X	X	X
Michigan	X	X	*	*	X		X	X	
Minnesota	X	X	*	X	*	X	X		X
Mississippi	*	X	*	X	X	X	X		X
Missouri	X	X	X	X		X	X		X
Montana	*	X	*	*	*	X			X
Nebraska	X	X	*	X	X	X	X	X	X
Nevada	X	X	*	X	X	X	X	X	X
New Hampshire	X	X	*	X	X	X	X	X	X
New Jersey	*	X	*	X	X				X
New Mexico	X	X	*	X	*	X	X	X	X
New York	X	X	X	X	X	X	X	X	X
North Carolina	X	X	*	X		X			
North Dakota	X	X	*	X	X	X	X		X
Ohio	X	X							
Oklahoma	X	X	*	X	X	X	X	X	X
Oregon	X	X	*	X	*	X	X	X	X
Pennsylvania	X	X	*	X	X	X	X		X
Rhode Island	X	X	*	X		X		X	X
South Carolina	X	*	*	X	X	X	X	X	X

(Continued)

BOX 4.11

Examples of Presentation Accommodations Allowed by States (Continued)

State	Format Braille Edition	Large Print	Read Test	Procedure Sign Directions	Read/Clarify Direction	Assistive Device Magnification	Amplification	Noise Buffer	Templates
South Dakota	*	X		*	*		X	X	X
Tennessee	X	X	*	X	*	X	X	X	X
Texas	*	X	*	X					
Utah	*	X	*	X	X				
Vermont	*	X	X			X			
Virginia	*	X	*	X	X	X	X	X	X
Washington	X	X	*	X	X	X	X	X	
West Virginia	X	X	*	X	X		X	X	
Wisconsin	X	X	*	X	*	X	X	X	X
Wyoming	X	X	*	X		X	X	X	X

X = acceptable; * = not acceptable in some cases or score may not be aggregated or reported. Information in this table is adapted from Thurlow, Lazarus, Thompson, and Robey (2002), "State Policies on Assessment Participation and Accommodations," with permission from the National Center on Educational Outcomes.

Although testing at a level below the student's actual grade level may be appropriate for making instructional decisions, it is generally not appropriate for accountability purposes. Testing at a lower grade level does not reflect the student's performance at the standard being assessed for the majority of students.

Despite our view on out-of-level testing, the number of states allowing it has jumped dramatically in recent years—a sign that tests may not be designed for the broad range of students now included in state and district tests. Hopefully, the advance of universally-designed assessments, combined with increased access to the general curriculum, will decrease the pressure to place students in out-of-level tests.

A program of research now underway is illuminating the complexities of out-of-level testing—when it might be appropriate, and what characteristics tests must have to support appropriate out-of-level testing (e.g., vertically equated levels). Such characteristics are most often found in norm-referenced tests, not standards-based tests. Still, test and measurement experts are equivocal about the advantages and disadvantages of out-of-level testing, often raising critical concerns about the expectations and lower-level instruction that may be reflected in the perception that we need to have out-of-level testing.

Motivational Accommodations

These comprise a set of accommodations that less clearly fits within the broad categories presented in this book. Motivational accommodations

BOX 4.12

Examples of Presentation Accommodations Allowed in National Tests

ACT	GED	SAT
Audiocassette	Audiocassette edition	Audiocassette version
Braille edition	Braille edition	Braille
Large-print version	Large-print edition	Interpreter for instructions
Reader	Sign language interpreter	Large-print test and answer sheet
Sign language interpreter for instructions	Video equipment	Test reader
Visual notification of test start, time remaining, and stop times	Vision-enhancing technologies	

encourage slow-to-begin students to start the test and also encourage "quitters" to continue working on the test and to refocus attention. It is our belief that these activities are indeed accommodations and as such should be discussed and noted on the IEPs of students needing them. They also comprise a need, however, that should be addressed through students' training. For example, self-monitoring techniques and other self-regulation interventions might be taught to students with attention or motivation difficulties.

Test Preparation

Another type of accommodation is test preparation. We have included test preparation as an accommodation here because it is often forgotten. Students without disabilities usually gain test-taking skills on their own without the need for explicit instruction. That often is not the case for students with disabilities, who may be less likely to pick up the skills on their own and who have had less practice in taking district and state assessments. Ideas for test preparation are discussed in Chapter 9, as well as in our book *Improving Test Performance of Students with Disabilities* (Elliott & Thurlow, 2000).

Computer-Based Accommodations

Computer-based accommodations fit within the "other" category of accommodations that we have discussed. For example, use of a computer for completing a writing test is frequently allowed. There are several other

BOX 4.13

Examples of Response Accommodations

Format Alterations	Procedure Changes	Assistive Devices
Mark responses in test booklet rather than on separate page	Use reference materials (e.g., dictionary, arithmetic tables)	Word processor or computer to record responses
Respond on different paper, such as graph paper, wide-lined paper, paper with wide margins	Give response in different mode (e.g., pointing, oral response to tape recorder, sign language)	Amanuensis (proctor/scribe writes student responses)
		Slantboard or wedge
		Calculator or abacus
		Brailler
		Other communication device (e.g., symbol board)
		Spell checker

computer-based accommodations, however, that are directly relevant for students with disabilities that probably will emerge as technology becomes more commonly used to accommodate students with disabilities. One example is a computer voice synthesizer, which allows any paper-and-pencil test to be translated easily and quickly by passing it through a scanner, so that the computer can read the test to the student. Another is a videodisc system that can show written text while it presents a corresponding insert showing a person translating the text into sign language. We expect that the potential for other computer-based accommodations will expand in the future.

Electronic and Online Testing

Technology has the potential to revolutionize district and state testing. It has not yet done so because of the real and perceived costs of making computers more widely accessible in general and accessible for testing purposes in particular.

Despite the initial cost investments of electronic and online testing, more and more states are undertaking the development of these assessments. Few states, however, have considered the interface of electronic testing and accommodations—how to incorporate accommodations into the electronic format and how to identify what are appropriate accommodations when electronic testing is used.

We do know a lot about the computer adaptive testing—the most broadly examined version of computerized testing. Adaptive testing allows

BOX 4.14

Examples of Response Accommodations Allowed by States

	Format		Procedure		Assistive Device	
State	Mark on Test	Special Paper	Point to Response	Dictate to Tape	Proctor/ Scribe	Communication Device
Alabama	*		*		*	*
Alaska	X		X	X	X	X
Arkansas	X				X	
Arizona				X	X	
California	X		*	X	*	X
Colorado	X		X		X	X
Connecticut	X				*	*
Delaware	X		X	*	X	X
Florida	X				X	
Georgia	X		X			
Hawaii	X				*	
Idaho	X		X	X	X	X
Illinois	X			X	X	
Indiana	X				*	*
Iowa	X				X	X
Kansas			X	X	X	
Kentucky			X	X	X	X
Louisiana	X		X	X	*	*
Maine		X			*	X
Maryland	X		X	*	X	*
Massachusetts	X			X	X	X
Michigan	X		X	X	X	X
Minnesota	X		X	*	*	
Mississippi	X			X	X	X
Missouri			X	X	X	X
Montana	X			X	X	X
Nebraska	X		X	X	X	X
Nevada	X		*	*	*	*
New Hampshire					*	X
New Jersey	X				X	X
New Mexico	X			X	*	*
New York	X		X	X	X	X
North Carolina	X				X	
North Dakota	X		X	X	X	X
Ohio					X	

(Continued)

BOX 4.14

Examples of Response Accommodations Allowed by States (Continued)

State	Format		Procedure		Assistive Device	
	Mark on Test	Special Paper	Point to Response	Dictate to Tape	Proctor/ Scribe	Communication Device
Oklahoma	X		X	X	X	X
Oregon	X		X		*	X
Pennsylvania	X			*	*	X
Rhode Island				*	X	X
South Carolina	X			X	*	
South Dakota				*	*	
Tennessee	X				*	
Texas	*			*	*	
Utah						
Vermont				X	X	*
Virginia	X				X	X
Washington	X		X		X	X
West Virginia	X		X		X	X
Wisconsin	X		X	X	X	X
Wyoming	X		X		X	X

X = acceptable; * = not acceptable in some cases or score may not be aggregated or reported. Information in this table is adapted from Thurlow, Lazarus, Thompson, and Robey (2002), "State Policies on Assessment Participation and Accommodations," with permission from the National Center on Educational Outcomes.

an individual student's response to influence which items are presented to the student, just as individualized testing does through basals and ceilings.

In other words, a student starts a test at the item difficulty assumed to be most appropriate for his or her grade. If the student gets most of the items incorrect at this level, the test administrator goes back to easier items. Computers can serve the same function, which allows the assessment to have a much broader difficulty range (from very easy to very difficult) than can be included in a test in which every student must complete every item.

The possibility that this approach to testing is a version of out-of-level testing is an important concern.

Do's and Don'ts in Testing Accommodations

Most of the do's and don'ts of testing accommodations relate to the purposes of the assessment, what happens during instruction, and common sense. But it is a good idea to run through these lists every now and again. Here are some of the don'ts:

BOX 4.15

Examples of Response Accommodations Allowed in National Tests

ACT	GED	SAT
Mark answer in test booklet	Scribe Talking calculator or abacus	Computer for writing Writer to record responses

---

- *Don't* introduce a new accommodation for the first time for an assessment.
- *Don't* base the decision about what accommodations a student will use on the student's disability category.
- *Don't* start from the district or state list of approved accommodations when considering what accommodations a student will use in an upcoming test.
- *Don't* pick accommodations once and then never again re-evaluate the need for them or for new ones.

Add your own don'ts to this list. Keep it in view when making decisions about accommodations. Also, keep in view a list of the do's:

- *Do* systematically use accommodations during instruction and carry these into the assessment process.
- *Do* base the decision about accommodations, both for instruction and for assessment, on the needs of the student.
- *Do* consult the district or state list of approved accommodations after determining what accommodations the student needs. Then, reevaluate the importance of the accommodations that are not allowed. If they are important for the student, request their approval from the district or state.
- Evaluate the student's accommodations periodically because the specific accommodations the student needs may change over time as a function of the student's age or skills.

It is a good idea to add your own ideas to the "do" list, just as you did for the "don't" list. Keep it at hand as you make accommodations decisions.

Considering the Effects of Testing Accommodations

As we have talked about accommodations, we have on occasion mentioned that controversy surrounds the use of certain accommodations. The controversy is about whether the scores that a student obtains when using accommodations mean the same things as scores obtained by students who do not use them—are the scores comparable? People may talk about accommodations invalidating scores. These kinds of concerns are reasonable in some cases but not in others.

How can you know the difference between accommodations that do not change what is measured and those that do? You may not be able to—yet. Even the psychometricians working on these issues do not agree with each other. And, like many other issues, most people's views on the use of certain accommodations vary with their fundamental beliefs about the importance of being accountable for all students. There is even disagreement on what criteria must be met for an accommodation to be considered appropriate. Thus, it may be some time before the controversy surrounding the use of accommodations abates. It is hoped that research on their effects may help reduce the controversy.

The issues related to the use of accommodations and threats to the meaning of a test score will surface again as we consider the reporting of test scores. The way it plays out most typically is that students are allowed to use the accommodations they need, but their scores do not count in school or district assessments if there are consequences attached to the scores. Sometimes, this means that a student is required to take the assessment without accommodations so that the score can count. Sometimes, it means that a student is encouraged to use accommodations so that the score will not count, without the student or the student's parents knowing this. Chapter 7 contains additional information on the topic of accommodations and reporting.

What the Research Tells Us

Although research has been conducted to examine the effects of accommodations, the "answers" are by no means simple or clear. As noted previously, an inappropriate effect can be defined in different ways, and the way in which it is defined influences the "answer" you get.

Research on accommodations has mushroomed in the past few years—both in response to the availability of federal funding and because states and testing companies have felt the need to have data on the effects of accommodations. Some of the research has been descriptive in nature, such as identifying the percentages of students with disabilities who used accommodations during particular assessments (e.g., Thurlow, 2001). Studies like this one have confirmed that there is tremendous variability in the percentage of students with disabilities from one state to the next, and probably from one district to the next. One of the major implications for practice is that there may be "over-accommodation" occurring—IEP teams may be selecting many more accommodations for a student than are needed.

Much accommodations research uses extant data—often data from the administration of the state or district test—to study how students with disabilities perform with and without the use of accommodations. While there are many problems that arise when trying to conduct research in this way, unique approaches have been tried to identify comparison groups to better understand the effects that might be observed. A study by Bielinski and his colleagues used this approach to demonstrate that the read aloud accommodation does not produce interference with the constructs measured in a math test, but does when the test is a reading test. The findings of this study, however, were not quite so simple, and also raised issues about the original decisions that had been made about who needed accommodations, as well as about the test itself—where there seemed to be interference with the constructs measured also for lower performing students who did not use accommodations.

The type of research that has been lauded as most desirable—experimental research that compares groups of students with and without disabilities who use and then do not use an accommodation—is very difficult to conduct. One reason is that to be pure, only one accommodation should be examined at a time. Yet few students need only one accommodation, so that when only one is provided there is already a potential problem with the measurement of the student's performance. Gerald Tindal and his colleagues (1998) at the University of Oregon have several examples of research on accommodations conducted using fairly stringent experimental designs.

A different approach that is being used with increasing frequency to study the effects of accommodations is single subject research, in which accommodations are provided and then not provided for a single student, and the effects of the presence and absence of the accommodation graphed and evaluated. This approach has been used by Stephen Elliott and his colleagues at the University of Wisconsin. This approach has also been used by Fuchs and colleagues to assist in making accommodations decisions.

There are now ways to get to the results of current research. The National Center on Educational Outcomes (NCEO) has a searchable accommodations research database on its website (www.education.umn.edu/nceo) that can be searched by specific accommodation, disability, test content area, or student grade level. The database provides a summary of each study, along with information on the accommodation, study participants, dependent variables, and major findings. This database is being updated every three months so that it has the latest research that has been conducted.

It is important to be critical of decisions based on opinions. Too often recommendations about whether accommodations affect the meaning or comparability of test scores are based on opinions and best guesses.

Summary

In this chapter, we identified types of accommodations and specific accommodations that might be used during assessments. Decision makers should become familiar with both the broad array of accommodations that might be used and the list that might be used by a district or state to indicate which accommodations are allowed. More important, they should identify the accommodations that an individual student needs. Box 4.16 lists student characteristics and possible accommodations for decision

BOX 4.16

Student Characteristics and Possible Accommodations

Student Characteristic	Possible Accommodations
Attention difficulties: Student has difficulty staying focused on the task at hand, frequently looking at other students, out the window, or at other areas away from the test.	**Setting:** Individual, small group **Scheduling:** Administer within 30 minutes of taking medication **Timing:** Provide frequent breaks during the usual time of administration, extend the administration time to compensate for the increased break time
Tracking and attention difficulties: Student has difficulty staying on the problem on which he or she is working, often looking at multiple-choice item responses for another question than the one on which working.	**Presentation:** Provide student with a template to reduce distraction from other items **Response:** Allow student to respond on the test booklet rather than having to track to a separate bubble sheet
Text processing difficulties: Student has difficulty decoding text at the same speed as other students.	**Presentation:** Orally present test directions or both test directions and test items
Low vision: Student has a visual impairment that does not quite meet the definition of legal blindness.	**Setting:** Individual setting, where extra-bright light can be provided to shine directly on the test materials **Scheduling:** Administer in morning to avoid end of day eye strain from day's work **Timing:** Administer with frequent breaks because of fatigue to eyes created by extra-bright light and intense strain at deciphering text **Response:** Scribe records responses to avoid extra time and eye strain trying to find appropriate location for a response and to give the response

makers to use. It is by no means a complete list and is one that might be added to within the context of a specific school, district, or state. Be sure to refer also to the interview on student needs in Chapter 9 and to the wealth

---

BOX 4.17

Myth or Truth Answers

TRUTH   Most states allow setting accommodations and presentation accommodations in their statewide testing programs.
Explanation: Setting accommodations and presentation accommodations are among the more frequently allowed accommodations [See Boxes 4.3 and 4.11]

TRUTH   The most controversial accommodations fall within the areas of presentation and response accommodations.
Explanation: Accommodations in the areas of presentation and response are most controversial because they raise the issues of (1) whether the accommodations provide an unfair advantage, and (2) whether the accommodations change what is being measured. [See page 52]

TRUTH   Most national college admissions exams allow a variety of accommodations with no penalty to the student.
Explanation: College admissions tests allow more accommodations now that in the past. And, those that are allowed no longer result in flagging of the test scores. [See page 56 and Boxes 4.4, 4.7, 4.12, and 4.15]

MYTH   Out-of-level testing is an appropriate accommodation for students with mental retardation in accountability assessments.
Explanation: Out-of-level testing is not an appropriate accommodation for any student when the assessment is being used for accountability purposes. This may be an appropriate accommodation for assessments used for instruction. [See page 63]

TRUTH   Electronic testing has tremendous potential for making assessments more accessible and meaningful for the full range of students in today's schools.
Explanation: Electronic and online testing is at the beginning stages of increasing accessibility and meaningfulness of district and state tests for many students with disabilities. [See page 67]

MYTH   Research findings are now available that define which accommodations invalidate test scores.
Explanation: While we now have some research findings on the effects of accommodations, they are often linked to specific assessments or conditions. Both research findings and better decision-making practices are needed to ensure appropriate accommodation practices. [See page 71]

of information in our book *Improving Test Performance of Students with Disabilities* (Elliott & Thurlow, 2000).

Now, check your knowledge about the myth/truth statements presented at the beginning of this chapter (see Box 4.17 for answers). Try to give an explanation of why each statement is correctly identified either as a myth or as the truth.

Resources for Further Information

Bielinski, J., Thurlow, M., Minnema, J., & Scott, J. (2000). *How out-of-level testing affects the psychometric quality of test scores* (Out-of-Level Testing Report 2). Minneapolis, MN: University of Minnesota, National Center on Educational Outcomes.

Bielinski, J., Thurlow, M., Ysseldyke, J., Freidebach, J., & Freidebach, M. (2001). *Read-aloud accommodation: Effects on multiple-choice reading and math items* (Technical Report 31). Minneapolis, MN: University of Minnesota, National Center on Educational Outcomes.

Elliott, J.L., & Thurlow, M.L. (2000). *Improving test performance of students with disabilities*. Thousand Oaks, CA: Corwin Press.

Elliott, S.N., Braden, J.P., & White, J.L. (2001). *Assessing one and all: Educational accountability for students with disabilities*. Arlington, VA: Council for Exceptional Children.

Elliott, S.N., Kratochwill, T.R., & McKevitt, B.C. (2001). Experimental analysis of the effects of testing accommodations on the scores of students with and without disabilities. *Journal of School Psychology, 39*(1), 3-24.

Fuchs, L.S., Fuchs, D., Eaton, S.B., Hamlet, C., & Karns, K. (2000). Supplementing teacher judgments of test accommodations with objective data sources. *School Psychology Review, 29*, 65-85.

Minnema, J., Thurlow, M., & Bielinski, J. (2002). *Test and measurement expert opinions: A dialogue about testing students with disabilities out of level in large-scale assessments* (Out-of-Level Testing Report 6). Minneapolis, MN: University of Minnesota, National Center on Educational Outcomes.

Minnema, J., Thurlow, M., Bielinski, J., & Scott, J. (2000). *Past and present understandings of out-of-level testing: A research synthesis* (Out-of-Level Testing Report 1). Minneapolis: University of Minnesota, National Center on Educational Outcomes.

Thompson, S.J., Johnstone, C.J., & Thurlow, M.L. (2002). *Universal design applied to large scale assessments* (Synthesis Report 44). Minneapolis: University of Minnesota, National Center on Educational Outcomes.

Thompson, S., & Thurlow, M. (2002). *Universally designed assessments: Better tests for everyone!* (NCEO Policy Directions 14). Minneapolis: University of Minnesota, National Center on Educational Outcomes.

Thompson, S.J., Thurlow, M.L., Quenemoen, R.F., & Lehr, C.A. (2002). *Access to computer-based testing for students with disabilities* (Synthesis Report 45). Minneapolis: University of Minnesota, National Center on Educational Outcomes.

Thurlow, M. (2001). *Use of accommodations in state assessments: What databases tell us about differential levels of use and how to document the use of accommodations* (Technical Report 30). Minneapolis: University of Minnesota, National Center on Educational Outcomes.

Thurlow, M., & Bolt, S. (2001). *Empirical support for accommodations most often allowed in state policy* (Synthesis Report 41). Minneapolis: University of Minnesota, National Center on Educational Outcomes.

Thurlow, M., Lazarus, S., Thompson, S., & Robey, J. (2002). *2001 state policies on assessment participation and accommodations* (Synthesis Report 42). Minneapolis: University of Minnesota, National Center on Educational Outcomes.

Thurlow, M., & Minnema, J. (2001). *States' out-of-level testing policies* (Out-of-Level Testing Report 4). Minneapolis: University of Minnesota, National Center on Educational Outcomes.

Tindal, G., Heath, B., Hollenbeck, K., Almond, P., & Harniss, M. (1998). Accommodating students with disabilities on large-scale tests: An experimental study. *Exceptional Children, 64*(4), 439-450.

Alternate Assessments

In this chapter, you will . . .

– find out what an alternate assessment is and who is eligible to take one.
– examine the status of state alternate assessments.
– learn about evaluating alternate assessments.
– study a variety of states' examples of alternate assessments.

In Chapter 4, we examined possible accommodations for a student to use during assessments. We also gave you just a hint of some of the technical issues that require consideration and what the research tells us. In this chapter, we address what to do for students for whom none of the accommodations discussed in Chapter 4 provide the support needed to participate in the regular assessment. These are students who are unable to meaningfully participate in the regular assessment, even with accommodations. These students often have different instructional goals, even though they are working toward the same content standards.

In this chapter, we examine the following questions: What is an alternate assessment? Who should participate in it? What do we do with the results? When you finish this chapter, you will be able to identify which of the statements in Box 5.1 are myths and which are the truth.

Box 5.1

Myth or Truth? Do You Know?

Read each statement below and decide whether it is a myth or the truth about current practice.

- There is still confusion about who should take an alternate assessment.
- Alternate assessments are performance events that allow students to show what they can do on a specific task.
- All teachers, including special education teachers, embrace the concept and practice of the alternate assessment for students with significant cognitive disabilities.
- The general impact of the alternate assessment has been positive.

What Is an Alternate Assessment?

An alternate assessment is a method of measuring the performance of students unable to participate in the typical district or state assessment. We have thus far identified several different ways in which students can participate in an accountability system: (a) in the regular assessment without accommodations, (b) in the regular assessment with accommodations, (c) in an alternate assessment, and (d) partially in an alternate assessment and partially in the regular assessment. It is estimated that approximately 10% of students with disabilities (about 1% of the total student population) should participate in the alternate assessment. For those students not in the regular assessment, the alternate assessment serves as a substitute way to gather information needed to measure and document the results of education.

There are many approaches to measurement that are appropriate for an alternate assessment system. For a district or state accountability system, however, it is critical that the data be "aggregated" (i.e., combined) to produce an overall estimate of performance for all students participating in the alternate assessment. That means that whatever is used for the alternate assessment must measure common elements so that data can be combined across students in the alternate assessment.

The first two states to have an alternate assessment were Kentucky and Maryland. Kentucky has the Alternate Portfolio System. Maryland has the Independence Mastery Assessment Program (IMAP).

Defining the common domains for which student data are to be combined is critical. Kentucky did this by first identifying domains for all students and then selecting those most relevant for students with significant disabilities. Maryland did it by gaining consensus on the important domains for students with significant disabilities, regardless of the domains for other students.

BOX 5.2

Possible Measurement Approaches for an Alternate Assessment

Observation	Interviews and Checklists
Marking occurrence of specific behaviors	Interviews: teachers, peers, parents, employers
Written narrative of what is observed	Rating scales or checklists: mobility and community skills, self-help skills, daily living skills, adaptive behavior, social skills
Notation of the frequency, duration, and intensity of behavior	
Videotape	Peer and/or adult rating scales or checklists.
Audiotape	

Testing	Record Review
Performance events	School records
Portfolios	Student products
Curriculum-based measures	IEP objectives and progress

There are a number of ways to think about what alternate assessments look like. Salvia and Ysseldyke (2001) identify several assessment approaches that provide a framework for thinking about what might work for an alternate assessment system. Using four general approaches (observation, interviews and checklists, testing, and record review) you can generate an array of methods for an alternate assessment (see Box 5.2).

When Should a Student Take an Alternate Assessment?

This is an appropriate time to revisit this question, which was first addressed in Chapter 2. In that chapter, the criterion that targeted a student for participation in an alternate assessment was that the student was working on different instructional goals from other students. Thus, if the goals of a student's instruction are focused on various life skills while the student's peers are working on specific content in English, mathematics, and science, then that student should be in an alternate assessment. In some cases, students will not be shifted into the alternate assessment until they are older.

The academic focus of students with disabilities will necessarily change as they progress through their school years. The degree or severity of a student's disability often will have a major impact on the academic path that student takes. The academic focus for students with more significant cognitive disabilities will differ from that for students with mild to moderate cognitive disabilities. Students with mild to moderate disabilities are typically those with learning disabilities, mild mental retardation, emotional disabilities, or those with multiple disabilities who are able, with assistance, to participate in the same course requirements and assessments as students without disabilities. Students with more significant cognitive disabilities are those who, because of their disability, need a more individualized curriculum. Generally, students who participate in an alternate assessment are those not working on requirements to earn a standard diploma.

The decision to participate in the alternate assessment may not be made for most students until they are approaching the age of transition planning (14 to 16 years). However, for some students with disabilities, the need for an alternate assessment will be more apparent and appropriate early in their schooling due to the significance of their cognitive disability and the highly individualized curriculum they are learning.

Factors to Consider

While it is easy to state that the alternate assessment is for students who are working on different instructional goals from those of the majority of students, distinctions like these are not always so clear-cut. There are a number of factors that complicate the situation.

Change Over Time. The most common factor, one that is to be encouraged, is that things change over time. When a student first enters school, it is in most cases appropriate to assume that the student will be taught the same things as other students. Even recognizing tremendous diversity in the abilities and skills that children bring to school, it is still appropriate to be teaching the same skill areas to all children.

As children progress through school and begin to enter the years when transition to postschool environments is under consideration, it is time to rethink the goals of instruction for the student. At some point, for some small percentage of students, there is the recognition that life skills are more important to target than is traditional content.

Nature of the Assessment. Another factor is the nature of the assessment that has been developed to measure students' progress towards the standards. Assessments can be developed to be very broad in difficulty levels or quite narrow. The narrower the assessment, in general, the easier it is to administer in a short amount of time.

Most district and state tests are not developed to be broad in the difficulty levels they assess. The result is that, for many students, the tests do not have any items on which they can successfully perform. This is a major problem for accountability systems. Needless to say, it is also a major

BOX 5.3

Examples of Kentucky's Academic Expectations and Indicators for Students in the Alternate Portfolio System

Academic Expectation	Indicator
Accessing Information: Students use research tools to locate sources of information and ideas relevant to a specific need or problem.	Requests assistance
Reading: Students construct meaning from a variety of printed materials for a variety of purposes through reading.	Reads environmental, pictorial print
Writing: Students communicate ideas and information to a variety of audiences for a variety of purposes through writing.	Constructs printed, pictorial messages, uses personal signature

problem for those making decisions about whether a student should participate in the general assessment or the alternate assessment.

Standards Assessed. The decision about participation in an alternate assessment is also complicated by the nature or breadth of the standards developed by the district or state. When standards are very broad, a student may be working toward those standards but still need to be in an alternate assessment. This is what has occurred in Kentucky, where quite broad standards were developed for all students. Teachers and others who worked with students with significant cognitive disabilities double-checked all standards for their appropriateness for these students and determined that 28 of the original 60 were the most appropriate and important (see Box 5.3 for a sample of these standards and the indicators that apply to students in the Alternate Portfolio System).

In Maryland, a slightly different approach underlies the state standards and thus the alternate assessment. Maryland started with a set of standards appropriate for the majority of students and then went back to identify desired educational outcomes for those students with significant cognitive disabilities (see Box 5.4 for a sample of these standards and indicators of them).

As pressure has increased for all students to have access to the general curriculum, and thus, work toward the same academic content standards, initial "alternate standards" have been revised to become extended or expanded standards aligned to the general standards. While we discuss

---

BOX 5.4

Examples of Maryland's Content-Domain Outcomes and Indicators for Students in the Independence Mastery Assessment Program

Content Domain	Indicator
Personal Management: Students demonstrate their ability in the following areas: personal needs, appropriate health and safety practices, managing household routines, and participating in transition planning with adult service providers.	Eating and feeding self Dressing appropriately for activities, season, and weather
Community: Students demonstrate their ability to access community resources and get about safely in the environment.	Shopping or browsing for variety of items Demonstrating safe pedestrian skills
Career/Vocational: Students demonstrate their ability to participate in transitioning to employment and in various employment opportunities.	Arriving at work appropriately dressed and on time Completing assigned duties with appropriate productivity and quality
Recreation/Leisure: Students demonstrate their ability to participate in recreational and leisure activities.	Engaging in hobbies Participating in clubs or organizations

---

these and other trends in alternate assessments later, it is important to recognize that alternate assessments are still evolving. This does not mean, however, that they are going to go away. It means, rather, that they should get better over time.

Both Kentucky and Maryland have developed accountability systems that include all students, but they have done so in different ways. The major advantage of having started from broad standards is that the merging of data for reporting may be easier (more on this in Chapter 7).

Eligibility Decisions

As states and districts continue to refine their alternate assessments, eligibility continues to be of concern. In fact, we think issues of eligibility for who takes the alternate assessment will be at the forefront of assessment issues for students with disabilities for some time to come. Bottom line—those students who participate in the alternate assessment should be those for whom the regular assessment is not appropriate for two major reasons:

(1) any and all accommodations that might be provided to students still do not enable them to participate, and (2) students are working on instructional goals that are not assessed by the assessment.

The tricky part in all this is making sure the folks who are making eligibility decisions—the IEP team members—are fully aware of these important distinctions. One of the best ways to do this is to have IEP teams complete a decision-making checklist that is part of a student's IEP. In the Long Beach (California) Unified School District, for example, IEP teams are required to do just that—complete an IEP page that documents the decision for a student to participate in the alternate assessment (see Box 5.5). In other words, every student's IEP team must discuss and document the alternate assessment participation decision on the IEP page.

In some states, eligibility criteria are published in assessment guideline documents (see Box 5.6). The criteria that are probably most familiar are the guidelines published in Kentucky (see Box 5.7).

Status of Alternate Assessments

Since July 1, 2000, most states have implemented an alternate assessment. The National Center on Educational Outcomes (NCEO) continues to gather information from states in the area of alternate assessment. In its 2001 state survey, NCEO published information on the status of alternate assessments. This status update reveals that alternate assessments are still evolving—as might be expected of an entirely new level of assessment. We highlight some of the survey findings here.

What Is Measured and How

Of particular interest in the NCEO update is the fact that what is assessed by state alternate assessments has changed over time (see Box 5.8). Most states are either using the same standards (with some expanded standards) or using functional skills that are linked to standards. An example of the second approach is:

Content Area: Health

Standard: Behaviors to Reduce Risk

Curriculum Objective: Students will develop and use appropriate behaviors to identify, avoid, and cope with dangerous situations.

A number of states now use both standards and an additional set of functional skills. During the three years since states knew that they needed to have alternate assessments, most have moved from developing alternate assessments based on the special education curriculum, to alternate assessments connected to state standards.

Assessment strategies used in state alternate assessments have also fluctuated. States continue to refine their approaches as the reality of who is being assessed and for what purpose is clarified. An evidence-based or portfolio approach continues to be the strategy of choice for most

Box 5.5

Student Name _____   IEP Date _____   Page 9 of _____
          Last   First

Sample IEP Page Documenting the Alternate Assessment Decision

XVI. ALTERNATE ASSESSMENT PARTICIPATION CRITERIA

☐ Student will participate in SAT9 and district assessment only. Stop here.

☐ Student may require participation in the Alternate Assessment. See Decision-Making Criteria below.

Eligibility in the LBUSD Alternate Assessment is based on a student's IEP that reflects significant modifications to the general education standards and whose curriculum emphasizes functional life and social skills. To be eligible for participation in alternate assessment, the response to each of the statements below must be 'Agree.' If the answer to any of these questions is 'Disagree,' the team should consider including the student in the district and state standard assessments.

Check 'Agree' or 'Disagree' for each item:

☐ Agree   ☐ Disagree   The student requires extensive instruction in multiple settings to acquire, maintain and generalize skills necessary for application in school, work, home, and community environments.

☐ Agree   ☐ Disagree   The student demonstrates cognitive ability and adaptive behavior that require substantial adjustments to the general curriculum. The student may participate in many of the same activities as their non-disabled peers; however, their learning objectives and expected outcomes focus on the functional applications of the general curriculum.

☐ Agree   ☐ Disagree   The standard assessments do not reflect the content taught to the student.

☐ Agree   ☐ Disagree   The student will require support for post-school living.

      ☐ The team agrees that participation in the alternate assessment is **not primarily** based on:

         – an administrative decision, but an IEP team decision
         – the amount of time receiving special education services
         – excessive or extended absences
         – social, cultural or economic differences
         – Deaf/Blindness, visual, auditory and/or motor disabilities
         – achievement significantly lower than his or her same age peers
         – a specific categorical label

IEP Team Decision: **is eligible for participation in LBUSD Alternate Assessment.**

IEP Team Decision: **is not eligible for participation in LBUSD Alternate Assessment.**

LONG BEACH UNIFIED SCHOOL DISTRICT Form #IEP9   Distribution: Special Education Office–Original; Special Education teacher – 1 Copy,
Revised 7/01. Used by permission.   Parent – 1 Copy, CUM –1 Copu.

Box 5.6

2001 MCAS Participation Guidelines for Students With Disabilities

Massachusetts addresses the participation of students with disabilities within its assessment manual. Noting that a separate decision is to be made for the student in each subject scheduled for testing, four options are provided.

Option 1 – If the student is: a) engaged in an instructional program guided by the Curriculum Framework learning standards in this subject; and is b) working on learning standards at or near grade level; and is c) generally able to take a paper-and-pencil test either under routine conditions, or with one or more test accommodations
Then: The student should take the **standard MCAS test** in this subject, either routinely or with accommodation(s) that are consistent with instructional accommodation(s) used in the student's educational program.

Option 2 – If the student is: a) engaged in an instructional program guided by the Curriculum Framework learning standards in this subject; and is b) working on learning standards that have been modified and are below grade level due to the nature of the student's disability(ies); and is c) generally able to take a paper-and-pencil test under routine conditions, or with one or more test accommodations
Then: The student should take the **standard MCAS test** in this subject, either routinely or with accommodation(s) that are consistent with instructional accommodation(s) used in the student's educational program.

Option 3 – If the student is: a) engaged in an instructional program guided by the Curriculum Framework learning standards in this subject; and is b) working on learning standards that are at, near, or below grade level; and is c) generally able to take a paper-and-pencil test under routine conditions, or with one or more test accommodation(s); **but** is d) presented with unique and significant challenges in demonstrating his/her knowledge and skills on a test of this duration
Then: The student should take the **standard MCAS test** in this subject, with accommodations if necessary. However: The team may recommend an **alternate assessment** for the student when the nature and complexity of the student's disability prevent him/her from demonstrating his/her knowledge and skills on the test. (See section f on page 7 for examples of unique circumstances in which a student in this category may require an alternate assessment.)

Option 4 – If the student is: a) engaged in an instructional program guided by the Curriculum Framework learning standards in this subject; and is b) working on learning standards that have been substantially modified due to the nature and severity of the student's disability; and c) requires intensive, individualized instruction in order to acquire knowledge, make generalizations, and/or demonstrate skills in this subject; and is d) generally unable to demonstrate knowledge on a paper-and-pencil test, even with accommodations
Then: The student should take the **alternate assessment** in this subject. (Participation in alternate assessment(s) is intended for a very small number of students with significant disabilities.)

SOURCE: Retrieved from Massachusetts Department of Education Web site, January 2, (2002).

Box 5.7

Alternate Assessment Criteria in Kentucky

In order for a student to participate in the Alternate Portfolio Assessment Program, he/she must meet ALL of the following criteria:

- The student has a current Individual Education Plan
- The student's demonstrated cognitive ability and adaptive behavior itself prevents completion of the regular course of study even with program modifications and/or accommodations
- The student's current adaptive behavior requires extensive direct instruction in multiple settings to accomplish the application and transfer of skills necessary in school, work, home, and community environments
- The student's inability to complete the course of study may NOT be the result of excessive or extended absences; or it may NOT be primarily the result of visual or auditory disabilities, specific learning disabilities, emotional-behavioral disabilities, or social/cultural economic differences
- The student is unable to apply or use academic skills at a minimal competency level in natural settings (i.e., home, community, or work site) when instructed solely or primarily through school-based instruction
- The student is unable to acquire, maintain, or generalize skills, and demonstrate performance without intensive, frequent, and individualized community-based instruction
- The student is unable to complete a regular diploma program even with extended schooling and program modifications/accommodations

Students who do not meet ALL of these criteria CANNOT participate in the Alternate Portfolio Assessment Program. Those students are assessed in one of two other ways

- Take part in the Commonwealth Accountability Testing System (CATS) as is
- Take part in CATS with modifications/accommodations.

Students for whom an alternate assessment format might be appropriate are evaluated every year (usually at the yearly Admissions and Release Committee meeting) according to the preceding criteria. They may change assessment formats (alternate assessment or general assessment) due to whether or not they meet the criteria at that point.

SOURCE: http:// www.ihdi.uky.edu/kap/faq.asp Retrieved 1.2.02

states. Interviews and checklists are used as the primary data collection technique by only a few states. It is likely, however, that these and other techniques (e.g., observation, adaptive behavior scales) are used as additional or supporting documentation for portfolios or evidence folios.

Box 5.8

**What Is Assessed in Alternate Assessments
(Number of States with Each Focus)**

Focus of Assessment	1999	2000	2001
State or Expanded Standards	19	28	19
Skills Linked to State Standards	—	3	15
Standards Plus Additional Skills	1	7	9
Skills Only	16	9	4
Other or Uncertain Focus of Assessment	24	3	3

This appropriately allows IEP teams to determine how they will collect data on individual students.

One the most difficult tasks facing states is the reporting of alternate assessment results. States have developed a variety of performance measures to use in arriving at scores that can be used to report alternate assessment performance. Because alternate assessments generally are for a group of students never before assessed via large-scale assessments, they often measure more than just student skills. Thus, in addition to (or instead of) student performance, states may measure system performance. As is evident in Box 5.9, all states use some measure of student performance for their alternate assessments, with about 40 states measuring skill or competence. Nearly half of the states measure degree of progress in addition to or instead of skill/competence. Several states use level of independence and students' ability to generalize skills. A few states allow IEP teams to determine performance levels.

In terms of system performance measures, most states consider the variety of instructional settings, the level of staff support, and the appropriateness of settings. The measures that states use are translated in various ways to describe the performance of alternate assessment students. About equal numbers of states use the same performance descriptors as use different descriptors (see Box 5.10). In 2001, several states were still determining how student performance on the alternate assessment would be described. Because state and district alternate assessments are still under construction and revision, it is important to stay informed on what is happening. In fact, it is important to take part in what is happening!

Aggregating Results

States and districts must report alternate assessment results to the public, and use the data in school accountability systems. To do this, data must be aggregated—added together in some way to give an indication of group

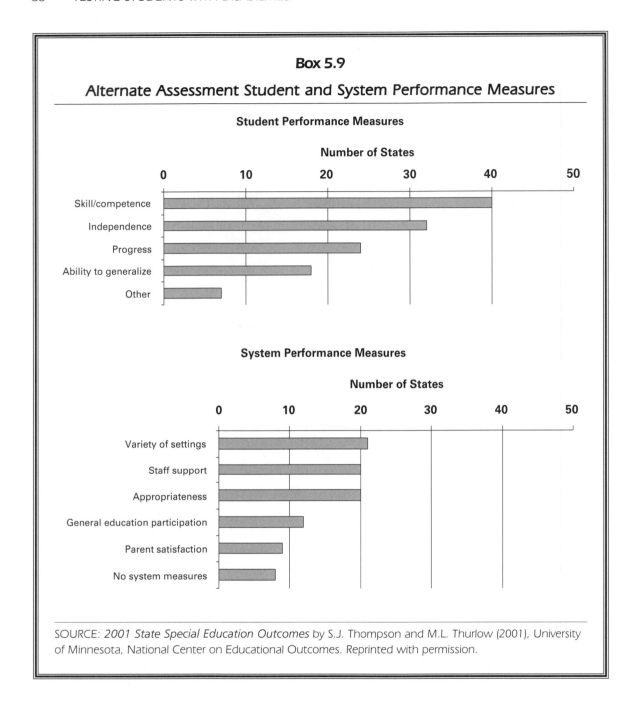

Box 5.9

Alternate Assessment Student and System Performance Measures

SOURCE: *2001 State Special Education Outcomes* by S.J. Thompson and M.L. Thurlow (2001), University of Minnesota, National Center on Educational Outcomes. Reprinted with permission.

results. In order to aggregate data, the alternate assessment must have a common set of domains or standards.

Here is an example to consider—two students in the alternate assessment are working on different skills within the content area of Career Development. The standard "Personal Growth and Development of Positive Peer Relations" is a general state standard that is not measured by the general assessment, but is considered an important target for the alternate assessment. The two students are instructed and work on this standard in different ways. Maria is working on mobility skills that include

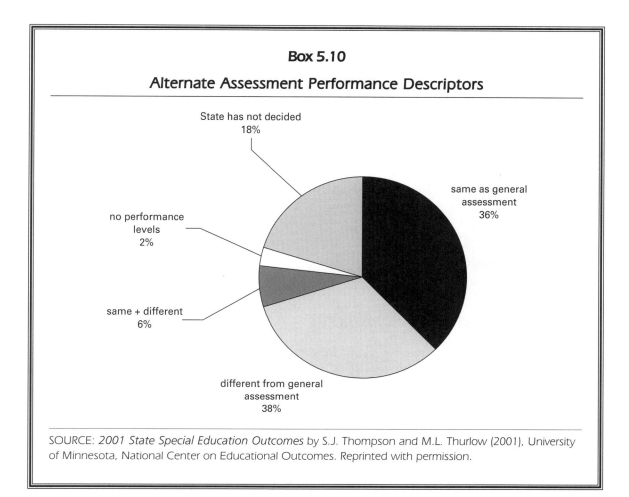

Box 5.10

Alternate Assessment Performance Descriptors

State has not decided 18%

same as general assessment 36%

no performance levels 2%

same + different 6%

different from general assessment 38%

SOURCE: *2001 State Special Education Outcomes* by S.J. Thompson and M.L. Thurlow (2001), University of Minnesota, National Center on Educational Outcomes. Reprinted with permission.

moving from the classroom to the bathroom, the lunchroom, and the door to the bus. At the same time, she is working on making needs known by communicating requests such as, "May I go to the bathroom?" "Is it time for lunch?" "Open the door," and "May I sit here?" Jose, on the other hand, is working on job skills. He is learning to maintain the cleanliness of the local health club. His job includes picking up old newspapers and magazines left near exercise equipment, vacuuming the carpet, and polishing the exercise equipment. Along with job skills, Jose is learning to get to work and leave work on time, punch in and out properly, and greet clients appropriately.

Despite differences in the focus of their instructional programs, both Maria and Jose can be assessed within the same areas and even the same standards. These standards are broader than just peer relations and include communication skills and reading skills. To aggregate results, states have had to clarify their standards, determine how to accurately score student and system performance, and set standards for proficiency level determinations. When this has been done, meaningful aggregation of scores can occur.

*Inclusive Accountability and
Reporting Alternate Assessment Results*

The way that student performance is described leads us directly into the discussion of how to report results. The goal of inclusive accountability is to have a single index for a school, district, or state that reflects the performance of *all* students. In order to be able to do this, proactive planning has to occur. Options must be considered. One option for reporting is to report scores from the general and the alternate assessment separately, but always to report both sets of scores. Another option is to use the same performance descriptors for both the general and alternate assessments, and then to simply put them together because they are equally valued. Although Kentucky was the first state to use such a method, several additional states have indicated that they have similar systems.

Examples of Alternate Assessments

In this section we provide you with examples of a few state alternate assessments and one district alternate assessment. We include them here to show a diverse sample of the types of alternate assessments thus far developed and implemented.

New York. The New York State Alternate Assessment (NYSSA) has been developed for students with severe disabilities ages 9-10, 13-14, and 16-17. NYSSA encompasses a datafolio of information in which students demonstrate their performance (3-5 pieces of evidence) on alternate performance indicators. Alternate performance indicators have been developed for each of New York's Regents' standards. These indicators are considered educational outcomes at a basic level. Performance that is collected over several months is documented through direct assessments that include student written work and other products, videotaping, audiotaping, or observation of the student demonstrating the performance task. A 4-point rubric is used for scoring. NYSAA also includes a parent survey that asks for the family's perception of student performance.

Eligibility Criteria. For students to participate in the NYSAA, they must have the following characteristics:

- A severe cognitive disability
- Significant deficits in communication/language and adaptive behavior
- AND, require a highly specialized educational program that facilitates the acquisition, application, and transfer of skills across natural environments
- AND require educational support systems such as: assistive technology, personal care services, or behavioral intervention.

Reporting Results. In 2000-2001, the number of students taking NYSSA was reported. In 2001-2002, both the number of students with disabilities participating in the NYSAA and their individual performance scores were reported.

General Comments. IEP teams are to identify what performance indicators will be targeted for each child. IEP teams are encouraged to identify indicators for each of the standards and assessments that are appropriate for each student. For example, some performance indicators may be at the alternate level and a few may be at the elementary level. IEP teams also decide how performance will be documented (e.g., locally developed assessments and other state assessments). For more information see http://web.nysed. gov/vesid/sped/AlterAssess/home.html

Oregon. Oregon has taken a two-pronged approach for its alternate assessment. Option 1 is an Extended Career and Life Role Assessment System (Extended CLRAS). Option 2 includes Extended Assessments.

The Extended CLRAS is a functional assessment approach for students with moderate to severe disabilities. These students are typically functioning in content areas that match Career and Life Role education standards of the Common Curriculum Goals. Two domains are assessed—Personal Management and Career Development. The Personal Management domain focuses on daily living activities. Five routines are selected for performance assessment from five categories: (1) Daily School: Living Skills; (2) Daily School: Transition; (3) Daily School: Academic Activities; (4) Leisure, and (5) Community. The Career Development domain focuses on vocational activities. Routines are selected from the following areas: (1) a School or Community Vocational Activity, and (2) Career Exploration Activity. At the same time that these routines are selected, the IEP team identifies other related skills from the student's IEP. All assessments in the Extended CLRAS are scored using a 4-point rating scale that measures independence (see Box 5.11).

Oregon's second alternate assessment option is the Extended Reading, Writing, and Mathematics assessments. These assessments assess academic content standards below the third grade benchmark level. They are one-on-one performance assessments. Oregon anticipates that one to two of every 10 students with IEPs will take the Extended Assessments. Most students on IEPs will take the general assessments with accommodations where necessary.

Eligibility Criteria. A student assessed by the extended CLRAS generally will meet the following criteria:

1. The student has previously been exempted from the available Certificate of Initial Mastery (CIM) assessments.

2. The student has IEP goals and objectives in the functional daily living skills area or participates in a functional daily living skills curriculum.

Box 5.11

Oregon's Independence Measurement Scale

---

4 = completes independently

3 = completes with visual, verbal, or gestural prompting

2 = completes with partial physical prompting (requires at least one physical prompt, but not continuous physical prompts)

1 = completes with full physical prompting (requires continuous physical prompts)

0 = does not complete even with physical prompting

N = not applicable (due to student's medical needs, the school environment does not provide an opportunity to perform, or the IEP team deems the routine/activity inappropriate for the student)

---

3. The student has been identified as having a moderate/severe disability (e.g., mental retardation, autism, multiple disabilities).

    a. The student is enrolled in grades 3, 5, 8, 10, or

    b. If the student's program is ungraded, as of September 1, the student's age is equivalent to other students in grades 3 (age 8), 5 (age 10), 8 (age 13) or 10 (age 15).

Students assessed by the Extended Reading, Writing, and Mathematics assessments are those judged to be performing below the third-grade level.

Reporting Results. The results of the Extended Assessments and the Extended CLRAS are reported in three ways: (1) individual student reports, (2) class rosters, and (3) districtwide reports. They are reported in a range from fully assisted to independent. They are not, however, reported in performance categories. They are reported separately for performance.

General Comments. Oregon is one of several states with a two-pronged alternate assessment. Like other states with this approach, Oregon has determined that this approach is needed to include all students in its assessment system. For more information see http://www.ode.state.or.us/asmt/faqs/faqextasmts.htm

Wyoming. Wyoming's alternate assessment is called the WyCAS-Alt (Wyoming Comprehensive Assessment System—Alternate). Students are assessed in grades 4, 8, and 11. Two standards areas are assessed in the WyCAS-Alt—Language Arts and Mathematics. The IEP team selects goals that meet a student's needs and which are aligned with expanded standards. At least two Language Arts and two Mathematics expanded standards must be addressed on a student's IEP (see Box 5.12). In addition, for

---

Box 5.12

Wyoming's Mathematics Expanded Standards

Number Operations and Concepts Expanded Standard: *Students use numbers, number sense, and number relationships in a problem-solving situation.*

Geometry Expanded Standard: *Students apply geometric concepts, properties, and relationships in a problem-solving situation.*

Measurement Expanded Standard: *Students use a variety of tools and techniques of measurement in a problem-solving situation.*

Algebraic Concepts and Relationships Expanded Standard: *Students use algebraic method to investigate, model, and interpret patterns and functions involving numbers, shapes, data, and graphs in a problem-solving situation.*

Tools and Technology Expanded Standard: *Students use appropriate tools and technologies to model, measure, and apply the results in a problem-solving situation.*

Problem-solving and Mathematical Reasoning Expanded Standards: *Students apply a variety of problem-solving strategies to investigate and solve problems from across the curriculum as well as from practical applications.*

---

each of these standards, a Real World Performance Indicator must be assessed. A minimum of two assessment strategies must be used to assess progress toward these four expanded standards. These strategies include assessment evidence such as recording sheets, observation forms, checklists, and videos. It is expected that these assessment strategies are not an add-on but part of the daily instruction-assessment process within the classroom. A scoring and reporting form is completed for each of the four expanded standards assessed. One of three performance levels is assigned to each expanded standard assessed—Skilled, Partially Skilled, or Beginner.

Eligibility Criteria. Students participating in the WyCAS-Alt must meet the following participation validation criteria:

1. The student's demonstrated cognitive functioning and adaptive behavior in home, school, and community environments are significantly below age expectations, even with program accommodations and adaptations.

2. The student requires extensive direct instruction and/or extensive supports in multiple settings to acquire, maintain, and generalize skills necessary for application in school, work, home, and community environments.

3. Decisions about participation have been made/reviewed within the past year, and were based on the student's curriculum, present level of educational performance, skill levels, and learning characteristics.

Reporting Results. Wyoming has common standards in Language Arts and Mathematics toward which all students need to be working. By expanding these two areas, Wyoming has provided a way to include all students and has linked its alternate assessment to the general education standards. While all students in WyCAS are reported in the state's accountability system, results of the WyCAS-Alt cannot be aggregated or combined because they are not on the same scoring scale. The results from the two assessment systems must be reported separately—but they are reported! Individual student reports are distributed to parents and schools. School-level results are produced for schools and districts in the state.

General Comments. By expanding Language Arts and Mathematic standards to include all students, Wyoming has linked its alternate assessment to the general education standards. Rates of non-participation of students with disabilities and the reasons for the non-participation are included in reports to the public. Wyoming believes that reporting the non-participation numbers will assist in pinpointing ways to increase participation of students with disabilities in assessments. For more information see http://measured progress.org/wycas/AltAssess/AltImplementation.html

Long Beach Unified School District (LBUSD). LBUSD is located in Southern California and is the third largest urban school district in the United States. With approximately 7% of the 97,000-student school district receiving special education, LBUSD has led the state in its development of the district's alternate assessment. LBUSD developed its alternate assessment around the following domains: Personal and Social Adjustment, Vocational, Self-Care, Communication and Self-Advocacy, Motor and Mobility, and Functional Academics. Within each domain are LBUSD's content standards. Each standard has a set of curriculum objectives. For each set of objectives, sample performance indicators were developed (see Box 5.13).

Secured performance events were developed to assess standards within each domain. These performance events are administered during the same testing window as the required statewide assessment. The secured prompts are administered across the following levels: Kindergarten, Primary, Intermediate, Middle School, and High School. The prompts are scored using a 6-point rubric. Each prompt renders two scores; one score for content and one score for independence. The content rubrics are task specific. In other words, for a student to receive a '6' for content, he or she must demonstrate all performance events listed in the rubric. To receive a '6' on the independence rubric, a student must demonstrate a specific level of behavior (see Box 5.14).

Eligibility Criteria. IEP teams use an assessment decision-making checklist to make eligibility decisions. As part of each student's IEP, the participation

---

Box 5.13

Sample Domain, Standards, and Performance Indicators

Domain: Personal and Social Adjustment

Content Area: Health

Standard 3: Behaviors to Reduce Risk Students will demonstrate the ability to use behaviors that reduce the risk of becoming involved in potentially dangerous situations and react to potentially dangerous situations in a way that helps to protect their health.

Curriculum Objectives:
- develop and use appropriate behaviors to identify, avoid, and cope with dangerous situations
- describe how to safely interact with strangers
- develop and use effective communication skills
- identify and respond appropriately to emergencies

Sample Performance Indicators:
Student will:
- know name and recognize it in print
- identify address and phone number
- know that dialing '911' will bring emergency assistance
- know that fire is dangerous and can be hurtful
- know to look both ways before crossing the street
- respond to signs in the community (e.g., exit, walk/don't walk, stop)

---

criteria checklist is completed every year as a part of the IEP process (see Box 5.5).

Reporting Results. Results of the LBUSD alternate assessment are available by student, classroom, school site, and district. All reports give results on all domains as well as content and independence scales. Parents receive individual student reports and peer comparisons. Teachers receive individual student, classroom, and district comparisons. School site administrators receive their building scores and district comparisons. District data for the general assessment and the alternate assessment are not aggregated.

General Comments. LBUSD was able to show that approximately 5% of its total special education population took the alternate assessment. All other students participated in the district and statewide assessment with and without accommodations. In spring 2002, a standards-based alternate portfolio will be added to the current alternate assessment developed in LBUSD. It will be fully implemented districtwide in 2003.

Box 5.14

Explanation of Scoring Rubric Used in Long Beach

Domain 1: Personal/Social Adjustment
Health
Standard 3: Behaviors to Reduce Risk

Middle School Performance Indicator: Student will simulate dialing 911 for emergency.

Content Score
To score a 6, student will
- ❑ identify an emergency situation via television clip, pictures etc.
- ❑ pick up the telephone
- ❑ push or dial 911
- ❑ verbalize "HELP!", "Emergency!", etc.

To score a 5, student will
- ❑ when given a choice of three different situations, identify an emergency situation
- ❑ pick up the telephone
- ❑ push or dial 911
- ❑ attempt communication on the telephone

To score a 4, student will
- ❑ when given a choice of two different situations, identify an emergency situation
- ❑ pick up the telephone
- ❑ push or dial 911

To score a 3, student will
- ❑ when directed to, pick up the telephone
- ❑ push or dial 911

To score a 2, student will
- ❑ when directed to, pick up the telephone
- ❑ push or dial any number(s) in 911

To score a 1, student will
- ❑ pick up the telephone
- ❑ dial random numbers

	0	1	2	3	4	5	6
Please circle One Independence Score	No Performance (describe reason)	Tolerates/ attempts engagement	Performs skill with intensive physical prompt	Performs skill with slight physical prompt	Performs skill with gesture and verbal/sign prompt	Performs skill with verbal/sign prompt	Performs skill independently

Expectations, staff development, and opportunities for buy-in are critical to the success of LBUSD's alternate assessment. District and school site administrators are now aware of the instruction and assessment expectations for all students with disabilities, including those with the most significant disabilities. Finally, the quality of the IEPs for all students has skyrocketed! For more information see www.lbusd.k12.ca.us, Office of Special Education.

Evaluating the Effectiveness of the Alternate Assessment

So in the big picture of assessment, what does the alternate assessment really mean to accountability systems, teachers, instruction, and kids? How do we know it is worth the effort? How do we know it works? "Seems like a lot of work for a few kids," someone recently said. The impetus for this "work" is, of course, grounded in IDEA 97.

A national study by Kleinert and Kearns (2001) looked at the impact of alternate assessment. Forty-four national authorities in best practices for students with more significant cognitive disabilities were asked to respond to a number of issues surrounding alternate assessments. The most important indicator identified by these authorities was the ability of students to function in integrated environments. In fact, over 20% of the respondents cautioned against the use of only functional domains. One reason is that the use of only functional domains often sends a message contrary to a student's participation in general education classes. In fact, many respondents indicated that general education classes were important vehicles for students to achieve functional outcomes.

The results of this national study showed that leading authorities in the field strongly believe that students with significant disabilities should take an alternate assessment that is based on the same standards or learner outcomes (or at least a subset of them) that all students should know and be able to do.

A Common Core of Questions. Questions continue to be raised about the use and impact of the alternate assessment. Some of these critical questions include:

What will schools and districts do with the alternate assessment results? We have provided you with a few examples of alternate assessments. The examples are diverse in how the alternate assessment systems conduct and report results. Still, we recognize that it is naive to think that everyone embraces the concept of assessing students with significant cognitive disabilities. At a special education pre-convention workshop, one teacher voiced her concern about the alternate assessment: "Why would my Superintendent care if my student has mastered catching drool on a tennis wrist band with 100% accuracy?" The discussion that ensued following this comment centered around the following: "What part of 'all' don't we understand?" All means each and every child. No child left behind. This means that the next step in many places really is to look at their alternate assessment results to make sure they mean something, and then, to try to have an impact on these results by improving the instruction provided to students with the most significant disabilities.

With all the paperwork special education teachers have, isn't the alternate assessment just another piece of paper on the pile? No! A recent survey conducted by the Council for Exceptional Children looked at the amount of time general and special education teachers spend in paperwork-related activity. The score: General education teachers – 5.* hours. Special education teachers – 5.* hours. Sure we have IEPs; however, general education teachers who have 130 students' writing portfolios to grade, for example, have the same load.

While general education teachers may complain about district and state assessments, they do it and realize the importance of preparing students for these assessments and the critical nature of test results. Sure it could be another task or piece of paper, but the bottom line is assessment drives instruction and lets all constituents know what students should know and be able to do.

Have instructional practices really changed as a result of including all students with disabilities, even those with significant disabilities, in assessments? It depends who you ask. Highly correlated with the answer is knowledge about the alternate assessment and the rationale behind its use and development. A survey completed by Costello, Turner, Kearns, and Kleinert (2000) found that there were strikingly different perceptions about these critical variables:

- Changes in school practices as a result of the alternate assessment
- Impact of the alternate assessment on the quality of IEPs and classroom instruction
- The extent to which teachers felt they were supported by the school

Like any innovation adopted in education, its success often is heavily reliant on administrative leadership. Even if the leadership is not there, we can all step up to the plate and advocate for not what might be, but for what always should have been—accountability for all students. No longer should we hear a special education teacher say "I feel like a second class citizen in my building," "I am looked at as a babysitter for these kids, not a teacher!" The law and strong leaders are moving inclusive accountability forward. Less and less often should we hear stories like the one about an uncooperative school board that years ago refused to support inclusive accountability for all students, including students with disabilities. Despite many board workshops and discussions of why, no progress was made. Then, a school board member's son was hit on the head by the ball during physical education. At that instant, he became a student with a Traumatic Brain Injury. From that day forward the Board of Education attended to inclusive accountability and quality programs for students with special needs. We no longer need to wait for tragic circumstances to lead to change and responsibility for the learning of all students.

What is in it for the students? Ask the students! In a survey conducted by the Long Beach Unified School District after its first administration of the alternate assessment, students and teachers were interviewed. The results were astounding. A resounding theme throughout the surveys was that for the first time both teachers and students felt that they were part of the school (and district). Teachers unequivocally indicated that "finally someone is paying attention to our kids!" One parent said, "I have never, in all the years that Sara has been in school, ever received an assessment report that showed how she was doing in comparison to other students her age. The parent report was just like the one I got for her brother on the SAT9." Student responses showed that, of the students who were interviewed, they really took "it" seriously. The fact that the entire school, including students of the alternate assessment, were geared up for the testing window that occurred for all students at the same time had a significant impact on all teachers' attitudes and appreciation for those teachers who teach students with cognitive and physical challenges.

Asking questions like those posed here is an important part of evaluating your alternate assessment. A critical aspect of any assessment system is evaluating it, and improving it as needed. The alternate assessment is no different. Because it is so new, evaluation and revision is perhaps even more important than for the general assessment. A sound evaluation plan—one that looks for input from varied stakeholders, and also looks for improvements in performance—is essential.

Summary

In this chapter, we have explored alternate assessments—the final piece of the assessment puzzle that enables states and districts to assess the performance of *all* students. We discussed who is eligible for the alternate assessment and the role of the alternate assessment in inclusive accountability and reporting. We also looked at several examples of alternate assessments. We concluded with common evaluation questions that need to be asked as alternate assessments are revised and improved.

Alternate assessments provide the opportunity to truly create an accountability system that includes all students. While states continue to establish, define, and refine how students' alternate assessment results will be used in state accountability systems, the potential for improved IEPs and instruction can be capitalized on right now. The fact that special educators do not understand or embrace the alternate assessment must be addressed immediately. Capitalizing on the instructional possibilities doesn't come without hard work to show the relevance of the alternate assessments.

The alternate assessment is but one additional tool to drive improved instruction and better standards-based IEPs. We know, because we have witnessed first hand and have spent an awful lot of time reviewing and discussing alternate assessment systems across the country. Attitude is everything!

Box 5.15

Myth or Truth Answers

TRUTH   There is still confusion about who should take an alternate assessment.
<u>Explanation:</u> Students who participate in the alternate assessment should be those for whom the regular assessment is not appropriate due for two major reasons: (1) any and all accommodations that might be provided to students still do not enable them to participate, and (2) students are working on instructional goals that are not assessed by the assessment. [See pages 82-83]

MYTH   Alternate assessments are performance events that allow students to show what they can do on a specific task.
<u>Explanation:</u> Many approaches are used for alternate assessments. Most states use a portfolio or body of evidence approach. [See page 86]

MYTH   All teachers, including special education teachers embrace the concept and practice of the alternate assessment for students with significant cognitive disabilities.
<u>Explanation:</u> Personnel across the country are still struggling to understand why all students need to be assessed, and why students with the most significant disabilities need to be assessed. [See page 97]

TRUTH   The general impact of the alternate assessment has been positive.
<u>Explanation:</u> It depends on who you ask. We say "Yes!" [See page 98]

Now, check your knowledge about the myth/truth statements presented at the beginning of this chapter (see Box 5.15 for answers). Try to give an explanation for why each statement is correctly identified either as a myth or as the truth.

Resources for Further Information

Costello, K., Turner, M., Kearns, J., & Kleinert, H. (2000). Teacher and principal perceptions of the impact of alternate assessments on school accountability and instructional practices. Manuscript in preparation.

Elliott, J., & Roeber, E. (1996). *Assessment accommodations for students with disabilities*. (Videotape recording). Alexandria, VA: National Association of State Directors of Special Education.

Kleinert, H., & Kearns, J. (1999). A validation study of the performance indicators and learner outcomes of Kentucky's alternate assessment for students with significant disabilities. *Journal of the Association for Persons with Severe Handicaps*, 24(2), 100-110.

Kleinert, H., & Kearns, J. (2001). *Alternate assessment: Measuring outcomes and supports for students with disabilities*. Baltimore: Brookes.

Olsen, K., & Ysseldyke, J. (1997). *Alternate assessment.* (Videotape recording). Alexandria, VA: National Association of State Directors of Special Education.

Salvia, J., & Ysseldyke, J. E. (2001) *Assessment* (8th ed.). Boston: Houghton Mifflin.

Thompson, S., Quenemoen, R., Thurlow, M., & Ysseldyke, J. (2001). *Alternate assessments for students with disabilities.* Thousand Oaks, CA; Corwin Press.

Thompson, S., & Thurlow, M. (2000). *State alternate assessments: Status as IDEA alternate assessment requirements take effect* (Synthesis Report 35). Minneapolis, MN: University of Minnesota, National Center on Educational Outcomes.

Thompson, S., & Thurlow, M. (2001). *2001 state special education outcomes: A report on state activities at the beginning of a new decade.* Minneapolis, MN: University of Minnesota, National Center on Educational Outcomes.

Thurlow, M., Olsen, K., Elliott, J., Ysseldyke, J., Erickson, R., & Ahearn, E. (1996). *Alternate assessments for students with disabilities: For students unable to participate in general large-scale assessment* (NCEO Policy Directions 5.) Minneapolis: University of Minnesota, National Center on Educational Outcomes.

Thurlow, M., Ysseldyke, J., Erickson, R., & Elliott, J. (1997). *Increasing the participation of students with disabilities in state and district assessments* (NCEO Policy Directions 5). Minneapolis: University of Minnesota, National Center on Educational Outcomes.

Ysseldyke, J. E., & Olsen, K. (1997). *Putting alternate assessments into practice: Possible sources of data.* Minneapolis: University of Minnesota, National Center of Educational Outcomes.

Ysseldyke, J. E., & Olsen, K., & Thurlow, M. (1997). *Issues and considerations in alternate assessments.* Minneapolis: University of Minnesota, National Center of Educational Outcomes.

Ysseldyke, J. E., & Thurlow, M. L. (1994). *Guidelines for inclusion of students with disabilities in large-scale assessments* (NCEO Policy Directions 1). Minneapolis: University of Minnesota, National Center of Educational Outcomes.

Ysseldyke, J. E., Thurlow, M. L., & Olsen, K. (1996). *Self-study guide for the development of statewide assessments that include students with disabilities.* Minneapolis: University of Minnesota, National Center of Educational Outcomes.

Including English Language Learners With Disabilities in District and State Assessments

In this chapter, you will . . .

- examine who these IEP/LEP students are
- identify the ways in which IEP/LEP students can participate in assessments
- become familiar with accommodations for IEP/LEP students
- learn what research says about the participation and performance of IEP/LEP students in state assessments.

The diversity of students in U.S. schools continues to increase. As it does so, more and more students are coming to school with limited English proficiency. And, with requirements that all students be included in assessments, these students now must be considered as decisions are made about participation and accommodations. The information in this chapter is derived from a chapter we developed for our book, *Improving Test Performance*

This chapter is an adaptation of Chapter 11, "Addressing the Assessment Needs of Students with Disabilities Who Are Learning English: The IEP/LEP Population," in *Improving Test Performance of Students With Disabilities On District and State Assessments* by Judy L. Elliott and Martha L. Thurlow (Corwin, 2000).

Box 6.1

Myth or Truth? Do You Know?

Read each statement below and decide whether it is a myth or the truth about current practice.

- *The disability issues of students with disabilities who also have limited English proficiency really cannot be addressed until the language limitations are addressed.*
- *Current demographic estimates confirm that the number of students considered to be IEP/LEP students will continue to increase over the years.*
- *Since academic language proficiency is limited in IEP/LEP students, they really cannot be included in testing that is presented in English.*
- *Accommodations are often needed by IEP/LEP students to address their needs related to both disability and limited language proficiency.*
- *It is critical that sufficient collaboration occur among the programs that work with IEP/LEP students, both for instruction and for assessments.*

---

of Students With Disabilities, where we first recognized the importance of addressing the issues that surround the assessment of English language learners with disabilities. (We use the shorthand IEP/LEP in this chapter.)

The number of IEP/LEP students varies from one place to the next, dependent to a great extent on the population of non-English speakers in communities across the country. The numbers are not directly related, however, because we do not yet know how to accurately diagnose disabilities in students who are learning to speak English.

In this chapter we intend to give some of the basic information that you need to begin to make good decisions about how these students participate in assessments—whether in the regular assessment or in an alternate—and the nature of accommodations that should be considered for these students. First, we describe who these students are—how many there are, what their characteristics are, and other similar information. Then we address how to make decisions about their participation in assessments, what accommodations they may need, and how their scores should be reported.

We do not have all the answers when it comes to students with disabilities who have limited English proficiency. But, we do have some basic assumptions for you to consider, and some starting steps for you to take as you include these students in district and state assessments. By the time that you finish this chapter, you will be able to identify which of the statements in Box 6.1 are myths and which are the truth.

Who Are IEP/LEP Students?

Let's start with some terminology. We often use the term "limited English proficient" student. We selected that term because it is the one used in federal legislation. But, there are many more terms used in schools, districts, and states today. Some of the more common terms, and the fine distinctions among them, are provided in Box 6.2. As you will note in this list of words, there are some terms that might be used interchangeably, such as English language learners, or ELLs, and limited English proficient students, or LEP students, because they generally refer to the same group of students. There are other terms that have very different meanings, and that may be misused by those who really don't understand the differences among the groups. A common mistake is to equate students whose home language is other than English (commonly referred to as NELB, or non-English language background) and students who are limited in their English language proficiency, or LEP.

Another complication related to terminology is that the same student may be considered to have limited English proficiency for some purposes and not for others. For example, a student may not count as having limited English proficiency when the school decides whether he or she is eligible for ESL (English as a Second Language) or Bilingual Education services. But the same student may count as having limited English proficiency when the state or district determines whether the student will participate in its assessment. In some states and districts, a test of English language proficiency may be used to determine participation in an assessment, while in other states, regardless of performance on a language proficiency test, the number of years that a student has been in the U.S. or in an English speaking school is the basis for determining whether the student participates in the district or state assessment. More about this later when we get into making decisions about participation in assessments, and the implications for instruction, but suffice it to say that limited English proficiency is not a simple thing.

One more complication needs to be mentioned before we move on to the LEP student who has a disability. Because students with limited English proficiency have different language backgrounds, there are associated differences in their educational histories. These students may or may not have been born in the United States. They may or may not have come from a country with an educational system. They may or may not have attended the educational system if one existed. They may have been in their home country's educational system for 10 years or 5 years or 1 year (and all the variations in between) before coming to the U.S. Not only are the educational systems varied and the amount of time that the student may have been in them varied, but other experiential factors may have varied as well. For example, many students in the U.S. who arrived from war torn countries may have spent considerable time in hiding or in refugee camps. All of these kinds of educational and experiential differences are intertwined with the language complexities that these students carry with them.

In a nutshell, IEP/LEP students are those students who have limited English proficiency (or who are English language learners) who also have been determined to have a disability. The complication, as you might guess, is in determining that a disability exists when there is a language difficulty that impedes our ability to identify a disability. That this is a problem is obvious, since we already have difficulty identifying disabilities

Box 6.2

Clarification of Terminology

Term	Definition	Equivalent Terms*	Non-Equivalent Terms
Bilingual Student	Student who speaks two languages; one of the languages may be English		LEP Student
Bilingual Education Student	Student in the process of learning English and at the same time content in his or her first language		ESL Student
English Language Learner (ELL)	Student in the process of learning the English language, either oral or written	LEP Student, LM Student	ESL Student, Bilingual Ed Student
ESL Student	Student learning English through English as a Second Language classes		Bilingual Ed Student
Language Minority (LM) Student	Student whose first language is in the minority in the educational setting in which he or she is located	LEP Student, ELL	ESL Student, Bilingual Ed Student
Non-English Language Background (NELB)	Student whose home language is other than English, regardless of whether the student is fully English proficient	LEP Student, ELL, LM Student	
Second Language Learner	An individual learning a second language; the first language may or may not be English		ELL, LEP Student

*Generally, fine distinctions are made between these terms. However, in practice they are often used interchangeably.

in those who are proficient in the English language. And, of course, the difficulty is not so much in identifying students who have physical disabilities or severe cognitive disabilities. The difficulties arise most often related to disabilities that are not outwardly evident, such as learning disabilities, emotional disabilities, and even sensory disabilities. The challenges of conducting sound psychoeducational assessments are considerable. And, these challenges are complicated, as we will note later, by the difficulty of convening IEP teams that recognize the complications and that can sort them out in the decision-making process.

How Many Are There?

It is difficult to say exactly how many there are of something that we don't have common definitions for, and that we don't have a counting system for. But, we can get some estimates, and we certainly know a lot about trends.

First, let's get a little handle on students with limited English proficiency (without the disabilities). Current estimates across the U.S. are that anywhere from approximately 3 to 10 million or more of all school-age children have limited English proficiency, however defined by the school, district, or state. The estimates vary greatly depending on where one lives. There are several states where the estimated percentage of school-age LEP students is close to 25%. Most of the largest states (California, Texas, Florida, New York) and less so some of the other large states (for example, Illinois) have the majority of students with limited English proficiency. Box 6.3 shows the 10 states with the largest number and largest percentage of total enrollment. It is interesting to note that when looking at the percentage of the total student population who have limited English proficiency, several additional states emerge in the list of "top 10," such as Utah and the District of Columbia, and other states disappear from the "top 10," such as Washington, New Jersey, and Massachusetts.

Looking at state distributions of students with limited English proficiency does not provide a completely accurate picture of the composition of school districts within the state. There are some states with relatively small populations of students with limited English proficiency overall, that have significant populations of these students within some of their large districts. Examples of these are in St. Paul, Minnesota. Minnesota is a state that is often viewed as a typical Midwestern, homogenous Caucasian state. Yet, even though the overall population of LEP students in the state is quite small, in St. Paul over 40% of its students are English language learners—and the increase in LEP students in the past 5 years has been over 200%.

When thinking about how many LEP students there are, it is also important to consider trends in numbers. It is not the case that these students are here now, but that as they learn English, we will have diminishing numbers of these students. Current demographic estimates confirm that the number of students with limited English proficiency will continue to increase over the years, not decrease. It is expected that there

Box 6.3

States With Largest Populations of LEP Students, By Number and By Percentage, 2002

Top 10 States by Number of LEP Students		Top 10 States by Percentage of LEP Students	
State	**Number**	**State**	**Percentage**
1. California	1,406,527	1. California	24.9%
2. Texas	554,949	2. New Mexico	23.6%
3. Florida	235,181	3. Alaska	14.8%
4. New York	228,730	4. Arizona	14.7%
5. Illinois	228,730	5. Texas	13.9%
6. Arizona	125,311	6. Nevada	12.4%
7. New Mexico	76,661	7. Florida	9.9%
8. Colorado	60,031	8. Utah	8.6%
9. Washington	55,709	9. Colorado	8.5%
10. New Jersey	49,847	10. New York, Oregon	8.0%

will be more than 100 different languages in many of our mid- to large-size school districts.

Given all this, how many IEP/LEP students are there? We don't know. But, we can guess. The presence of disabilities would be expected to be fairly evenly distributed across language groups. That would mean, given current estimates of disability, that approximately 10% of all students with limited English proficiency also have a disability. The percentage of students actually receiving special education services may be smaller since we have a more difficult time identifying disability in students with limited English proficiency. Of course, you can see where this is going. Even if we are talking about only 5% of students with limited English proficiency also having a disability, then as the numbers of LEP students increase, so will the number of students who are IEP/LEP students. The numbers should skyrocket in the next 10 to 20 years!

What Is the Language of LEP Students?

Overall, Spanish is the most prevalent first language of students with limited English proficiency in the United States. That is true in the largest states, as well as in many large districts regardless of the state. But, it is not universally true. For example, in St. Paul, the most common language is Hmong, followed by Vietnamese, Cambodian, and Laotian; then comes Spanish. In many states and districts there are over 75 different languages represented among the students in the schools. Of course, this brings in lots of complications!

But, the home language is only the tip of the proverbial iceberg. Students who receive instruction in U.S. schools typically receive their content instruction in English, perhaps supported by something in their first language. It is pretty commonly accepted that students learning English first learn social English—that is, they learn to communicate with their peers and perhaps their teacher about social topics. Learning social English typically (complicated by all the other factors mentioned earlier) takes 3 to 5 years. Social English is not the same as academic English—the language of instruction. Academic English may take 7 to 10 years to master. Yet, it is the language in which most students receive instruction. So, the answer for assessment may be not to provide a translated version of a test, because the student has not learned the content in his or her first language.

The differences between social and academic language have been studied extensively by language learning theorists. The terms that may be heard are "BICS" for "Basic Interpersonal Communication Skills" and "CALP" for "Cognitive Academic Language Proficiency." It is generally accepted that students must reach a threshold of BICS before CALP can develop. In addition, however, the development of CALP is dependent on academic reasoning skills, which are more likely to exist or develop more quickly if the student has strong language skills in his or her first language, which in turn is facilitated by coming from a literate home background. To further complicate the issues, certain content areas may require a longer time for CALP to develop than others. For example, reading, social studies, and science are generally considered to require more time for CALP to develop, while math and language arts may take less time.

These language issues, of course, complicate not only the diagnosis of disability, but they also complicate how to make good decisions about participation in district and state assessments, accommodations that are needed, and whether some type of alternate assessments are needed.

What Comes First—IEP or LEP?

This question may be unanswerable. In terms of legal rights, if a student has an IEP, all the rights that are connected to that IEP are held by the student. Yet, all the issues and difficulties created by the student's limited proficiency in English also apply.

When most people ask questions about what comes first, they are really asking about who is responsible for the dollars required to meet the student's needs. This is especially true if there are special accommodations needed—either for instruction or for assessment. What we know is that this type of question does little to help the student. It is likely that there needs to be an integration of dollars and services, so that the needs of all are met equally.

We suggest that the question of "what comes first" is a non-question. Even if we could come up with an answer, it would be of little benefit to the student or to anyone else in the system.

Participation of IEP/LEP Students in District and State Assessments

The participation of students with limited English proficiency in district and state assessments is not something that is covered by federal law, other than through the Elementary and Secondary Education Act (ESEA). This act requires that Title I programs be evaluated by reporting the performance of students on state and district assessments tied to standards, and that the performance of students with limited English proficiency (like the performance of students with disabilities) be disaggregated from the overall performance of all students. The intent of this requirement is to enable us to examine the performance of these traditionally low-performing groups. In the 2001 reauthorization of ESEA, Title III requires that there also be assessments of the English proficiency of LEP students. This is a new requirement that is designed to ensure that students are learning English.

Despite federal laws, states and districts differ on their requirements for the participation of students with limited English proficiency in their assessments. This confusion, when coupled with IDEA requirements for students with disabilities means that we have a muddy set of guidelines for determining whether or how an LEP student with a disability should participate in state and district assessments. So, does this mean that all students with disabilities are supposed to participate in either the regular assessment or an alternate assessment, or does the complication of limited English proficiency automatically qualify that student for the alternate assessment? Does a policy that LEP students are exempted from district or state assessments for a period of time supersede the disability requirements that students participate in state and district assessments? Can primary language tests, which assess students in their own language (generally Spanish), provide adequate measures of what the state or district test attempts to measure? Does the IDEA requirement that students be assessed in their native language apply to state and district assessments?

Looking at state policies gives us little guidance for how things should be for IEP/LEP students. Only a few states now address these students specifically in their assessment policies. One states that does is Texas. It has a description of how to make appropriate testing decisions for IEP/LEP students and a description of which accommodations these students are eligible to receive on state tests. The guidelines are available on the Texas Web site in both Spanish and English.

We believe that if a student has a disability, that student should participate in the regular or alternate assessment, under the same guidelines as other students with disabilities. The caveat is that the assessment must occur in the language of instruction, or perhaps even better, in the student's language of choice. We use the term "language of choice" because of the problems with social language versus academic language, and all the other complications of educational and experiential background. The IEP team should take into consideration the language characteristics of the IEP/LEP student.

Of course, things are not always ideal, and "language of choice" may not always be a viable option. There are tests, such as English tests, that preclude allowing the student to use his or her language of choice. Similarly there are now many states that insist that the student demonstrate English skills in all content areas in order to earn a high school diploma. This situation makes it much more difficult to develop and implement what might be considered "best practice" in the assessment of IEP/LEP students.

It is also important to think about the goals of the students' instruction. These goals should include both academic content (or functional skills, as appropriate) and the learning of the English language. Thus, state and district assessments for IEP/LEP students perhaps should encompass more than they do for those students for whom we are not worried about assessing their language acquisition. This is the thinking behind the new requirement that states assess the acquisition of English, to ensure that the student is making progress in this essential skill at the same time that the state/district is measuring acquisition of content knowledge and skills.

Accommodations

IEP/LEP students often need accommodations to address their needs related to both their disabilities and their limited English proficiency. You may wonder whether the accommodations needed would be the same. It seems logical that these students may need extra time, and maybe a separate setting. But, are there some accommodations that might be needed for their language concerns and others for their disability concerns?

Since we are dealing with humans, whose needs don't nicely separate between those related to disability and those related to language, it is probably not beneficial to analyze a student's needs separately. Instructionally, this kind of division makes little sense. However, lists of accommodations that are allowed for assessments may or may not be separated for students with disabilities and students with limited English proficiency. Sometimes when the listed accommodations are divided, they just say the same things but have different labels. But, more often now, the lists are divided and different kinds of accommodations are included in each list. If this is the case, you will need to have both lists at hand, and you will need to be able to justify the need for accommodations in one or the other list. A list of some common LEP accommodations is included in Box 6.4. These are ones taken from state-level accommodations policies for LEP students.

Making decisions about the accommodations that IEP/LEP students need should follow the same basic procedures as decisions about accommodations for any student—they should be related to what happens in

Box 6.4

Common LEP Accommodations

Setting	Scheduling/Timing
Bilingual Education or ESL classroom Individualized setting	Extended time Frequent breaks

Presentation	Response
English dictionary/glossary Familiar examiner Translated test items	First language responses acceptable Scribe writes responses

instruction and they should meet the specific needs of the student. Setting up a questionnaire that gets at needs works for IEP/LEP students.

Reporting Scores

The reporting of scores on state and district assessments becomes even more complicated when we are talking about students with disabilities who have limited English proficiency. Should the scores of these students be included with the scores of all other IEP students? Should these scores be included instead with the scores of LEP students? Or, should a separate group of students be formed—those students with limited English proficiency who are on IEPs.

Answering the question of how scores should be reported is less difficult if we go back to some basic assumptions and some considerations about the type of data needed to make good decisions for instruction. First, our assumptions. If we assume that all students can learn, and that the learning of all students is the responsibility of educators, then there is no question that the scores of IEP/LEP students must be included in the scores reported—somewhere.

When we consider what kind of information is needed to make good instructional decisions—decisions about programs for students—then it becomes clear that we need the data reported for the subgroup of students with limited English proficiency who are on IEPs. This approach, however, does not preclude the reports from also including students in with those students with limited English proficiency, and in with those students on IEPs.

The reason that it is important to have data just on IEP/LEP students is that this level of information will help us to more clearly see how these students are doing—relative to other students with disabilities, and relative to other students with limited English proficiency. The exception for public reporting, of course, is that if the number of students in this group is too small, it should not be reported. The fact that data are not reported publicly, however, should not preclude those educators working with the students from seeing how they are performing so that programs and instruction can be changed as needed.

With the passage of the Title I legislation (Improving America's Schools Act) in 1994, it became clear that students with disabilities and English Language Learners have the disadvantage of being subjected to little research. This is changing. Recent work within the Office of Bilingual Education and Language Minority Affairs (OBEMLA) is identifying expected gains in LEP student achievement and ways to achieve and document those gains. Other research is examining ways to ensure the accurate scoring of LEP assessments. Recently the Office of Special Education Programs provided funding for research on the issues involved in including IEP/LEP students in assessments and in using assessment data to improve instruction for these students. In the next several years, more and more information should be available on how best to include these students in assessments, reporting, and accountability systems.

As we await research-based information, discussions about what to do assessment-wise for these students also have been initiated. Suggestions made by the National Research Council in *Testing, Teaching, and Learning* (see Box 6.5) are a first step in thinking about LEP students in assessments. For example, exposure of students to assessments in the classroom is one way to familiarize LEP/IEP students with the process. Another is to develop and then use specific procedures for deciding what accommodations individual students need to participate in assessments. These suggestions, and others, of course, may need to be adapted for IEP/LEP students.

Instruction for IEP/LEP Students

Back to the bottom line! Students must be taught in order to perform well on tests. This is particularly true for students with disabilities who are limited in their English proficiency. While our knowledge base on how best to teach IEP/LEP students is limited, we do know something. Applying even this little bit of knowledge will help students go much farther than before toward improved test performance.

According to a comprehensive literature review conducted by Minnesota Assessment Project researchers within the National Center on Educational Outcomes (NCEO) at the University of Minnesota, there are a variety of factors that affect their test scores. Among the factors identified by the literature were:

- Degree of acculturation in the student—the extent to which the student has acquired the customs and values of a culture.
- Level of first and second language proficiency—the level of social and academic language skills in both the first and language.

Box 6.5

Considerations for Assessing LEP Students

- Teachers should regularly and frequently administer assessments, including assessments of English-language proficiency, for the purpose of monitoring the progress of English-language learners and for adapting instruction to improve performance.
- States and districts should develop clear guidelines for accommodations that permit English-language learners to participate in assessment administered for accountability purposes. Especially important are clear decision rules for determining the level of English-language proficiency at which English-language learners should be expected to participate exclusively in English-language assessments.
- Students should be assessed in the language that permits the most valid inferences about the quality of their academic performance. When numbers are sufficiently large, states and districts should develop subject-matter assessments in a language other than English.
- English-language learners should be exempted from assessments only when there is evidence that the assessment, even with accommodations, cannot measure the knowledge or skill of particular students or groups of students.
- States and districts should describe the methods they use to screen English-language learners for accommodations, exemptions, and alternate assessments, and they should report the frequency of these practices.
- Federal research units, foundations, and other funding agencies should promote research that advances knowledge about the validity and reliability of different accommodations, exemption, and alternate assessment practices for English-language learners.

SOURCE: Reprinted, with permission, from the National Research Council (1999) report entitled, ''Testing, Teaching, and Learning,'' edited by Richard Elmore and Robert Rothman. Washington, DC: National Academy Press, page 63.

- Extent of cognitive development and literacy in the native language—the extent to which the student has been exposed to schooling and other factors related to cognitive development.
- Attitudinal factors—beliefs about a variety of topics related to assessment, including attitudes about demonstrating knowledge, verbal communication, use of time, and so on.
- Test bias—in addition to language or cultural bias, there may be bias in communicative style, cognitive style, or test interpretation.

Some of these factors are alterable, and affected by instruction, while others are not. It is important to identify those factors that are alterable in one's own situation, and then to systematically identify ways to address the factors. These factors, of course, will also affect how students react to and profit from instruction.

Box 6.6

Instructional Strategies for IEP/LEP Students

- Procedures and strategies that are appropriate for elementary-age students should be continued into secondary school. . . . Classrooms should be "print rich" environments.
- The classroom climate should show value for the skills and knowledge students have from the home culture.
- Teaching acculturation is part of the goal of instruction. This includes familiarizing students with the expectations of the school and other social environments within the community.
- No assumptions should be made about what a student knows. Always give sufficient background information to establish a context for new information.
- Linguistic interference may affect all areas of learning.
- It is normal for students to make certain errors as they acquire English skills. Overcorrection of linguistic errors will reduce the student's motivation to communicate.
- The student should be spoken to at a normal rate and volume, using natural intonation.

SOURCE: Reprinted with permission from the Minnesota Department of Education (1991). Service delivery guidelines for LEP students with special education needs. St. Paul, MN: Unique Learner Needs Section.

When a student both has a diagnosed disability and limited English proficiency, there are at least three programs that need to collaborate—general education, special education, and the ESL/Bilingual program. It is critical that the three programs work with each other to form a seamless system for the student, one that does not have duplicated supports, or gaps in support.

It is generally believed that effective instruction is good practice for all students (see Chapter 9 in our book, *Improving Test Performance of Students With Disabilities*, for more information on instruction). Many state and local-level materials have been developed to guide educators in ways to make sure that effective instruction really does occur for students with disabilities who are limited in their English proficiency. In general, these materials develop the following principles (taken here from Minnesota's Special Delivery Guidelines for LEP Students with Special Education Needs):

- Instructional preparation takes into account student needs, learning styles, and available resources.
- Flexible grouping patterns based on student needs are exhibited in the school and classroom
- Effective models of teaching are employed to increase academic learning time and student achievement
- Parents are involved in the child's education and support the goals and expectations of the school.

In addition to these principles, Minnesota (like other states) identifies important instructional strategies (see Box 6.6).

Box 6.7

Myth or Truth Answers

MYTH The disability issues of students with disabilities who also have limited English proficiency really cannot be addressed until the language limitations are addressed.
Explanation: It makes little sense to try to determine that one characteristic—disability or limited proficiency in English—needs to be addressed before the other. Students on IEPs have all the legal rights connected to the IEP. For the benefit of the student, both disability and language issues must be addressed at the same time. [See page 104]

TRUTH Current demographic estimates confirm that the number of students considered to be IEP/LEP students will continue to increase over the years.
Explanation: Although no one has specifically counted IEP/LEP students enough to determine whether the number is increasing, or will continue to increase, estimates for students with limited English proficiency clearly confirm the increases, and since a percentage of these students can be expected to have disabilities, it is a safe guess that the number of IEP/LEP students will continue to increase as well. [See page 107]

MYTH Since academic language proficiency is limited in IEP/LEP students, they really cannot be included in testing that is presented in English.
Explanation: Distinctions between BICS (Basic Interpersonal Communication Skills) and CALP (Cognitive Academic Language Proficiency) are not necessarily helpful in making assessment participation decisions. The language of instruction for most students is English, and this often means that a translated version of the test is not the answer, nor is simply excluding the student from all assessments. [See page 108]

TRUTH Accommodations are often needed by IEP/LEP students to address their needs related to both disability and limited language proficiency.
Explanation: Assuming that either accommodations designed for disabilities or those designed for limited English will address the testing or instructional needs of IEP/LEP students is not appropriate. Consideration of both types of accommodations is needed. [See page 110]

TRUTH It is critical that sufficient collaboration occur among the programs that work with IEP/LEP students, both for instruction and for assessments.
Explanation: At least three programs that work with IEP/LEP students must use collaboration to ensure that the best instructional and assessment decisions are made—general education, special education, and the ESL/Bilingual program. [See page 114]

An important part of preparing IEP/LEP students to perform their best on state and district assessments is giving them the same advantages that other students have. As noted previously, general education students generally have picked up test-preparation and test-taking strategies on their own. This is generally not the case for students with disabilities, and doubly so for students who have limited English proficiency.

Thus, it is even more critical that sufficient energy be devoted to ensure that IEP/LEP students know what to expect in the state or district test, and that they know how to prepare and take tests to their greatest advantage. Also as noted before, this energy should not occur in place of regular instruction but rather should be integrated into it. Still, there need to be checks to make sure that the students are learning testing procedures as well as content.

Summary

The IEP/LEP population – students with disabilities who are learning English – is perhaps one of the more challenging groups for our schools today. This is no excuse, however, for failing to give them the best education possible. And, now is the time to quickly learn how to do this because the number of IEP/LEP students is increasing and will continue to do so.

From what we now know, good instruction for any student is also good for IEP/LEP students. However, additional considerations must be given to these students because they have additional challenges. These challenges are related to language, the major way that we communicate the information we want students to learn. Thus, as educators, we need to rely on principles that ease the burden of language, while still educating the child.

Now check your knowledge about the myth/truth statements presented at the beginning of this chapter. Try to explain each of the answers that you gave. Correct answers and possible explanations are given in Box 6.7.

Resources for Further Information

August, D., & Hakuta, K. (Eds.). (1998). *Educating language-minority children* (National Research Council report). Washington, DC: National Academy Press.

Elliot, J., & Thurlow, M. (2000). *Improving test performance of students with disabilities . . .On district and state assessments.* Thousand Oaks, CA: Corwin.

Elmore, R. F., & Rothman, R. (Eds.). (1999). *Testing, teaching, and learning* (National Research Council report). Washington, DC: National Academy Press.

Kopriva, R. (2001). *Ensuring accuracy in testing for English language learners.* Washington, DC: Council of Chief State School Officers.

Liu, K., Thurlow, M., Erickson, R., & Spicuzza, R. (1997). *A review of the literature on students with limited English proficiency and assessment* (Minnesota Report 11). Minneapolis: University of Minnesota, National Center on Educational Outcomes.

Minnesota Department of Education. (1991). *Service delivery guidelines for LEP students with special education needs.* St. Paul, MN: Unique Learner Needs Section.

National Research Council. (1998). *Educating language-minority children* (D. August & K. Hakuta, Eds.). Washington, DC: National Academy Press.

National Research Council. (1999). *Testing, teaching, and learning: A guide for state and school districts* (R.F Elmore & R. Rothman, Eds.). Washington, DC: National Academy Press.

Ortiz, A. (1984). Choosing the language of instruction for exceptional bilingual children. *Teaching Exceptional Children, 16*(3), 202-206.

Thurlow, M. L. & Liu, K. K. (2001). Can "all" really mean students with disabilities who have limited English proficiency? *Journal of Special Education Leadership, 14*(2), 63-71.

Thurlow, M., & Liu, K. (2001). *State and district assessments as an avenue to equity and excellence for English language learners with disabilities* (LEP Projects Report 2). Minneapolis: University of Minnesota, National Center on Educational Outcomes.

Internet Resources

National Association of Bilingual Education (NABE): *http://www.nabe.org*

National Clearinghouse for Bilingual Education (NCBE): http://www.ncbe.gwu.edu/index.html

Office of Bilingual Education and Minority Language Affairs (OBEMLA): http://www.ed.gov/offices/OBEMLA

Teachers of English to Students of Other Languages (TESOL): http://www.tesol.edu

Using Assessment Results

Topics

- ☐ Reports of District and State Data
- ☐ Using District and State Data
- ☐ Adding Data of Your Own Data
- ☐ Good Data Use and Reporting Practices

In this chapter, you will . . .

- explore the issues in understanding district and state test reports.
- find out how to use district and state data to make decisions about programs and instruction.
- identify other data to use to make better decisions.
- review best practices in accountability and reporting.

In several of the chapters thus far, we have mentioned the reporting of scores. Reporting is an area that brings up lots of issues because even if educators are willing to have students with disabilities take assessments, with or without accommodations, they are less likely to want the scores of these students included within the scores that are reported. It is assumed that if the scores of student with disabilities are included, average scores will be pulled down. Opinions differ about the validity of merging scores from accommodated and nonaccommodated assessments, and about merging indices of performance on the regular and alternate assessments. Furthermore, data that are reported are not being used to make programmatic and instructional decisions. These and related topics are the focus of this chapter.

Reporting the scores of students with disabilities is one element of a truly inclusive accountability system. This is reinforced by the 1997

BOX 7.1

Myth or Truth? Do You Know?

Read each statement below and decide whether it is a myth or the truth about current practice.

- If a student takes an assessment, that student automatically is included in average scores because of the way that test developers set up reporting programs.
- There are specific steps that can be followed to dig deeper into the data that are reported by states and by districts.
- Among the elements that should be examined in looking at longitudinal data is the flow of students in and out of special education.
- State and district data are all that are needed to make good programmatic and instructional decisions for students with disabilities.
- District and state reporting practices limit what educators can do to improve the educational results of students with disabilities.

---

amendments to IDEA, which require public reporting of scores of students with disabilities with the same frequency as for other students. It is further supported by Title I of the Elementary and Secondary Education Act (ESEA), which requires not only the reporting of disaggregated scores of students with disabilities, but also the inclusion of the scores of students with disabilities in its accountability system. Until we recognize that all students count, and back it up with data on the success of our programs for students with disabilities, we will continue to not be accountable for all students.

In this chapter, we clarify the issues involved in reporting. We also look at ways in which state and district level data can be used to make good decisions about programs and instruction, including how to identify when other data are needed to make good decisions. Finally, we provide examples of good accountability and reporting practices that help you ensure that you are doing the best you can for each and every student with a disability. When you finish this chapter, you will be able to identify which of the statements in Box 7.1 are myths and which are the truth.

Issues in Understanding District and State Test Reports

There are many reasons why it may be difficult to look at district and state test reports and really understand how students with disabilities are performing. First, it is often difficult to determine who really is included in the results when they are reported. Second, data may not be disaggregated in ways that are helpful to local administrators and educators. Finally, data systems themselves may make it difficult to obtain data that are useful.

Difficulty in Determining Who Is Really Included in Reports

The fact that students with disabilities take assessments in more than one way (with or without accommodations, through an alternate assessment) apparently makes it more challenging for districts and states to report their scores. To some extent, the challenges reflect concerns about reporting anything not considered to be a "standard" test administration. The difficulty for those looking at the data included in reports is that the reports often do not make clear who is actually included in them.

The National Center on Educational Outcomes (NCEO) has been examining state reporting on the participation and performance of students with disabilities in statewide assessments since 1998. Over time, the data on students with disabilities that NCEO has found in state reports have changed dramatically. In reports from 1995 to 1997, only 11 states included any test-based data on students with disabilities. In 2001, 35 states included test data on students with disabilities. Despite the dramatic changes in the number of states reporting data, in many states it was just as difficult in 2001 to determine which students with disabilities really were included in reports as it was in the mid 1990s.

It is very clear that states have not figured out how to report on the performance of students with disabilities on their alternate assessments. As of 2001, no state had yet publicly reported alternate assessment performance data; only one state had reported alternate assessment participation data. Indications were, however, that more states were reporting on their alternate assessments in 2002. For other aspects of reporting, there still is great variation in the extent to which states are clear in their reporting practices. This variability relates primarily to practices in reporting on participation in assessments and on accommodated test performance.

Participation Reporting. In the early days of state reporting on students with disabilities, it was often the case that assessment scores were reported without any indication of the number or percentage of students with disabilities whose scores were reflected in the reports. This has changed. Now, it is generally the case that when states report on the performance of students with disabilities, they also report on participation. Still, probably because it is all that is required by law, states usually report only the number of students tested—without also providing enrollment numbers that would allow the reader to determine whether all or some students with disabilities participated.

Even when states calculate a participation rate, they do so in different ways. The number of students with disabilities tested may be counted by starting from a list of students with disabilities and determining whether a test form was received from each of these students. The number tested may also be counted by simply having teachers identify students with disabilities on their test forms when they are handed in to the teacher before being sent to the test coordinator.

To determine a participation rate, some states divide the number of students with disabilities who took the test by annual child count numbers.

Some obtain an enrollment count during the week of testing, then use that as the denominator for the number of students who took the regular test and the alternate assessment. Others develop a test form for every student with a disability and require that they be turned in regardless of whether the student participated in testing—so that the number of test forms is the denominator used to calculate participation rates. Because of these differences in ways to count students with disabilities who participate in testing, the numbers may be more or less accurate in different places.

To really understand data from your state or district, it is important to know how participation data are obtained and how students are counted. As you dig deeper into your data, having in mind the number of students with disabilities who should have been accounted for in reporting will be an essential part of being able to determine the meaning of the results that you are seeing.

Accommodated Test Performance. In most district and state reports, the scores of students with disabilities who take regular assessments under standard conditions are both aggregated with the scores of students without disabilities and disaggregated so that we can see how these students are performing. It is not always a simple matter, however, to determine whether the scores that are aggregated and disaggregated include all of the students who might have been reported elsewhere as participating in the assessment.

A concrete example is what happens to the scores of students who use "non-approved" or "nonstandard" accommodations during testing. These students generally are counted when reporting test participation numbers. However, whether these scores are reported is a different matter. The map in Box 7.2 shows the states that aggregate the scores from tests taken with "nonapproved" accommodations in with other scores. Some states report the scores from nonstandard accommodations separately but do not aggregate them with other scores. Some states simply do not report these scores, and do not indicate that they are not reporting them.

All of this points to the importance of really knowing what is in the information that is reported. It also highlights the need to figure out what additional information is needed to understand what the data tell you about students in your district or classroom.

Data Not Disaggregated in Useful Ways

Most states and districts that report on the participation and performance of students with disabilities simply report on the two elements defined in IDEA 97—the number of students with disabilities participating and their performance. These two elements should be reported for both the regular assessment and the alternate assessment. It is often useful for district administrators and other personnel to have more in-depth information than this. For example, information on the percentages of students with different categories of disabilities might provide extremely helpful participation information. Similarly, the number of students

Box 7.2

States' Plans for Reporting Scores from Tests Taken with Non-Approved Accommodations

Ways in Which States Report Data for Non-Approved Accommodations

○ Not Reported*

● Aggregated**

◐ Separate

◯ Aggregated and Separate

* States that indicated they "counted" scores, but did not explicitly indicate that they reported them were depicted as "not reported" in this figure (California, Ohio, Washington).
** Although scores are to be aggregated in Indiana and New Hampshire, the scores that are aggregated will be the lowest score possible rather than the actual score obtained with the nonapproved accommodation. In Wyoming, a zero score will be used for students using nonapproved accommodations.

receiving accommodations, perhaps by category of disability, also would provide information that would be relevant for evaluating whether decision making is producing expected results.

Data Systems Make It Difficult to Obtain Useful Data

Some data systems are set up in ways that make it easier to produce useful data than do other systems. Those data systems that have student identification numbers generally allow for greater digging because different data sets can be connected to each other. Data systems that are very limited in the amount of data they include (for example, whether student category of disability is available at the individual student level) make it more difficult to obtain useful data.

The message here is that it is very important to know what data elements are included in the data system that exists. This information should be easily obtained from the state or district assessment office.

Using District and State Data

There are several critical questions to ask to get you on the road to making better use of the results that are provided in district and state reports. First is the question of why it is important to look at data. If you don't answer this question, it will be difficult to move to the next step even though there is a commitment to do so. Next, where do you want to start in your efforts and how deep can you dig into the data should you decide that you want to dig deeper? Answering this question involves knowing the data elements that are included in the data system that is used to generate district or state reports. Information on available data elements will help you identify additional information that you might be able to request when trying to use district and state data. A third question to answer is whether you can look at data over time and what it will mean, of course, combined with the question of whether you want to do this. The basis for "improvement" data, particularly for students with disabilities, will help you understand what "growth" or "nongrowth" in performance means. It will also enable you to determine the extent to which you need other information to really understand changes in the performance of students with disabilities.

Why Look at Data?

Books have been written about the importance of examining data in order to know what is happening and to make better decisions. Districts and states produce many reports, supposedly with the intent that these meet consumers' needs for looking at the data. Unfortunately, many school improvement leaders have found that this is not necessarily true— and there are reasons why it is true. Some of them (from the perspectives of two different authors) are shown in Box 7.3. While we do not dwell on the barriers to data use here, they are important and valid and must be addressed to move forward. The following comment from Deborah McDonald, a Distinguished Educator in Kentucky, which was made in her introduction to Edie Holcomb's book on using data, is also important to keep in mind:

By analyzing what is and is not working to improve student learning, educators can focus scarce resources on goals and strategies that make the most impact on achievement. Time is the most critical resource. . . . The time invested in "data work" can generate a net savings if it

Box 7.3

Perceived Barriers to Using Data

Edie L. Holcomb[a]	Victoria L. Bernhardt[b]
Director of Standards and Assessment Seattle Public Schools	**Professor California State University-Chico**

<table>
<tr>
<td>

- Lack of proper training: . . . how to involve others in decision making. . . . how to use data in appropriate ways to guide the decision making . . . .
- Lack of time
- Feast or famine: . . . where are we going to get [the data]. . . . what are we going to do with all [the data]? . . .
- Fear of evaluation: . . . how can we keep this from being used against us? . . . .
- Fear of exposure: . . . anxiety that our inadequacies will be exposed if we try something new that we realize we should know . . . .
- Confusing a technical problem with a cultural problem: . . . barriers that have to fall are not just barriers of lack of training. Cultural norms like "Let me close my classroom door and do my own thing" have to be replaced by more systemic thinking.

</td>
<td>

- Work culture does not focus on data. . . .
- Gathering data is perceived to be a waste of time . . . .
- Computer systems are outdated and inadequate . . . .
- Teachers have been trained to be subject oriented, not data oriented . . . .
- From the state level down to the regional and local levels, data are not used systematically, or are not used well.
- School personnel have only had negative experiences with data.
- There is a perception that data are collected for someone else's purposes.
- There are not enough good examples of schools gathering, maintaining, and benefiting from the use of data.

</td>
</tr>
</table>

a Reprinted with permission from E.L. Holcomb (1999), *Getting Excited About Data: How to Combine People, Passion, and Proof*, Thousand Oaks, CA: Corwin Press, pages 20-24.

b Reprinted with permission from V.L. Bernhardt (1998), *Data Analysis for Comprehensive Schoolwide Improvement*, Larchmont, NY: Eye on Education, page 5.

guides the school toward decisions that pay dividends in student achievement. (Holcomb, 1999, p. xiii)

Digging Into Existing Data

Districts and states often publicly report less than they could—simply because the general public would find it too confusing to have all the data that could be reported. For example, many districts have information on each student's ethnic group as well as disability. While test results may be reported for students with disabilities and for various racial/ethnic groups, they rarely are reported for each category of disability broken down by all the ethnic groups. If districts and states did these kinds of data analyses and reported them in their public reports, the reports would be several hundred pages—or even a thousand or more pages long. This is way too long. You don't need extra information unless you are trying to specifically understand assessment results so that you can improve your programs and the results of instruction for your students with disabilities.

The first step that must be taken before digging into the data is to determine how far you want to dig. It is often best to just take a quick dip before plunging headlong into the data digging. And, for districts or schools that are smaller, the quick dip may be all that is possible without extra funding or a special grant. No matter how small the first steps, they are better than no steps at all. So, as we think about digging into the data, we will address it in three steps: (1) Getting more out of what you are given; (2) Understanding data elements that make it possible to get more than what you are given; and (3) Exploring trends in performance.

Getting More Out of What You Are Given. The first step in using data is knowing how to look at what you are given—what you have in hand—without having to look for additional information or having to collect additional data. When the scores of groups of students are reported in school and district reports, it is helpful to look for surprising and expected results in those reports. This is the first level of using the data that are provided to you.

Another level of using data is to look at the nature of errors that significant numbers of students have made. Test companies produce error reports, and these reports are generally provided along with the group results. If you haven't been provided with error analyses, or performance data at the level of specific standards or objectives, talk to the principal or talk to your evaluation department, if you have one. The data are there—somewhere. If you benchmark your district's curriculum and instruction to the errors that many students have made, you are likely to produce significant improvements in student achievement. This can be done year after year, with likely the same effects.

Understanding the Data Elements. There are many data elements and coding options might already be incorporated into your district or state data management system. Some of these are listed in Box 7.4. These elements are ones that we think might be useful in digging into existing data systems—so that you can better understand what is happening for the students with disabilities with whom you work.

Box 7.5 is a case study of a district that started to dig into its data to find information that could help it address staff development and how IEP forms might be changed to encourage changes that the data indicated were needed. This case study is an excellent example of how administrators, teachers, and other school personnel can ask questions of data to help improve the assessment decision-making process.

Exploring Trends in Performance. There are many ways to explore trends in student performance. Most state and district data systems are set up so

---

BOX 7.4

Data Elements and Coding Options That Facilitate the Development and Implementation of Appropriate Reporting Procedures

Data Element	Coding Option
How student participated in the accountability system	Whether student took the regular assessment
Student's primary disability	Name of the federal category for which student receives primary special education services
Student's related services	Type of related services a student receives (e.g., occupational therapy, physical therapy)
Student's placement	Placement of student's special education services (e.g., regular, resource, self-contained)
Student's functional learning characteristics (e.g., estimated reading level)	Any one of an array of variables that provides information about the student's learning and functional characteristics that goes beyond a mere categorical label
Accommodations used during the assessment (by category or by specific accommodation)	Indication of the accommodations used by a student during assessment

---

that it is possible to look at changes in test scores across grades within a given year (for example, the scores of students in grades 5, 6, and 7 in 2001 can be compared). Data systems are also often set up so that changes in the scores of students within specific grades can be examined across years (for example, the performance of grade 4 students can be compared in 1999, 2000, and 2001).

Another way to look at performance is to look at the performance of the same students as they progress across grades. If these data are available, it is important to look at them in addition to the other ways to explore trends. This is particularly the case for students with disabilities because a recent study by Bielinski and Ysseldyke has shown that some students in special education move to general education, and others who are enrolled in general education move to special education, and this movement affects the trends in performance of special education students. Those students who move to special education are among the lowest performers in general education, and those who move from special education to general education are among the highest performers in special education. Looking

Box 7.5

Case Study of a District Digging into State Data

District L is a large urban school district in a state that reports limited data on its students with disabilities. Yet, the state has a number of elements coded into its data system, so that District L can explore the results in greater detail. This is exactly what District L did.

After the first administration of the state assessment, District L asked for a breakdown of its participation data by category of disability. This breakdown revealed that almost all of the students in the speech/language disability category had not participated in either the reading or the math part of the assessment. District-level staff looking at the numbers (and rates) determined that it was highly likely that the decisions for these students to not participate in the regular assessment were inappropriate. As a result, the district decided to institute extensive staff development—primarily on the legal requirements for all students to be included in state assessments—either in the regular assessment or in the alternate assessment. In the year after this staff development effort, the participation rate of speech/language students was over 99%.

only at class averages will produce distorted data when the mobility described here exists. It is important both to keep track of mobility in and out of special education, and to look at data in varied ways. This is especially true when trying to reach conclusions about improvements in the performance of students with disabilities.

Identifying and Obtaining Other Data

What if the state or district database doesn't have the elements needed to answer questions that you have. For example, say that you want to look at the extent to which students are using accommodations during testing, but the state or district does not collect data on accommodations used during testing. It is at this point that it may be important to collect your own data to connect to the state or district data.

Box 7.6 provides a case study of a district in which additional data were collected to increase the usefulness of the data that the district received from the state assessment. As is evident in this case, there needed to be a common student identification number for the district to be able to connect student-level data provided by the state to the student-level data that the district had collected on accommodations used during testing.

Teachers and administrators shouldn't be analyzing the data. But, they should be asking the questions—and these involve questions that may involve collecting other data. There are many excellent resources available to assist in identifying what kinds of additional data might be needed to contribute to school improvement efforts.

Box 7.6

Case Study of a District Identifying and Using Other Data

After another year of assessments, District L decided to look at the use of accommodations during state testing. However, information on accommodations used during testing was not collected by the state. Unless the district could figure out a way to collect that information itself, it could not determine the extent to which accommodations were being used during the assessment. The district already had decided that this was important information for it to have—both to look at the potential effect on the inclusion of scores in the state reporting system (because only scores from tests taken without accommodations or with "standard" accommodations were reported)—and to look at whether there seemed to be indications of under- or overuse of accommodations.

District L devised its own accommodation data collection form, which was filled out by teachers during the administration of the state assessment. Student identification numbers were entered on the forms and the forms were scanned into a database system so that when the state sent the individual student test data to the district, it could merge the two databases.

When the two databases were merged, and the data printed out for examination by district administrators, large variability in the number of accommodations used from student to student was found. Many students did not receive any accommodations during state testing, whereas others received every possible accommodation. These data were considered worthy of further investigation.

The next step in delving into the data was to take a sample of the students with accommodations data and to compare those data to the students' IEPs. This comparison revealed a startling lack of agreement between the two, and prompted the district to undertake another round of massive staff development and to institute a change in its IEP form so that IEP teams had to specifically indicate both instructional accommodations and specific assessment accommodations for each student with an IEP. The district is looking forward to examining the extent to which the range of accommodations used by students during state testing has narrowed (to produce fewer, all, or none sets of accommodations), and to again checking the agreement between accommodation information on the IEP and accommodations used during testing.

Good Data Use and Reporting Practices

Several years ago, NCEO gathered a group of state department personnel, special education representatives, state assessment specialists, and researchers to develop a list of necessary and desirable characteristics of good state and district educational accountability reports. The group started from the work of LaPointe, who argued (among other things) that all reports need to include information on factors that describe the context of learning and school (e.g., socioeconomic status, family size and involvement in school, parent education level, per pupil expenditures). NCEO's meeting

---

BOX 7.7

Myth or Truth Answers

MYTH   If a student takes an assessment, that student automatically is included in average scores because of the way that test developers set up reporting programs.

Explanation: Because many places do identify students with disabilities and specifically indicate that their scores are excluded from reports, this is a myth. However, even in those places where all students are included in reporting, it may not be known whether any of the students had disabilities. [See page 120]

TRUTH   There are specific steps that can be followed to dig deeper into the data that are reported by states and districts.

Explanation: Although the steps might not be the same for every state or district, it is possible to systematically look at the data provided, then ask questions to "dig deeper." [See page 124]

TRUTH   Among the elements that should be examined in looking at longitudinal data is the flow of students in and out of special education.

Explanation: A study by Bielinski and Ysseldyke demonstrated the dramatic effect that movement in and out of special education can have when looking at performance across time. While the same amount of movement may not characterize all districts or states, it is important to know the extent to which it occurs and whether it is having an impact on performance data across grades. [See page 126]

MYTH   State and district data are all that are needed to make good programmatic and instructional decisions for students with disabilities.

Explanation: Just as it is the case for students without disabilities, it is important to collect and look at data other than state and district assessment data. Classroom tests and other frequent measures are needed to make good instructional decisions. [See page 127]

MYTH   District and state reporting practices limit what educators can do to improve the educational results of students with disabilities.

Explanation: While district or state reporting practices may be less than what they could be to be really useful, there is no reason not to ask additional questions, to dig deeper into the data, or to collect additional data to make that which is reported richer in meaning. [See page 127]

---

produced a checklist that included: *content* that is clear, comprehensive, comparative, and concise and that includes cautions and maintains confidentiality; and *format* that is readable, responsive to intended audiences, has a good layout, provides links, and includes a bulleted executive summary. The group concluded that the most important overall questions were:

- Is the report readable?
- Is the report fair?
- Is the report concise?
- Is the report visually attractive?
- Is the report accurate?

These criteria for good reporting were general—in the sense that they apply to all reports, regardless of whether they include students with disabilities.

Since its initial attempts to clarify good reporting, NCEO has become more specific in what constitutes reporting in an inclusive accountability system:

- A written policy exists about who is included when calculating participation or exclusion rates.
- Rates of exclusion that are specific to students with disabilities, and reasons for the exclusion, are reported when assessment results are reported.
- Data reports include information from all test takers.
- Records are kept so that data for students with disabilities could be reported separately, overall, or by other breakdowns.
- Records are kept of the use of accommodations by students with disabilities, by type of accommodation, so that the information could be reported separately either by individual student or in aggregate.
- Parents are informed about the reporting policy for their child's data.

With the revision of this book, we became increasingly aware that we no longer needed to focus just on the characteristics of good reports but, instead, needed to move on to what constitutes good use of assessment results. We have attempted to describe some of the steps toward this end in this chapter. But, there is one thing more that needs to be said about presenting data to your advantage.

Presenting Data to Your Advantage

Whether arguing for a specific program that is needed, attempting to change a policy, or simply presenting what you know about (such as increased student learning and performance), how you present your information is as important as what you present.

While numbers are good, pictures often communicate more. There are a variety of graphic formats—such as bar graphs and pie charts—that are more engaging and convincing than simply the numbers. The resources that we have listed at the end of this chapter provide numerous examples of different ways to look at and present data. When you commit to using assessment results, you should also commit to sharing them with others in ways that are easy to understand. A picture really is worth a thousand words (or a thousand data points).

Summary

In this chapter, we described several aspects of reporting. We went beyond the issues that surround reporting as it exists in districts and states today, to look at how you can use the data that are reported. We explored looking in different ways at the data presented to you, as well as digging deeper into those data and even collecting additional data. We concluded by revisiting criteria for good reports, then expanding those to criteria for reporting that are aligned with inclusive accountability systems. Finally, we talked about the ways in which you can use data to your advantage.

Now, check your knowledge about the myth/truth statements presented at the beginning of this chapter (see Box 7.7 for answers). Try to give an explanation for why each statement is correctly identified either as a myth or as the truth.

Resources for Further Information

Bernhardt, V. L. (1998). *Data analysis for comprehensive schoolwide improvement.* Larchmont, NY: Eye on Education.

Elliott, J., Thurlow, M., & Ysseldyke, J. (1996). *Assessment guidelines that maximize the participation of students with disabilities in large-scale assessments: Characteristics and considerations* (Synthesis Rep. 25). Minneapolis: University of Minnesota, National Center on Educational Outcomes.

Erickson, R., Ysseldyke, J., & Thurlow, M. (1996). *Neglected numerators, drifting denominators, and fractured fractions: Determining participation rates for students with disabilities in statewide assessment programs* (Synthesis Rep. 23). Minneapolis: University of Minnesota, National Center on Educational Outcomes.

Erickson, R., Ysseldyke, J., & Thurlow, M., & Elliott, J. (1997). *Reporting the results of students with disabilities in state and district assessments* (NCEO Policy Directions 8). Minneapolis: University of Minnesota, National Center on Educational Outcomes.

Holcomb, E. L. (1999). *Getting excited about data: How to combine people, passion, and proof,* Thousand Oaks, CA: Corwin.

Jaeger, R. M., & Tucker, C. G. (1998). *Analyzing, disaggregating, reporting, and interpreting students' achievement test results: A guide to practice for Title I and beyond.* Washington, DC: Council of Chief State School Officers.

McGrew, K. S., Thurlow, M. L., & Spiegel, A. (1993). An investigation of the exclusion of students with disabilities in national data collection programs. *Educational Evaluation and Policy Analysis, 15*(3), 339-352.

Quinn, D., Greunert, S., & Valentine, J. (1999). *Using data for school improvement.* Reston, VA: National Association of Secondary School Principals.

Thurlow, M., Olsen, K., Elliott, J., Ysseldyke, J., Erickson, R., & Ahearn, E. (1996). *Alternate assessments for students with disabilities* (NCEO Policy Directions 5). Minneapolis: University of Minnesota, National Center on Educational Outcomes.

Thurlow, M. L., Scott, D. L., & Ysseldyke, J. E. (1995). *A compilation of states' guidelines for including students with disabilities in assessments* (Synthesis Report 17). Minneapolis: University of Minnesota, National Center on Educational Outcomes.

Ysseldyke, J., Thurlow, M., & Olsen, K. (1996). *Self-study guide for the development of statewide assessments that include students with disabilities.* Minneapolis: University of Minnesota, National Center on Educational Outcomes.

An Important Tool: The IEP

Topics

- [ ] Role of the IEP
- [ ] Tools for Making Inclusive Accountability Decisions for Assessment and Accommodations
- [ ] Rethinking the IEP Format
- [ ] Logistics, Training, and Implementation of Accountable Decision Making

In this chapter, you will . . .

- learn what IEP members should know about assessment and accommodation decisions.
- discover critical components of the IEP.
- examine checklists used during the IEP process to make informed decisions about participation and accommodations for instruction and assessment.
- learn how to use district and state assessment results in the IEP process.

In Chapter 5, we discussed alternate assessments needed for a small percentage of students with disabilities unable to participate in the general assessment regardless of accommodations given. Even with an alternate assessment, the challenge is how to make informed and documented decisions about who participates in what assessment and with what accommodations. We need a clear systematic decision-making process that is documented on the IEP. In this chapter, we rethink the IEP so that it becomes a useful tool and process for *accounting* for all students' learning and progress.

BOX 8.1

Myth or Truth? Do You Know?

Read each statement below and decide whether it is a myth or the truth about current practice.

- The purpose of an assessment and what it sets out to measure is a critical variable in deciding assessment accommodations for a student.
- IEP forms require the same basic assessment and accommodation information from district to district.
- Most IEP formats allow for the documentation of district/state tests, but not accommodations needed for instruction and classroom tests.
- IEP team members are fully informed decision makers about which tests allow what accommodations and the process of making assessment accommodations decisions.
- If older and able, students can be helpful in making decisions on what accommodations are needed both for instruction and assessment.

When you finish this chapter, you will be able to identify which of the statements in Box 8.1 are myths and which are the truth.

Role of the IEP

Originally, the IEP was to be the federally-required document that served as a blueprint for the instruction of students with disabilities. In reality, it has become the very document on which due process and compliance issues are based. But what happen to instruction? It seems to have been lost. The IEP is more often about frequency and duration of related services, and whether each letter written on the IEP has been dotted and crossed. As one district superintendent said, "It is a good idea gone very wrong." This comment was made during a recent triumph in which the district had reduced the requirements of the IEP so that it could go from 26 pages to down to 12 pages!

Talkin Turkey

So is it a wonder that IEPs are written and placed in desk drawers until the annual review? It probably doesn't happen in your backyard, just in your neighbor's! How many times have you read goals and objectives that made no sense? What the heck are they related to? And if there are 50 of them, who tracks the progress made on them? (One district representative told us that its IEP was 55 pages long!) We need to revisit what IEPs are really about. How can we use them to plan, manage, deliver, and evaluate instruction to special needs students?

Present Levels of Educational Performance

We think that the answer to many IEP issues lies in tightly written and explicit Present Levels of Performance. Present Levels of Educational Performance (PLEP) is just one of many mandated parts of the IEP. When well written, PLEPs include how a student's disability affects involvement and progress in the general education curriculum. PLEPs typically fall into four domains: academic, social, physical, and management. PLEPs should be considered separately for each student and show individual strengths and needs in each of the four domains. From PLEPs, corresponding goals and benchmarks (referred to as objectives in some places) are written to address each area of need. And of course the goals and benchmarks are standards-based.

The *academic* domain deals with any academic skill that may be in need of acquisition, remediation, or compensatory skill development. Students who have a reading disability, for example, may have several goals and objectives written specifically in the area of reading. Each of these reflects the student's current instructional need.

Any need that a student has in the areas of social skills, peer relations, adult relations, independence, ability to initiate conversation, and so on are listed in the *social* domain. Again, it is important to remember that the needs under each of these areas will vary widely.

Physical needs or medical conditions that a student might have that may have an impact on the learning and instruction process are listed in the *physical* domain. For example, a student with Chronic Fatigue Syndrome may require a change in the daily schedule to allow late arrival to or early dismissal from school. This same student may be physically unable to sit for a test or exam that exceeds 30 minutes. Another student may have allergies that have a significant impact on learning and attendance during specific times of the year, and yet another student may need to avoid certain foods.

The *management* domain includes behavioral needs and structural considerations (e.g., ability to function in small and/or large group instruction, independent work habits) that the student may require to successfully participate in the educational process. For example, a student with a visual or hearing impairment or behavioral disability may need to be seated in close proximity to the teacher or board to learn best. For some students, teachers need to ascertain what instructional formats work best to facilitate and maintain engaged learning with the least behavioral interference. This may include providing incentives, contracts, or modified assignments.

Clearly articulated PLEPs are critical to identifying accommodations for classroom instruction, classroom tests, and district/state assessments.

Other Important Components of the IEP

Although needed accommodations should be documented in a student's IEP, many IEPs do not provide a specific place for these to be recorded. As a result, they often do not appear on IEPs. In most cases, there is general reference to the type of changes or modifications a student needs for assignments or tests, but accommodations are not specifically identified for instruction or classroom tests. While IDEA 97 required that IEPs include individual modifications and accommodations needed to participate in district and state assessments, it did not technically require the documentation of instructional accommodations.

In a 2001 analysis of IEP forms by the National Center on Educational Outcomes (NCEO), most of the 41 states with recommended or required IEP forms "strongly encouraged" districts to use the state-designed IEP form for ease of monitoring and compliance with state and federal requirements. (Six states had no state-level forms, and the other three were revising their forms.) Interestingly enough, only 5 of the 41 states made reference to state and district standards on their IEP forms. Only 30 state IEP forms listed three or more options for assessment, generally standard participation in general state and district assessments, accommodated participation, or alternate assessment participation.

Since IDEA and Title I both require all students to learn toward common content standards, it makes sense that special education services designed to help students work toward these standards would be referenced or addressed on IEP forms. According to IDEA 97 regulations (300.26(b)(3)(ii)), the purpose of special education is "to ensure access of the child to the general curriculum, so that he or she can meet the educational standards within the jurisdiction of the public agency that apply to all children." In other words, we must show not only that students with disabilities have access to the general curriculum but also that they are provided necessary modifications and accommodations to allow them to fully participate.

Simple access to the general curriculum, of course, does not mean that students are working on the same standards. Until there is pervasive belief that all students with disabilities should be working toward the same standards as other students, in addition to working on their own personal goals, true access does not exist. Since the IEP has, in many places, become synonymous with due process, it only makes sense that students with disabilities not only have access, but also the opportunity to learn to standards. Can you see how critical this consideration is to what and how students will be assessed?

The requirement to document accommodations for classroom instruction and assessment does exist in some locations, even though it may not be required or recommended in state guidelines. For example, California and New York do not indicate that the IEP should document classroom instruction and test accommodations. However, we know that in both states local districts require IEP teams to document both instructional and assessment accommodations (see example in Box 8.2).

There are least three kinds of tests that students take throughout their K-12 education:

1. Classroom (e.g., Formative and Summative)

2. District (e.g., Achievement)

3. State (e.g., Achievement and Graduation, Exit, or Competency)

Box 8.2

Student Name _____ _____ IEP Date _____ Page 8 of _____
Last _First_

XIV. INSTRUCTIONAL ACCOMMODATIONS

Supplementary aids, services and other support required to access general education curriculum:

	Timing of Instruction	Scheduling of Instruction	Presentation of Instruction	Response to Instruction	Setting of Instruction	Other
Subject:						
Subject:						

XV. DISTRICT/STATE ASSESSMENT

Students will participate in the:

- ☐ SAT-9   ☐ Without Accommodations   ☐ With Accommodations (see below)
- ☐ District Assessments   ☐ Without Accommodations   ☐ With Accommodations (see below)
- ☐ Alternate Assessment (must use IEP page-9 Participation Criteria)

SAT 9 Participation

STANDARD ACCOMMODATIONS	All Content Areas	Reading (All Grades)	Math (All Grades)	Language (All Grades)	Spelling (Grades 1-8)	History (Grades 9-11)	Science (Grades 9-11)
Flexible Setting	☐	☐	☐	☐	☐	☐	☐
Large Print Test	☐	☐	☐	☐	☐	☐	☐
Out of Level Testing (one grade level only)	☐						
Revised Test Directions	☐	☐	☐	☐	☐	☐	☐
NON-STANDARD ACCOMMODATIONS	**All Content Areas**	**Reading (All Grades)**	**Math (All Grades)**	**Language (All Grades)**	**Spelling (Grades 1-8)**	**History (Grades 9-11)**	**Science (Grades 9-11)**
Braille Test	☐	☐	☐	☐	☐	☐	☐
Flexible Scheduling	☐	☐	☐	☐	☐	☐	☐
Use of Aids and/or Aides to Interpret Test Items	☐	☐	☐	☐	☐	☐	☐
PARTIAL PARTICIPATION	**All Content Areas**	**Reading (All Grades)**	**Math (All Grades)**	**Language (All Grades)**	**Spelling (Grades 1-8)**	**History (Grades 9-11)**	**Science (Grades 9-11)**
Partial Participation	☐	☐	☐	☐	☐	☐	☐

OTHER ASSESSMENTS

Test	Timing	Scheduling	Presentation	Response	Setting

LONG BEACH UNIFIED SCHOOL DISTRICT Form #IEP9
Revised 7/01

Distribution: Special Education Office – Original; Special Education teacher – 1 Copy; Parent – 1 Copy; CUM – 1 Copy

It is important that all IEP teams know which tests are required and what accommodations are allowed. It is critical for IEP teams to understand that if a student needs an accommodation to show what he or she knows and can do, then the student should indeed get it. It is also important for teams to know the potential consequences of these decisions. Sure, once you put something on the IEP, it legally must be provided.

Controversy surrounds IEP team decisions that are inconsistent with district or state assessment policies. It has been agreed that district or state policy cannot prevent a student receiving and using a "nonapproved" accommodation or modification. But it can alter the ways in which the district or state reports or aggregates the scores of students who use them. In other words, if Jim needs a certain accommodation that has been deemed nonstandard by the testing company or state department of education and you allow Jim to use it during assessment, then in fact his test scores could be rendered nonmeaningful and might not be reported. This is a big "heads up," especially if this test is a required graduation test. In Chapter 12 we talk more about recent court cases that have and continue to challenge the practice of denying students with disabilities needed accommodations on high-stakes tests.

Tools for Making Inclusive Accountability Decisions for Assessment

Student-centered decisions about program, service, and evaluation of students with disabilities are made by the IEP team. Clearly, the charge of this team is expansive and extremely important. Decisions about which student with a disability takes an alternate assessment or a general assessment with accommodations and what, if any, assessment accommodations are needed to provide a student equal footing during a testing situation are the responsibility of the IEP team. Having the tools and knowledge to makes sound decisions that are accountable for all students, including those with disabilities, again, is necessarily the responsibility of the IEP team—and a big one it is!

In Chapters 2, 3, and 7, we provided you with criteria to use in making thoughtful decisions around participation, accommodation, and using test results for all students, regardless of disabilities. The first two areas are within the jurisdiction of IEP teams, but reporting and using the test results is a broader policy issue to be determined by school district administration and the states' Departments of Education. However, it is important to review students' district and state assessment results at each annual review.

Using the criteria presented earlier, we constructed a checklist that integrates the issues of participation and accommodation (see Box 8.3). This checklist can be used during IEP development or review. While this certainly is not the only way to make decisions, it does provide a reliable framework from which accountable assessment decisions can be made. It is important to find out what guidelines and policies already exist in your

BOX 8.3

**Checklist of Criteria for Making Decisions About
Participation and Needed Accommodations for
Classroom, District, and State Assessments**

Participation and Accommodation Decisions

Student Name: **Grade:**

School/Program: **Date of Meeting:**

The following accommodation decisions were made by person(s) who know
_____'s learning needs and skills. These decisions were based on _____'s current
level of functioning and learning characteristics as follows:

Yes   No

SETTING

_____ _____ 1.   Can work independently

_____ _____ 1a.   Can complete tasks with assistance or with the
following accommodation(s):
___ One-to-one assistance to complete written tasks
___ On-task reminders
___ Directions repeated and/or clarified
___ Other_____

_____ _____ 2.   Can complete tasks within a large group but quiet
setting

_____ _____ 2a.   Can complete tasks if provided the following
accommodation(s):
___ Test administered in a separate location with
minimal distractions
___ Test administered in a small group, study carrel, or
individually (circle one)
___ Special lighting
___ Adaptive furniture_____specify_____
___ Noise buffer (e.g., earplugs, earphones, other)_____
___ Other_____

TIMING

_____ _____ 1.   Can work continuously for 20- to 30-minute
periods; if not, specify the average length of time
student is able to work continuously

_____ _____ 1a.   Can work in a group without distracting other test takers

(Continued)

Box 8.3

Checklist of Criteria for Making Decisions (Continued)

Yes   No

SCHEDULING

____ ____ 1.   Can complete tasks if provided periodic breaks or other timing consideration(s)/accommodation(s):

___ Test administered over several sessions, time per session not to exceed_____minutes

___ Allowed to take breaks as needed, not to exceed_____ breaks per 20- to 30-minute period

___ Test administered over several days, each session not to exceed _____minutes in duration

___ Test administered in the morning, early afternoon, late ___ afternoon (circle one)

___ Extended time to complete the test in one session
Other _____

PRESENTATION

____ ____ 1.   Can listen to and follow oral directions given by an adult or on audiotape

____ ____ 1a. Can listen to and follow oral directions with assistance or the following accommodation(s):

___ Visual cues or printed material to facilitate understanding of orally given directions

___ Directions repeated, clarified, or simplified

___ Directions read individually

___ Visual magnification device

___ Auditory amplification device

___ Other _____

____ ____ 2.   Can read and comprehend written directions

____ ____ 2a. Can comprehend written directions with assistance or the following accommodation:

___ Written directions read

___ Directions repeated, clarified, or simplified

___ Key words or phrases in written directions highlighted

___ Visual prompts (e.g., stop signs, arrows) that show directions to start, stop, and continue working

___ Written directions presented in larger and/or bold print

___ Written directions presented with one complete sentence per line of text

___ Visual magnification device

___ Auditory amplification device

___ Other _____

(Continued)

Box 8.3

Checklist of Criteria for Making Decisions (Continued)

Yes   No

____ ____ 3.   Can read, understand, and answer questions in multiple-choice format

____ ____ 3a. Can understand and answer questions in multiple-choice format with assistance or the following accommodation(s):
___ Reader to read the test
___ Pencil grip
___ Access to prerecorded reading
___ Test signed
___ Test presented in Braille or large print
___ Auditory amplification device
___ Increased spacing between items and/or limited items
___ presented per page
___ Templates or masks to reduce visible print
___ Other____

RESPONSE

____ ____ 1.   Can use paper and pen/pencil to write short answer or paragraph-length responses to open-ended questions

____ ____ 1a. Can respond to open-ended questions when provided assistance or the following accommodation(s):
___ Pencil grip
___ Word processor
___ Scribe (someone to record verbatim oral responses to questions)
___ Brailler
___ Copy assistance between drafts of writing
___ Write an outline to a question and, using a tape recorder, dictate the body of the response, per the written outline
___ Dictate answer into a tape recorder
___ Visual magnification devices
___ Touch Talker or other communication device
___ Calculator
___ Abacus
___ Arithmetic tables
___ Spell checker or spelling dictionary
___ Other___

(Continued)

Box 8.3

Checklist of Criteria for Making Decisions (Continued)

RESPONSE (Continued)

Yes   No

____ ____ 2.   Can use pencil to fill in bubble answer sheets

____ ____ 2a.   Can use pencil to fill in bubble answer sheets with assistance or the following accommodation(s):

      ___ Pencil grip

      ___ Bubbles enlarged

      ___ Bubbles presented on the test itself next to each question

      ___ Bubbles enlarged and presented on the test itself next to each question

      ___ Scribe

      ___ Calculator

      ___ Abacus

      ___ Arithmetic tables

      ___ Spell checker or spelling dictionary

      ___ Other____

Use the following section to guide decisions about participation in assessments.

LEVEL OF PARTICIPATION

____ ____ 1.   _____'s current level of skill and noted accommodations allow him/her to meaningfully participate in all/part (circle one) of the following assessments;

      ___ Classroom

      ___ District___specify which one(s)

      ___ State/national___specify which one(s)

If partial participation is considered more appropriate, specify which part of the assessment. The decision for partial participation on the assessment is based on the following:

____ ____ 2.   _____ is incapable of meaningfully participating in the assessment, regardless of accommodation. This decision is based on the following:

(Continued)

Box 8.3

Checklist of Criteria for Making Decisions (Continued)

___ ___ 3. Consideration has been given to how _____'s learning will be assessed. An alternate assessment of learning will be conducted as follows:

___ ___ 4. The consequences of alternate assessment participation and/or use of accommodations (if applicable) have been discussed with _____'s parent/guardian.

___ ___ 5. Proactive planning is under way to provide _____ the opportunity to meaningfully participate in the assessment cycle (either entire or partial) next year as follows (specify who is involved in the planning process):

___ ___ 6. _____'s parent/guardian is fully aware of these participation and accommodation decisions and has been a part of the process. Explain, if necessary.

Your signature on this form indicates that you were a part of the participation and accommodation decision-making process for _____. You are in agreement with the decisions.

_____   _____   _____
IEP Team Chair   Building Administrator   Student

_____   _____   _____
Parent/Guardian   Student's Teacher(s)   Others

Date of Meeting: _____

* Careful consideration must be given to the purpose of the test for which these accommodations are provided.

state and district regarding assessment and accommodations. Some may exist but are broadly discussed and lend little information about how building-level IEP teams are to operationalize them into day-to-day practice. The purpose of this and other checklists included in this book is to promote the participation of students with disabilities in assessment and accountability systems.

The tool for the participation decision-making process makes clear the thoughtful consideration needed for assessment decisions. Box 8.4 provides a form to guide your decision about which assessment a student takes. Each

Box 8.4

**Example of a Checklist for the Participation
Decision-Making Process**

Checklist for Deciding Assessment Type

Name: **School year:**

School: **Special Education Teacher:**

Grade: **Date:**

The purpose of this checklist is to facilitate and justify what district or state assessment program _____ will be a part of. Three options are being considered: general (or the name of the district/state assessment), alternate, or both (general/alternate) assessments. The final decision must be justified and validated by several parties including, but not limited to _____ (student, if deemed appropriate), parent/guardian, special and general education teachers, and involved related personnel.

On _____ (date), the IEP team, after much discussion and consideration, has decided that _____ is a candidate for:

_____1.   General assessment (or the name of the district/state assessment)
                _____ a.   Without accommodation
                _____ b.   With the following accommodation(s):

_____2.   Alternate assessment eligibility form is completed

_____3.   General/Alternate.* List the content areas _____

*This decision is based on the following (list any and all factors that led to the above decision—be specific):

While this decision was made based on the above factors, we recognize that the decision is not a permanent one and may change, if warranted and appropriate, at another scheduled IEP meeting.

Parent/Guardian _____   Other   _____

Administrator _____   Special Educator   _____

IEP Chair _____   General Educator   _____

Related Service Providers: _____   _____   _____

decision is an extensive one and may need to be tailored to the type and kind of assessment administered. As you make the participation decision, you should also be considering the accommodations that the student needs.

For some students, decisions about what assessment they will take can be made as early as elementary school. Students with more significant cognitive disabilities will probably need an alternate assessment, or partial assessment, that better reflects the individualized goals, objectives, and curriculum they are learning. We recognize that not all decisions are clear cut. If you are unsure of the academic path a student will take, regardless of age, have the student participate in the general assessment with needed accommodations.

Where appropriate, include older, able students in these discussions. Students need to be aware that these types of decisions are being made and should participate in them, for they can provide valuable input to the process. It is important to keep in mind that as these students move from the K-12 education system and into postsecondary settings, they will be in charge of these kinds of decisions.

Rethinking the IEP Format

It is time to rethink the content and structure of the IEP. While the mandated parts of the IEP will remain intact, additional areas are needed to document assessment decisions about participation and accommodation on tests and to document accommodations needed during instruction. The key is to align accommodations provided during the instructional process with those needed for classroom, district, and state assessment. As discussed earlier in this chapter, not all accommodations provided during instruction are appropriate during an assessment process. However, some types of assessments—for example, performance tests—are more amenable to a wider range of accommodations.

In Box 8.5, we identify those states that have written guidelines suggesting that accommodations used on state assessments be consistent with those used in the classroom. Colorado, Kentucky, and Wyoming require assessment accommodations to be written into a student's IEP at least three months prior to the state assessment window.

Additional IEP Components

At minimum, two sections must be clearly delineated on IEPs: instructional accommodations and testing accommodations.

One possible IEP format would require that the IEP team create its own list of the student's needed instructional accommodations (see Box 8.6). Another possible format would provide a checklist of allowed instructional accommodations (see Box 8.7). In this format, it is important to provide an "Other" option as students' needs vary. This option allows for the provision of an accommodation that may not be listed on the checklist. Instructional accommodations may vary according to content area of

Box 8.5

Making the Instruction to Assessment Accommodation Link: The Instruction to Assessment Flow

State	Accommodations Include Those Used in Classroom Instruction	State	Accommodations Include Those Used in Classroom Instruction
Alabama	×	Montana	×
Alaska	×	Nebraska	×
Arizona		Nevada	×
Arkansas	×	New Hampshire	×
California		New Jersey	×
Colorado	×	New Mexico	×
Connecticut	×	New York	
Delaware	×	North Carolina	×
Florida	×	North Dakota	
Georgia	×	Ohio	×
Hawaii	×	Oklahoma	×
Idaho	×	Oregon	×
Illinois	×	Pennsylvania	×
Indiana	×	Rhode Island	×
Iowa	×	South Carolina	×
Kansas	×	South Dakota	×
Kentucky	×	Tennessee	
Louisiana	×	Texas	×
Maine	×	Utah	×
Maryland	×	Vermont	×
Massachusetts	×	Virginia	×
Michigan		Washington	×
Minnesota	×	West Virginia	×
Mississippi	×	Wisconsin	×
Missouri	×	Wyoming	×

instruction. Some students may require accommodations for one area but not for another. Regardless of format, the emphasis is on thinking about what is needed by individual students to actively participate in the instructional process and show what they know.

Teachers instruct many different students each day. Most students have different individual needs, some more substantial than others. And, there are those students who, without instructional accommodations, will not learn or be able to participate fully in instruction. By documenting on the IEP the instructional accommodations a student with special needs requires, teachers can be kept informed of what needs to be done to include all students in the education process.

Box 8.6

**Example of a Format in Which the IEP Team
Creates Accommodations List**

IEP Form for Identifying Accommodations

Student: **Grade:**   **School/Teacher:**

Date:

Instructional Accommodations:

General accommodations needed for instruction.

List specific instructional accommodations needed for applicable content areas.

The examples in Boxes 8.6 and 8.7 are not meant to be exhaustive. Rather, they are a starting point for developing additional components of the IEP. These kinds of formats are necessary for inclusive accountability and assessment, not to mention good individualized instruction. (Don't forget, in Box 8.2, we provided you with one district's IEP page that requires documentation of accommodations for both instruction and assessment.) The case study presented in Box 8.8 gives you some practice in generating instructional and assessment accommodations for an individual student.

Making It Happen: Training and Implementation of Accountable Decision Making

Clearly, much learning, information exchange, and dissemination must take place among teachers, parents, administrators, students, and community members. Training IEP team members is a logical place to start. Do not assume that IEP teams understand and embrace inclusive assessment, accountability, and issues for students with disabilities (see Box 8.9 for a quiz!). The participation of students with disabilities in assessments at the school, district, and state levels requires a shift in thinking for all those involved in the IEP and assessment process. Consideration must be given to the purpose of the assessment and what it is trying to measure. Decisions to provide accommodations must be made while keeping the purpose of the assessment in

Box 8.7

**Example of an Instructional Accommodation
Format to Add to the IEP**

IEP Form for Identifying Accommodations

Name: **Grade:**   **Date:**

Use the following checklist to guide decisions about what instructional
accommodations are needed by this student.

Instructional Accommodation Checklist:

Setting
_____ Distraction-free space within classroom (e.g., doorway, windows, other
students, front of class, back of class)
_____ One-to-one assistance to complete written tasks
_____ On-task reminders
_____ Several verbal prompts to initiate a task
_____ Verbal encouragement, praise, or recognition to continue a task
_____ Directions repeated and/or clarified
_____ Small group or partner instruction, especially when learning or practicing new
facts, concepts, and strategies
_____ Adaptive furniture
_____ Other_____

Timing
_____ Periodic breaks during work sessions (specify)
_____ Other_____

Scheduling
_____ Extended time to complete class/homework assignments
_____ Length of assignments shortened to complete as overnight homework
assignments
_____ A daily assignment sheet
_____ A weekly quick strategic assignment meeting
_____ A weekly or monthly assignment calendar
_____ A weekly or monthly assignment calendar with check-in and due dates posted

Presentation
_____ Visual cues or printed material to facilitate understanding of orally given
directions
_____ Directions repeated, clarified, or simplified
_____ Directions read individually
_____ Visual magnification device

(Continued)

Box 8.7

Example of an Instructional Accommodation Format to Add to the IEP
(Continued)

_____ Auditory amplification device

_____ Written directions read

_____ Key words or phrases in written directions highlighted

_____ Visual prompts (e.g., stop signs, arrows) that show directions to start, stop, and continue working

_____ Written directions presented in larger and/or bold print

_____ Written directions presented with one complete sentence per line of text

_____ Reader to read the text

_____ Pencil grip

_____ Access to a prerecorded reading

_____ Test presented in sign language

_____ Written information presented in Braille or large print

_____ Increased spacing between items and/or limited items presented per page

_____ Templates or masks to reduce visible print

_____ Papers secured to desk (e.g., magnets, tape)

_____ Calculator*

_____ Abacus

_____ Arithmetic tables*

_____ Spell checker or spelling dictionary*

_____ Manipulatives

_____ Other_____

Response

_____ Text-talker converter

_____ Speech synthesizer

_____ Pencil grip

_____ Word processor

_____ Scribe (someone to record verbatim oral responses to questions)

_____ Brailler

_____ Copying assistance between drafts of writing

_____ Option to write an outline to a question and, using a tape recorder, dictate the body of the response, per the written outline

_____ Option to dictate answer into a tape recorder

_____ Visual magnification device

_____ Touch Talker or other communication device

(Continued)

Box 8.7

**Example of an Instructional Accommodation Format to
Add to the IEP (Continued)**

_____ Calculator*
_____ Abacus
_____ Arithmetic tables*
_____ Spell checker or spelling dictionary*
_____ Other_____

*Based on the purpose of the assignment and what and how the skill(s) will be assessed.

Additional Instructional Accommodations Needed for Specific Content Areas

List content area and any additional instructional accommodations needed.

mind. To avoid making accommodation decisions that could invalidate the test results, IEP teams must be able to answer some tough questions:

- What is the test measuring? Do some subtests measure different skills? For example, a reading test will test different skills in different subtests.
- What accommodations do students need in order to meaningfully participate and show what they know without the impediment of disability?
- Of the needed accommodations, which, if any, directly challenge what the test is attempting to measure?
- How will these same skills be measured validly if needed accommodations challenge the validity of the test?

Rolling Out the Good Stuff

We are all in agreement that getting folks to buy in to the practice and belief of inclusive assessment is easier said than done. Sure, federal law says that this must occur, but in reality many places are not yet there. Many places still look for loopholes so they can keep students with disabilities out of accountability indices. One popular way is to decide that nonstandard accommodations make a student's test results invalid. One teacher recently commented, "All of a sudden my principal is letting us give our students any and every accommodation we think our students need, even those that are nonstandard! Isn't that cool?" From our perspective, it is sad—this

BOX 8.8

Case Study to Practice Generating Instructional and Assessment Accommodations

Student: Yu Kanduit

Yu Kanduit is an eighth grader who was retained in first grade. Yu has been identified as a student with a learning disability in the area of written communication/basic reading skills. Yu attends school regularly. Yu has an integrated special/general instruction schedule. He receives resource room services and in-class support for mathematics. Science and social studies are taken in the general education classroom.

Yu reads on a third-grade level. His writing is hampered by his inability to spell. He has wonderful ideas and communicates them well. With the use of a tape recorder, Yu is able to record his ideas. His writing skills are improving with his reading skills. Yu shows excellent auditory comprehension, and his attention to task is above average. He actively participates in class activities and discussions.

Yu exhibits low self-esteem toward school. However, he will ask for and accept help from teachers. Yu is well accepted by his peers and is "looked up to" within the school context.

Instructional Accommodations
Using the above information, suggest instructional accommodations for Yu.

Assessment Accommodations
Now that you have identified possible instructional accommodations, suggest accommodations that would be needed for assessment.

Setting: **Presentation:**

Timing: **Response:**

Scheduling: **Other (specify):**

Box 8.9

**Test Your Knowledge:
IEP Team Evaluation of District and State Assessments**

Read and answer each of the following questions based on your knowledge of current district and state assessment requirements.

District Assessment(s)

1. What test or tests are used for your district assessments (e.g., running records for reading, etc)?

2. What areas are assessed on your district assessments?

3. What accommodations are allowed on your district assessments?

4. Do different district assessments allow different accommodations?

5. What, if any, accommodations are not allowed on your district's assessment?

LOGISTICS:

6. When are the district assessments administered?

7. How long does it take to administer each district assessment (e.g., days or minutes per session for each required assessment)?

8. If a student is absent, which of the following happens:

_____ a make-up session is scheduled
_____ no make-ups are allowed
_____ parent/guardian must request a make-up
_____ other (please specify)

USE OF RESULTS:

9. TRUE or FALSE: Grade level promotion depends on passing district assessments. If TRUE—Which assessment is required to be passed and with what score?

10. TRUE or FALSE: The high school diploma in your district depends upon passing district assessment(s). If TRUE—Which assessment requires passing and with what score?

11. TRUE or FALSE: The results of district assessments are used for instructional planning.

12. TRUE or FALSE: The results of district assessments are used for report card grading.

13. All test takers' scores are included and reported in the results published by the district.

State Assessments

1. What tests are used for the statewide assessment?

(Continued)

Box 8.9

Test Your Knowledge: IEP Team Evaluation (Continued)

2. What subject areas are tested by these assessments?

3. Is there a state graduation, competency, or exit exam? If yes, what subject areas are assessed?

4. What accommodations are allowed or considered standard for each state test?

5. What are the consequences of using a nonstandard accommodation for these tests?

6. Alternatives to the state assessment are available for students who are unable to take the state assessment(s) even with accommodations. They are:

    _____ a waiver can be applied for part or all of the assessment(s)
    _____ there is an appeals process that can be followed
    _____ students can take an alternate assessment
    _____ the state has an alternative assessment option for students
    _____ never heard of such an thing!

LOGISTICS:

7. What is the testing window for the state assessment? When does it start? End?

8. How long does it take to administer the state assessment (e.g., days or minutes per subtest)?

9. If a student is absent, which of the following happens:

    _____ a make-up session is scheduled
    _____ no make-ups are allowed
    _____ parent/guardian must request a make-up
    _____ other (please specify)

USE OF RESULTS:

10. TRUE or FALSE: Grade level promotion is dependent upon passing state assessments. If TRUE—Which assessment is required to be passed and with what score?

11. TRUE or FALSE: Earning a high school diploma depends on passing the state assessment(s).

    If TRUE—Which assessment requires passing and with what score?

12. TRUE or FALSE: The results of the state assessments are used for instructional planning.

13. TRUE or FALSE: The results of state assessments are used for report card grading.

14. TRUE or FALSE: All test takers' scores are included and reported in the statewide assessment results published by the state.

BOX 8.10

Try Your Skill: Roberta's Case

Roberta is currently a seventh grader who has a significant reading disability. When provided a reader or someone to read and/or clarify written text, Roberta is able to complete work on assignments in an exemplary fashion. Throughout this year and next, Roberta will continue to receive accommodations during instruction and on classroom tests. A reader, usually her resource room teacher, will be provided for Roberta.

Next year, Roberta will be required to take and pass the eighth-grade benchmark reading test, which purports to measure decoding, comprehension, and ability to answer literal and inferential questions on the passages.

It is annual review time, and the IEP team is faced with the decision of making participation and accommodation decisions for Roberta's eighth-grade year, including the benchmark test. What should the IEP team do regarding the benchmark reading test? Should Roberta participate? If so, with what accommodations? If not, why not?

---

principal had learned the loophole—nonstandard accommodations mean scores were not going to be counted in building or district test scores and the big accountability index that principals are held to. This principal is denying responsibility for some students in the school building.

The bottom line — it really is about ethics and the belief that all kids count. The way in which the message is delivered is critical. It isn't just principals making these decisions, but also IEP teams. In the first year of tracking accommodations in the Long Beach Unified School District, 33% of students with disabilities who took the SAT9 used accommodations that kicked their scores out of the accountability index. After a year of inservices for administrators, teachers, and parents, combined with a significant change in the IEP format, the next year's accommodation data showed a drop to 27% of students using accommodations that eliminated their scores.

Ways to Deliver the Message

Think of the many vehicles of effective communication you have. Use one or all of them to get your message across to your constituents. Administrators can present at principals' meetings, host administrative roundtables, or work with the curriculum and instruction office and the assessment or research office to deliver the message about the importance of inclusive assessment. Host Open Houses for teachers to come and ask questions. Focus staff development on areas of assessment and accommodations. Create a Q & A document that is disseminated to all and put it on your

---

Box 8.11

Decision and Explanation for Roberta's Case

Roberta should continue to receive reading accommodations during instruction and on classroom tests. The issue of the eighth-grade benchmark test is a more difficult decision. There should be a natural flow between what accommodations Roberta is receiving during instruction and what she is provided on tests. However, it appears that having a reader for the benchmark test may invalidate the test because decoding seems to be part of the skills measured.

More information is needed about the test. Often, reading tests measure different reading skills. Therefore, it may be that a reader could be provided for some parts of the test but not others. In addition, consideration needs to be given to the type of diploma Roberta is targeted for and the curriculum she is learning. Clearly, if she is on the same academic path as other students, she should participate in the benchmark test.

If in fact the entire test is attempting to measure Roberta's reading ability—both decoding and comprehension—then a decision about her participation must be made.

We believe it is better to include Roberta in the test with needed accommodations than to exclude her and have no data at all. If in fact the test results could be invalidated by the needed accommodations, it is the charge of the IEP team to decide on an alternate means of assessing the same skills, perhaps using a different or alternate test. Certainly, Roberta's scores may need to be disaggregated from the scores of other students to avoid introducing an inaccurate representation of results. In this case, the issue really becomes one of reporting.

---

district's web page. Develop fliers and present them at parent meetings and other events. Getting the word out is half the battle. Once the awareness level is raised, you can expect more inquiry into this inclusive assessment thing. How do we know? We have done it! It takes thoughtful and systematic planning and buy-in from folks in the district office to those at the school sites. Top-down and bottom-up works if done in a collaborative way.

How skillfully you make decisions is an important part of accountable decision making. Try your skills on the example provided in Box 8.10 and then see Box 8.11 for an example of a supportable decision and an explanation of it.

Another shift is that needed by teachers. Providing students with instructional and assessment accommodations within the classroom may

---

BOX 8.12

Myth or Truth Answers

TRUTH   The purpose of an assessment and what it sets out to measure is a critical variable in deciding assessment accommodations for a student.
Explanation: To provide assessment accommodations that do not invalidate what the test is attempting to measure, it is critical to know what the test purports to measure. [See page 146]

MYTH   IEP forms require the same basic assessment and accommodation information from district to district.
Explanation: There are fundamental components that, by law, must be on all IEPs. However, over and above the mandated IEP components, the information on both assessments and accommodations vary tremendously. [See page 135]

MYTH   Most IEP formats allow for the documentation of district/state tests, but not accommodations needed for instruction and classroom tests.
Explanation: IEP formats are all over the map. Most do not necessarily provide for the documentation of instructional accommodations, much less those for classroom assessment. [See page 135]

MYTH   IEP team members are fully informed decision makers about which tests allow what accommodations and the process of making assessment accommodations decisions.
Explanation: To date, the primary responsibilities of IEP teams have been to make eligibility and programming decisions for special education students. [See page 146]

TRUTH   If older and able, students can be helpful in making decisions on what accommodations are needed both for instruction and assessment.
Explanation: It is always good practice to involve students when they are able to participate in their educational program. [See page 144]

---

conflict with beliefs about what is fair and what will be required of students in society. The role of the IEP team is to embrace the practice of inclusive accountability and assessment and then disseminate and exchange information to parents and other staff. Chapter 10 provides an overview of what should be considered when designing a faculty meeting or staff development session on inclusive assessment and accountability systems.

Summary

In this chapter, we provided you with several resources for making decisions about participation and accommodations. We have provided frameworks to guide IEP team decisions for participation and accommodation, as well as examples of components to add to the IEP. The need to align instructional practices and accommodations with what a student is required to know and show on a test is of great importance and falls into the roles and responsibilities of the IEP team.

Now, check your knowledge about the myth/truth statements presented at the beginning of this chapter (see Box 8.12 for answers). Try to give an explanation for why each statement is correctly identified either as a myth or as the truth.

Resources for Further Information

Bateman, B. (1996). *Better IEPs: How to develop legally correct and educationally useful programs* (2nd ed.). Longmont, CO: Sopris West.

McGahee, M., Mason, C., Wallace, T., & Jones, B. (2001). *Student-led IEPs: A guide for student involvement*. Arlington, VA: Council for Exceptional Children.

Office of Special and Rehabilitative Services (2000). *A guide to the individualized education program*. Washington, DC: U.S. Department of Education.

Parent Advocate Coalition for Educational Rights. (1995). *What makes a good Individual Education Program?* Minneapolis, MN: PACER Center.

Parent Advocate Coalition for Educational Rights. (1996). *A guide for parents to the Individual Education Program.* Minneapolis, MN: PACER Center.

Thompson, S., Thurlow, M., Quenemoen, R., Esler, A., & Whetstone, P. (2001). *Addressing standards and assessments on state IEP forms* (Synthesis Report 35). Minneapolis: University of Minnesota, National Center on Educational Outcomes.

Collaboration for Success in Testing Students With Disabilities

In this chapter, you will . . .

– know the roles of general and special education teachers.
– know the roles of the paraeducator and related service providers.
– learn how to plan for the alignment and flow of instructional accommodations to assessment accommodations.
– learn how to plan for the logistics of implementing assessments for students with disabilities who need accommodations.
– know how to prepare students for different types of assessments.

In Chapter 8, the IEP and the role of the IEP team were examined. The federal requirement to include information about participation in assessments and accommodations in the IEP, for both instruction and assessment, is critical for providing students equal access to success. The IEP is the vehicle that affords students with disabilities a cohesive and consistent opportunity to learn and show what they know without being impeded by their disability.

Box 9.1

Myth or Truth? Do You Know?

Read each statement below and decide whether it is a myth or the truth about current practice.

- There should be a link between accommodations provided during instruction and those provided for classroom and district/state assessments.
- Special education teachers are in the best position to make decisions about what accommodations students with disabilities need.
- Paraprofessionals can be key players in the logistical planning and delivering of instructional and assessment accommodations.
- Related services personnel (e.g., occupational and physical therapists, speech/language pathologists) can provide insight into what, if any, instruction/assessment accommodations are needed by a student they are delivering service to.
- In some places, all students are eligible for assessment accommodations.
- Students need to be taught test-taking skills for an assessment (e.g., format of test, time limits, directions).

In this chapter, we discuss how school personnel can collaborate in assessing students with disabilities, from making decisions about the type of assessment these students take to determining the accommodations needed. We also look at the roles of general and special educators and paraprofessional involvement and assistance. There are many factors involved in the assessment of all students, including those with disabilities. However, as discussed elsewhere in this book, students with disabilities have been left out of assessment and accountability systems in school building, school districts, and states. In this chapter we examine the planning and collaboration that need to take place among educators for schools, districts, and states to be accountable for all students enrolled in schools. When you finish this chapter, you will be able to identify which of the statements in Box 9.1 are myths and which are the truth.

Instructional and Assessment Accommodations

It is important to consider the alignment of accommodations used during instruction with those provided during assessment when preparing students for assessments (see Chapter 4). There should be a natural flow from instructional accommodations to assessment accommodations. While we recognize that some accommodations delivered during instruction will not be appropriate for assessment, it is important to identify those accommodations that students need to show what they know without being impaired by their disabilities. Many different types of school personnel need to contribute to this shift from the classroom to the assessment. Often, classroom teachers are in the best position to help do this because they work with students on a daily basis. For this reason, classroom teachers and other personnel need to understand why it is important that students with disabilities participate in district and state assessments. They also need to understand accommodations and their appropriateness.

The IEP team and administration play a big role in helping facilitate the necessary shift in thinking. For some people, it is the lack of information about the definition of inclusive accountability and assessment that creates resistance. It is important that all staff members have information on the reasons why students should be provided with accommodations during classroom, district, and state assessments. Providing a guideline or list of questions to ask in determining the need for accommodations, as well as a list of possible accommodations for individual students, will help (see Chapters 3 and 4 for questions and possible accommodations).

The process of providing instructional and assessment accommodations is a top-down, bottom-up process. Policy or guidance is set at the state and district level, which in turn is to be implemented at the local school level by teachers and administrators. Sometimes there is resistance to policies sent down from above. Often this is due to lack of understanding of purpose. Another reason is the simple fact that school personnel are incredibly busy and need easy-to-understand and implementable directives. Teachers and other staff members are key to this process. The roles of all team players cannot be underestimated.

Roles and Responsibilities

Role of the General Education Classroom Teacher

Depending on the service needs of a student with a disability, a general education classroom teacher may see a student with special needs more than the special educator does. For example, if a student receives resource room services one time per day, the remainder of the day is spent in general education classes and, depending on the grade level, with one or several general education teachers. In the same manner, if the student is mainstreamed for a few classes or is in a self-contained special education program, the special education teacher is in a better position to help make assessment and accommodation decisions. Finally, inclusive schooling is the option that affords students an education in the general education setting for the entire day. This means that students with a variety and range of disabilities receive all their education with appropriate support while in the general education setting. In this case, both the general and special education teachers are in the best position collaboratively to coordinate decisions about inclusive assessment and the accommodations these students will need to maintain an equal footing with their peers without disabilities.

Even if students are mainstreamed for only a few classes, it is critical that teachers who teach students with special needs be involved in collaborative discussions on instruction, assessment, and accommodations. After all, these are our students—not yours, theirs, his, hers, or mine. Together with the special education teacher, the general educator can identify the needs of each special-needs student in the class. Together, the teachers can explore what instructional provisions or accommodations need to be considered, how they can be provided, and what assistance is necessary. Finally, teachers can examine how instructional accommodations naturally flow into the classroom assessments and district and state assessments.

Role of the Special Education Teacher

The role of the special education teacher is wide and varied. Depending on job responsibilities (e.g., resource room, self-contained, or consultant teacher), contact and collaboration with students and general education teachers will vary. The primary responsibility of a special education teacher is to make sure that students in special education are educated in the least restrictive environment (LRE) and are provided the instructional and behavior supports to achieve success. Over the years folks have begun to accept that special education is a service, not a place, and this fact has opened the doors for students with disabilities to participate in general education classes and activities.

Special education teachers are in the best position to support general education teachers and collaboratively plan for special education students' instruction, behavior management, and assessments. Although the focus of most of this book is on district and state assessments, collaboration really begins at the classroom level. Classroom teachers, especially special education teachers, are in the position to interpret a student's IEP and what it means in terms of classroom instruction. It is not uncommon to hear from general education teachers that "I have seven resource room students in my fifth-period class." Often, they may not know the needs or the IEP goals of these students or that they have mild disabilities, so mild in fact that they only require a 45-minute period of support once per day. It also is not uncommon to hear, "I've never even seen my students' IEPs!" Best practice dictates that both general and special education teachers who share instructional responsibilities for the same students communicate to be sure that goals are being met with necessary supports and needed supplemental services.

Another role of a special education teacher is to advocate for special education students. At the classroom level, special educators must talk with general education teachers about the needs of enrolled students and the accommodations that may be needed to afford them success in class during both instruction and assessment. Here again is where the "fair argument" may be raised. For example, how often have you heard "Why should Paco get extended time limits when José could also use them but he does not have an IEP?" This argument is a valid one. Some states are addressing this by providing accommodation to any student who needs it both in instruction and in assessment. There are English-language learners and others who need accommodations. Yet, until now, the only students eligible for accommodations by law, have been students with disabilities (those with IEPs and 504 accommodation plans). Recently, six states (Colorado, Kansas, Maine, Oregon, Rhode Island, Wyoming) have opened accommodations up to all students, at least for their performance assessments. It is important that special educators communicate the purpose of need versus benefit to those who raise the fairness argument. At the same time, this is a policy issue that needs to be dealt with at both the state and district levels.

Role of the Paraeducator

There are approximately 500,000 instructional paraeducators or paraprofessionals working in public schools across the country (Pickett, 1996). The recent surge of paraeducators can be attributed to several factors—ongoing collaborative efforts to integrate special needs students into the general education system, the increasing enrollment of second-language learners or students with limited English, expanding remedial programs (e.g., Title I), and the increasing demands placed on the classroom teacher (e.g., site-based team involvement, co-teaching, collaboration).

The role of the paraeducator in the education and assessment of students with disabilities is important. Paraeducators are in fact school employees who either work in an instructional role or deliver direct service to students. They work under the supervision of teachers or other school personnel who have the ultimate responsibility for designing, implementing, and evaluating education programs and related service programs for students. Paraeducators are valuable to both general and special education teachers faced with the charge of delivering and evaluating quality instruction to diverse student populations. In the arena of instruction and assessment, the word *diverse* brings to mind the need for additional hands and help in the classroom.

Once general and special educators have met to discuss the instructional needs, strengths, and accommodations necessary to allow students to be successful both in instruction and assessment, paraeducators are in the position to help carry out the plan of implementation. They may serve as supervisors of students taking classroom tests. For example, they can deliver needed accommodations such as reading a test to students or modifying or reworking the format of a test to better meet the needs of a student. Furthermore, some students simply need fewer problems or items per page, directions reworded, or the test given and supervised in a separate location. Paraeducators, under the supervision of a teacher, are fully capable of taking on these tasks. They also can be given responsibility for organizing and supervising test administration. For example, every time a math test or quiz is scheduled, the paraprofessional knows what to modify and what accommodations specific students require.

Box 9.2

Test Accommodation Planning Chart for Upcoming Tests

Test Accommodation Planning Chart					
Student Name	Class/ Teacher	Test Format	Needed Accommodation or Modification	Test Date	Actions

Using a chart like that in Box 9.2, paraeducators can meet with teachers to learn the dates of class tests and testing formats and then accommodate or modify the tests for individual students. This, of course, is done in collaboration with, and under the supervision of, the classroom teacher. No test should be accommodated or modified until all parties are aware of each student's needs and strengths.

We recognize that not all schools are able to provide paraeducators for special needs children. In these cases, it becomes even more important for general and special education teachers to team up to plan and pool energies and resources to meet the needs of the increasingly diverse student population.

Role of Related Service Providers

Related services are those corrective or supportive services required to assist a student with a disability in benefiting from education. Related services include speech-language pathology and audiology services, psychological services, physical and occupational therapy, recreation, early identification and assessment, counseling services, orientation and mobility services and medical services for diagnostic or evaluation purposes.

Related service providers are those professionals who provide any of the above services. Any or all of these related service personnel may be working with students with disabilities at one time or another. It is important to gather input from these personnel as well as from classroom teachers before making assessment and accommodation decisions. Each of these providers works with students for specific purposes, but all are working toward teaching the skills a student needs to be successful in his or her educational program and daily life. Related service providers can lend a different perspective and add information needed to make decisions about what accommodations could be used.

For example, a student with cerebral palsy may have physical and communication needs that can be addressed best by the physical therapist and speech pathologist who deliver direct services to the student. These related services personnel are in the position to suggest those assessment accommodations that are reasonable and functional, given the student's disability. Remember, a student with cerebral palsy may be quite capable of taking the traditional district or state assessments with accommodations. Alternate or partial assessment options may not be appropriate. The school psychologist may be in the position to help proactively plan for students with behavior disabilities. Often, these students receive counseling by a school psychologist. Together with teachers, the testing situation and potential reactionary behavior can be contained.

Coordination Among Service Providers

The need to coordinate all the team players for making decisions about any student is no small task. Scheduling meetings where all can attend is a major accomplishment, especially when many personnel travel and provide services in several sites. In many cases, each student with a disability has a lead special education teacher or a case coordinator who is responsible for the student's day-to-day and overall management. Typically, the responsibility of this teacher is to take the lead in communicating with all instructional teachers.

It is important that instructional teachers know a student's strengths and needs. Also, discussion about the student's IEP and the need to identify or implement already identified accommodations must occur at the start of a new school year and enrolled class. Gathering input from all players, including service providers, can be simplified by using documentation forms. These can be placed in service provider mailboxes. When returned, input can be summarized and follow-up planned, if needed. The key is to gather as much information as necessary to determine that decisions to provide instructional accommodations are warranted. Once instructional accommodations are in place, and written in a student's IEP, continue the discussion for assessment accommodations. What does the student need to be able to show what he or she knows? What currently provided instructional accommodations need to flow to the assessment, and which do not? And, in the bigger picture, of those classroom assessment accommodations provided, which will be applicable to the district or state assessment? The worksheet in Box 9.3 is useful for identifying instructional and assessment accommodations for content area classes.

The process of identifying instructional accommodations, classroom assessment accommodations, and district/state accommodations is both important and necessary. It opens up communication among all service providers. It allows a student's strengths and needs to be known. It sets the tone for accommodations based on need and observation of classroom performance rather than an IEP team handing down a decision that may have been made in isolation.

We recognize that this process may not necessarily make the acceptance of providing accommodations to students with disabilities easier. However, we do know that the more people know, and the more they are involved in the process, the more likely they are to have a stake in it.

The Planning Process

In this section, we discuss the many facets of collaborative planning for the logistics of assessment at both the classroom and district levels. We provide you with variables and issues to consider and questions to ask.

Where to Start?

The range and severity of disabilities are vast. For example, you may know a student with disabilities who requires extra time to complete assignments due to a writing deficit (dysgraphia), another one who requires modifications in spelling or accommodations for math calculations, and still another student who is more physically involved and unable to hold a writing tool or one who requires a communication device. Students with behavior or emotional disabilities also present challenges. They may exhibit behaviors that promote their removal from a setting, often because they do not want to be there or take part in a particular activity or task. Medically fragile students with head injuries and visual and hearing impairments also present unique needs. Our point is that all students with disabilities are a part of our education system. They have, for the most part, always been in our schools, whether segregated or integrated. Until now, unlike the situation for general education students, little interest or investment has been directed toward monitoring the learning, achievement, and progress of students with disabilities. New federal laws and the school reform movement have brought about necessary, but not sufficient, changes in standards, assessment, and accountability. States, districts, and school sites must examine current assessment and accountability systems to guarantee the inclusion of all student populations, including students with disabilities.

Knowing the Purpose of Your State and District Assessments

Find out exactly the purpose of your state or district assessment. If students must take a reading test, find out what skills are measured on the

---

BOX 9.3

Worksheet for Identifying Instructional and Assessment Accommodations

---

Instructional and Assessment Accommodations Worksheet

Student: _____   Grade: _____   Date: _____

Teacher/Class: _____   Class/Content Area: _____

Service Provider: _____

Student's Content-Related Strengths   Student's Content-Related Needs

Based on student need, list below the instructional accommodations that will be provided. Then list which of these naturally flow to classroom tests. Mark (**) those test accommodations that apply to the district/state assessment.

Instructional Accommodation(s)   Classroom Test Accommodation(s)

---

test. For example, is the purpose of the reading assessment to find out how well students can read or decode words, comprehend what they read, or interpret the meaning of written language? The answer to this question will influence the kinds of accommodations that a student needs. For example, if the goal of a math assessment is to find out a student's ability to problem solve and apply algorithms and formulas, the use of a calculator is appropriate. The assessment goal in this example is the application of skills, not merely the ability to perform basic calculations. If the purpose of a writing assessment is to have students compose a piece of writing around a theme, then dictating thoughts to a scribe or a tape recorder for later transcription would also be appropriate.

We advocate strongly that assessment accommodations be provided on the basis of need. However, we know that the use of some accommodations may raise questions about the validity of assessment results. For example, the accommodation may interfere with the skills or constructs the test purports to measure. Perhaps the most controversial accommodation is reading a reading test to a student. If the test is measuring a student's decoding and comprehension, this accommodation would change what is being measured. However, if the reading test is measuring a student's ability to comprehend written language, then a reader for the test may indeed be appropriate. It is absolutely imperative that the purpose of the test be known, as well as the consequences of providing certain accommodations. We believe that if a student needs an accommodation to show what he or she knows and can do, and has consistently used it during the instructional process, then that accommodation should be allowed during the state or district assessment. (See Chapter 12 for recent legal issues and cases.) This way, all students are assessed and reported (and, hopefully, counted) in results and accountability reports.

The worksheet in Box 9.4 is useful for identifying reasonable accommodations specifically for your district or state assessment.

Making Your Needs Known

Make requests of your district assessment personnel or administration to provide teachers, IEP teams, and any other persons involved in making these kinds of decisions with information about the assessments that are to be administered to all students. On the surface, a test may appear too difficult for a particular student.

For example, Gino can't take the reading test because he is a poor reader. You must ask and answer the following questions: What is the purpose of the test? Could Gino take the test if provided an appropriate accommodation? Be careful. Often, not enough information is known about the purpose of assessment and/or assessment accommodations by everyone involved in the decision-making process. Some argue that any accommodation will invalidate test scores if these same accommodations were not used in the standardization or norming procedures. As pointed out in Chapter 4, little research currently exists on the impact of assessment accommodations and test results. When in doubt, include and accommodate students. For these and many other reasons, you, the IEP team, and your district must be prepared to educate those you work with on the purpose of specific assessments, accommodations, and inclusive accountability systems. It is important to know, however, what alterations

BOX 9.4

Worksheet for Identifying District or State Assessment Accommodations

District/State Assessment Accommodations Worksheet

Use this worksheet to identify the skills measured on specific tests. Based on this information, identify accommodations that need to be provided. Keep in mind that these accommodations should be taken/recommended from those being currently provided during instruction.

Student: _____   Grade: _____   Date: _____

Test: _____

Skill(s) Measured   Needed Accommodation*

Comments/Further Action Needed:

*Indicate potential for compromising the construct assessed.

Completed by:

are available to students who need a nonstandard accommodation, and the consequences—if any—of providing one.

Deciding Who Takes What Test With What Accommodation

Once you have secured all the necessary information about the purpose of the assessment, needed accommodations, test-taking skills, and any other details, it is time to decide which students take what test. All students should be working toward the same content standards.

Even though decisions should not be based on category or placement, there are some general guidelines for decisions related to the course of study. Students receiving resource room or consulting services are, in most cases, those who are working toward a regular high school diploma. These students should be taking the same required assessments as other students. Students who are not working on the same requirements as others in order to receive a regular diploma will most likely need another consideration, namely, an alternate assessment.

Currently, there are several states that allow students who achieve their IEP goals and objectives to graduate with a regular high school diploma. These students typically are not working on the same requirements as other students who are on the regular diploma path. However, these students should not automatically be slotted to take the alternate assessment. Depending on the student and the state, these students may be able to take the general assessment. In Chapter 8, we provided checklists to guide these decisions. Although we have come a far way in making decisions about which accommodations and what tests, students' learning profiles and state requirements (e.g., diploma requirements) both play important roles in the IEP decisions.

Talking to Students

It is important to discuss with students the district or state-level assessment well in advance of its administration. These discussions will vary in depth and breadth depending on students' cognitive, developmental, and chronological ages. Such discussions should occur with all students, but they are particularly important for students with disabilities. These can take place within the regular classroom as part of the larger class or independently to discuss any concerns about participation, expectation, and preparation.

It is important to work with older students so that they can begin to identify their own needs related to assessments. When they enter postsecondary training institutions or employment situations, they will need to take care of their own needs for participation in assessments and to advocate for themselves for needed accommodations [see Chapter 3].

Discussing Recommended Accommodations

Students should be aware of accommodations recommended by the IEP team and the reasons for their selection. We strongly advocate the involvement of students in accommodation decisions. Students are often the best source of information in helping to decide what accommodations are needed and will be used. We have seen assessment situations in which accommodations provided to students were not used. For example, students often are provided extended times as an accommodation. Yet when they are sitting in a large group, say 50 students, they almost never make use of the extra time they are allowed. When asked, some students say it is because they do not need extra time. Others indicate that they are embarrassed to continue working when all their classmates and friends have left the testing situation. In the latter case, unintended peer pressure affects students' motivation to show what they know. It is not difficult to understand this student behavior. However, if indeed extended time is an accommodation that the student needs to complete an assessment and there is hesitation about using it, this is the time to discuss it. Most students do not want to be different from their peers. However, each student has a different interpretation of what makes him or her appear different. By talking about each accommodation and its purpose and use, it is possible to identify ways to adjust the accommodations for students. For example, arrangements might be made for the student to take the assessment in a different setting.

Discussing Student-Desired Accommodations

Age and developmental level are key to the issue of student-desired accommodations. Students should be fairly knowledgeable about their own accommodations needs. This is more likely to be the case if they have been included in discussions about accommodations throughout their school careers. To guide these discussions, it may be wise to use a set of questions (see Chapter 3, Box 3.5). You may find that some students, usually older students, avoid using accommodations at all costs even though the IEP team has appropriately identified them. These cases take more discussions. It is always important to include or enlist parental support in such cases. The role of a parent/guardian is an important one (see Chapter 11). Parent/guardians may help point out to their child what accommodations they see around the home (e.g., how they interact, carry out household tasks, and complete their homework). Students may automatically accommodate themselves and be unaware of it. Of course, the ideal time to have discussion is during the IEP meeting.

Identifying Needed Student
Preparation for Participation in Assessment

A student may not be prepared to take an assessment even though the decision has been made that the student is able and should participate. Given the history of excluding students with disabilities from assessments, it is likely that not enough instruction, thought, or planning has been given to preparing these students to participate in testing. There are three things to keep in mind when talking with all students, including those with disabilities, in preparation for the assessment experience:

Tailor the conversation to the student's age, skills, and posttesting experiences. Students will need to know why they are taking the assessment, the purpose of the assessment, and its importance.

Describe the test. Regardless of the student's background experiences, it is a good idea to describe the test. Review why the assessment is used, what it is like, and what can be done to prepare for it. Generate the understanding that students take these assessments to help people figure out whether school is doing what it needs to do to help all students learn. Do not assume that any of the students who take the assessment have this information.

Plan ways to prepare for the test. Over and above study skills and test-taking skills are other important variables in test preparation. They include eating meals, getting adequate sleep, and using relaxation techniques, among others. As simplistic as these sound, many students do not understand the impact that nutrition and sleep have on their ability to perform to their potential.

Teaching Test-Taking Skills

What skills do students need when taking specific assessments? Who teaches students these test-taking skills? Most of us have taken the Graduate Record Exam (GRE), the National Teachers Certification Exam (NTCE), or some other certification test. Think about your experience. What skills did you need to take the test? How difficult were the directions? How much time and frustration did you save or could you have saved by preparing for the test (e.g., being familiar with its format, knowing the directions for the test or subtest, and noting time limits)? If you went into the test cold without any preparation or completion of review books, how did you feel? Cold! If you were prepared for it, how did it feel when you found the format, time limits, and directions relatively close to what you expected?

These examples are what we mean when we refer to students having the necessary test-taking skills. Others include the ability to follow directions, complete specific sections of a test, stop at the end of the sections, fill in bubble sheets so that marked answers correspond to questions, and so on. On the classroom level, think about the number of times students are told to "study" for the test. Who shows them how to do this? For example, do they know the format of the test? Are they emotionally prepared (e.g., understand the purpose of the test, relaxed)? Have they received adequate sleep and nutrition?

A checklist like the one in Box 9.5 should be completed at least once a year for each student. As noted, this form can be used for both classroom and district/state assessments. It is important to note which, since the timeline for preparation will differ for each.

BOX 9.5

Checklist for Determining Study/Test-Taking Skills

Student: _____   Grade: _____   Date: _____

Teacher: _____

Test: _____

Test Skills Needed	Taught (Date/Initials)	Acquired (as evidenced by:)

Comments:

Completed by:

Effective educators take the steps necessary not only to instruct, but to prepare students for classroom tests and find that students perform better when these steps are in place. It is also important to make sure the students are taught what they are expected to know. Students should be instructed in all the areas that will be on the assessment. We are not suggesting teaching to the test but, rather, making sure that what students are expected to know and do has been thoroughly instructed in the class. This goes for both classroom and district/state assessments. We also are not advocating replacing regular instruction with test preparation. A good balance must be obtained.

Coordinating the Logistics of Assessment Administration

Once decisions have been made about who takes what assessment with what, if any, needed accommodation, the logistics of who does what, when, and where must be mapped out. In Box 9.6, we provide an example of a timeline of planning that could be used for a spring cycle of testing. Months will vary. The key is to list all the things that must be completed to ready students, parents, teachers, and other school personnel for the upcoming assessment cycle. A timeline such as this keeps everyone informed about what is expected by whom and when.

As the spring or fall cycle of assessment gets closer, providing for students who are taking the regular assessment with accommodations, participating in an alternate assessment, or both, requires coordinated planning by several parties. Much of this planning depends on how many students (and teachers) are involved, the degree to which accommodations for the regular and partial assessment are needed, and the sophistication of the alternate assessment. Plans will look different for the three assessment options.

General Assessment

For those students with disabilities who participate in the district/state assessment without accommodation, it is important that they know where to report and what materials/instruments they need and are allowed to use, especially if the instructional accommodation is one the assessment does not allow. For these students, their ability to take tests is important. Be sure to familiarize them with format and demands. If possible, use a previous version of the assessment to show students what to expect. Have them practice.

General Assessment With Accommodations

Along with the above provisions, students with disabilities needing accommodations require more coordination. Logistics of providing the actual accommodations (setting, timing, presentation, response, scheduling) must be planned. Who will arrange for the needed accommodations to be provided? A student requiring a reduced number of items per page will demand more advance planning than one who needs extended time or a separate environment. Accommodations that require use of assistive devices over and above what has been provided in classroom instruction must be arranged (e.g., Braille versions or enlarged print, increased spacing between items, reduced number of items per page).

BOX 9.6

Timeline for Planning the Assessment Cycle
Timeline for Assessment Cycle*

September	January	March	May
• IEP implemented • Meet with teachers • Instructional accommodations reviewed • Assessment accommodations reviewed • Complete Instructional and Assessment Accommodations Worksheet	• Plan logistics of district testing • Review accommodations • Who will coordinate planning cycle?	• Review test type • Complete Study/Test Skills Checklist • Complete Logistics and Strategic Plan for Providing Assessment Accommodations	• Complete Final Arrangements for Assessment Accommodations Form

* Forms mentioned here are provided both in this chapter and in the Resources section.

These types of accommodations require that the assessment booklets be adapted. Of course, to do this you must obtain a copy of the assessment. These kinds of arrangements introduce the issue of test security, which rightfully creates concern. Therefore, test contractors, or the test company that provides your district or state with the assessment itself, need to know well in advance the accommodations required for some students. While this may introduce a cost issue, the result of a student not participating in an assessment who is capable of doing so with accommodation is discriminatory. The cost of a due process hearing or court appearance will no doubt outweigh that of providing the assessment accommodations that some students with disabilities are entitled to and need to participate in the assessment. Using the checklists in Boxes 9.7 and 9.8 will help you coordinate a plan for providing assessment accommodations.

It is not uncommon for members of the IEP team, most often special education teachers, to be given the responsibility for arranging, coordinating, and providing assessment accommodations for all students in the building who may need them, whether or not they have disabilities. These may be Section 504 students, those with special circumstances, or English-language learners. Often, special educators are seen as most qualified and knowledgeable about providing accommodations. While this may be true for classroom instruction and tests, district and state assessments introduce a variety of different variables. Do not assume that special education teachers have the answers! It is the responsibility of the IEP team. It is imperative that all IEP team members know and understand the requirements and consequences of district and state assessments, including the use of accommodations. It is important to involve as many or as few personnel as needed to successfully plan for the logistics and provision of assessment accommodations.

Alternate Assessments

In Chapter 5, we discussed decisions surrounding students who need an alternate assessment. The logistics of administering an alternate assessment will depend on your state or district assessment. In many places, depending on the assessment method used, the alternate assessment is administered during the same testing window as the other state required assessments. In other places, district testing coordinators are in charge of the logistics of the alternate assessment right along with the required testing programs. It is important for you to know how yours works.

Be sure that only those students who need an alternate assessment take it. Your state and district are required by law to have specific criteria for who is eligible to take the alternate assessment. In most places, students taking the alternate assessment do not receive regular diplomas.

Finally, we know that there are those of you who work with students who are medically fragile. The simple act of breathing or coordinating muscle groups to hold one's head up or roll over is a huge learning task! We want to reinforce this learning and count it.

Partial General Assessment and Alternate Assessment

Students who are able to take part of the regular assessment but require an alternate one for the remainder of the assessment present similar considerations as those described above. Some students are able to take partial assessments without accommodations, whereas others need them. It is important to identify these and use the checklists to arrange for the logistics of providing them. Be sure to find out how partial assessment works in your state or district.

Evaluating the Planning and Assessment Process

Once the assessment cycle is complete, it is important to evaluate what worked, what did not, and how the students performed. Did they feel prepared? What went well? What needs work? It is important that feedback is solicited from students involved in all three types of assessment. And if

BOX 9.7

Checklist for Logistics and Strategic Planning for Providing Assessment Accommodations

Name: School year:

Assessment: Special Education Teacher:

Day/Time of Test:

Case Coordinator: Building Administrator:

Assessment accommodations student needs for this assessment and date arranged:

1.
2.
3.
4.

Comments:

Person responsible for arranging accommodations and due date:

1.
2.
3.
4.

Comments:

Room Assignment for Assessment:

Planners for This Process (Signatures/Dates):

BOX 9.8

Checklist for Making the Final Arrangements for Assessment Accommodations

---

Final Arrangements for Assessment Accommodations

Name: School Year:

Case Coordinator: Assessment:

Special Education Teacher: Date/Time of Test:

Building Administrator: Room Assignment:

The following assessment accommodations have been arranged (initial and date):

Setting:

Timing:

Scheduling:

Presentation:

Response:

Other:

---

there truly has been an effort devoted to the instruction-assessment process, these types of postevent data-gathering activities will be routine. It is important to gather similar information after tests or quizzes given at the classroom level to help better prepare the students for the challenges of the content and assessment. There are basically two parts to post-assessment

---

BOX 9.9

Suggestions for Alternate Assessments

Below is a list of possible data sources for developing or providing supporting documentation for an alternate assessment.

Checklists for:
___ Daily living skills
___ Community mobility skills
___ Social skills
___ Self-help skills
___ Adaptive behavior skills

Interviews:
___ Service providers
___ Parents/guardians
___ Peers
___ Employers

Observation:
___ Note the frequency, intensity, and/or duration of target skill
___ Informal observation of student in a variety of settings
___ Formal or systematic observation using checklists, criteria, rubrics
___ Videotaping of performance
___ Application of skill(s) in varied settings (natural or staged)
___ Demonstration of community mobility skills in real setting
___ Use of technology (specify)

Tests:
___ Portfolios
___ Performance based
___ Quantitative or qualitative

Record Review:
___ School cumulative records
___ Student products
___ Anecdotal records (IEP objectives and general progress)

---

data gathering: debriefing the implementation and assessment procedures and interviewing students.

Debriefing

Along with the IEP team that began the decision process of participation and accommodation of special needs students, discuss how things went. Keep in mind that providing accommodations to students on three

BOX 9.10

Form for Obtaining Feedback
From Students on the Assessment

Student Feedback/Interview Form

Student: Grade:

Assessment: Case Coordinator:

Date of Assessment: Special Education Teacher:

Date of Interview: Interviewer:

1. How did you think the test went? What was easy? What was hard?

2. How prepared were you for the

        Test format:

        Test content:

        Timing of the test:

        Any surprises?

        Other:

3. What (if any) testing accommodations did you use?

    a. Were they helpful?

    b. If so, how? If not, why?

    c. What, if any, other accommodations did you feel you needed?

(Continued)

BOX 9.10

Form for Obtaining Feedback From Students on the Assessment (Continued)

4. Was there any information that was "new" to you? Specify.

5. Did this test allow you to show what you know? Was it a good demonstration of what you know and can do?

    a. If yes, why and how?

    b. If no, why? What kind of test or method would allow you to better show what you know?

6. Anything else you would like to share about your testing experience?

different types of tests in different content areas, most likely given at different times and days, can be a logistical nightmare. Celebrate the successes and rework rough spots. Refer back to the completed checklists and note any changes needed on the form(s) or additional information that must be included.

Interviewing Students

Find out from students what was helpful, easy, hard, confusing, and so forth about the assessment process. A form to use for doing this is presented in Box 9.10. To obtain specific information, you will likely need to ask specific questions. It may be of interest to gather information about their attitude toward taking tests, the usefulness of provided accommodation(s), and their feeling of preparedness. Encourage students to make suggestions for improvement.

Summary

In this chapter, we discussed the role of the general educator, special educator, related services personnel, and paraprofessional. We also discussed the

BOX 9.11

Myth or Truth Answers

TRUTH   There should be a link between accommodations provided during instruction and those provided for classroom and district/state assessments.
Explanation: Assessment accommodations should be those a student is familiar with prior to the test and not introduced at the time of the test. Therefore, the logical link is to that which is used during instruction. [See pages 158-159]

MYTH   Special education teachers are in the best position to make decisions about what accommodations students with disabilities need.
Explanation: Those who teach students with disabilities are in the best position together with other school personnel to make decision about accommodations. [See pages 159-160]

TRUTH   Paraprofessionals can be key players in the logistical planning and delivering of instructional and assessment accommodations.
Explanation: When available, paraeducators can be vital to the instruction and assessment process. [See pages 161-162]

TRUTH   Related services personnel (e.g., occupational and physical therapists, speech/language pathologists) can provide insight into what, if any, instruction/assessment accommodations are needed by a student they are delivering service to.
Explanation: Anyone who provides services to students with disabilities can provide valuable input during the process of making decisions about instruction and assessment accommodations. [See pages 162-163]

TRUTH   In some places, all students are eligible for assessment accommodations.
Explanation: While a few states (currently six states) allow all students to be eligible for accommodations on the state performance test, most do not. This topic is being discussed with increasing frequency, however. [See page 161]

TRUTH   Students need to be taught test-taking skills for an assessment (e.g., format of test, time limits, directions).
Explanation: Levels of concerns as well as anxiety can be dissipated by helping students become more familiar with the test and its format. [See pages 170-171]

necessary steps to be taken for an inclusive assessment to take place, namely, (a) consider and decide on the purpose of the assessment, (b) decide on the type of assessment option for each student with a disability, (c) decide and delineate what accommodations, if any, are needed, (d) talk with the student to identify acceptance of accommodations and understanding of the assessment, and (e) plan for the logistics of the administration of the assessment.

Now check your knowledge about the myth/truth statements presented at the beginning of this chapter (see Box 9.11 for answers). Try to give an explanation for why each statement is correctly identified either as a myth or as the truth.

Resources for Further Information

Archer, A., & Gleason, M. (1992). *Advanced skills for school success*. North Billerica, MA: Curriculum Associates.

Archer, A., & Gleason, M. (2002). *Skills for school success*. North Billerica, MA: Curriculum Associates.

Brolin, D. E. (Ed.). (1991). *Life centered career education: A competency-based approach* (3rd ed.). Reston, VA: Council for Exceptional Children.

Council of Chief State School Officers. (1998). *Questions and answers about assessment accommodations and students with disabilities: A guide for parents and teachers.* Prepared by the State Collaborative on Assessment and Student Standards, Assessing Special Education Students Project. Washington, DC: Author.

DeBoer, A. (1995). *Working together: The art of consulting and communicating.* Longmont, CO: Sopris West.

DeBoer, A., & Fister, K. (1995). *Working together: Tools for collaborative teaching.* Longmont, CO: Sopris West.

Dettmer, P., Thurston, L., & Dyck, N. (1993). *Consultation, collaboration, and teamwork for students with special needs.* Needham Heights, MA: Allyn & Bacon.

Elliott, J.L., & Thurlow, M.L. (2000). *Improving test performance of students with disabilities in district and state assessments.* Thousand Oaks, CA: Corwin Press.

Friend, M., & Cook, L. (1996). *Interactions: Collaboration skills for school professionals* (2nd ed.). White Plains, NY: Longman.

Kleinert, H. L., & Kearns, J. (2001). *Alternate assessment: Measuring outcomes and supports for students with disabilities.* Baltimore: Brookes.

McGahee, M., Mason, C., Wallace, T., & Jones, B. (2001). *Student-led IEPs: A guide for student involvement.* Arlington, VA: Council for Exceptional Children.

Pickett, A. L. (1996). *State of the art report on paraeducators in education and related services.* New York: City University of New York, National Resource Center for Paraeducators in Education and Related Services, Center for Advanced Study in Education.

Pickett, A. L. (1999). *Strengthening and supporting teacher/provider – paraeducator teams: Guidelines for paraeducator roles, supervision, and preparation.* New York: City University of New York, Center for Advanced Study in Education Graduate Center.

Sugai. G. M., & Tindal, G. A. (1993). *Effective school consultation: An interactive approach.* Pacific Grove, CA: Brooks/Cole.

Thompson, S., Quenemoen, R., Thurlow, M., & Ysseldyke, J. (2001). *Alternate assessments for students with disabilities.* Thousand Oaks, CA: Corwin Press.

Thurlow, M., Olsen K., Elliott, J., Ysseldyke, J., Erickson, R., & Ahearn, E. (1996). *Alternate assessments for students with disabilities* (NCEO Policy Directions 5). Minneapolis: University of Minnesota, National Center on Educational Outcomes.

10

Gaining Support From Above:
What Needs to Happen?

Topics

☐ Roles and Responsibilities
☐ Putting It All Together: Monitoring the Integrity of Implementation
☐ Organizing Staff Development

In this chapter, you will . . .

– learn about the roles and responsibilities of boards of education, district- and building-level administrators, coordinators, and supervisors.
– know what steps and procedures are needed to implement a systemic inclusive assessment system.
– learn about a model of staff development for training staff.

In Chapter 9, we discussed the roles of teachers, related service providers, and paraeducators. We also examined the logistics of planning, preparing the student, implementing assessment, and the need for coordinated collaboration. In this chapter, we discuss, in relation to the assessment of students with disabilities, the roles and responsibilities of the administrator, both building and district level; boards of education; district assessment coordinators; special education administrators; and department chairpersons. Although we address them individually, they are not mutually exclusive. And although there may not be overlapping roles and responsibilities by different players at the policy level, there most certainly is overlap in practice. Bringing inclusive accountability and assessment policies into practice requires the work and coordination of several key players. In this chapter, we also describe how to plan staff

---

Box 10.1

Myth or Truth? Do You Know?

Read each statement below and decide whether it is a myth or the truth about current practice.

- Most schools and districts have a mission statement for both learning and assessment.
- Staff development is provided to prepare staff for inclusive assessment, its purpose, and how to implement it with diverse student learners.
- Most administrators have a working knowledge of testing, assessment, and accountability and can distinguish among them within the broader context of inclusive accountability.
- There is uniform implementation of participation, accommodations, and reporting for students with disabilities from building to building and department to department within a school district.
- There are many loopholes in assessment practices that allow students with disabilities to be left out of accountability reports.

---

development and make reference to the section of this book titled "Resources: Staff Development," which is full of materials for actually conducting staff development and engaging people in activities that will lead to inclusive assessment and accountability systems.

When you complete this chapter, you will be able identify which of the statements in Box 10.1 are myths and which are the truth.

Roles and Responsibilities

As inclusive assessment programs and accountability systems continue to become the reality of school-based reform, state and local education agencies must work together to find ways to measure the learning progress of all students, including those with disabilities. The need for communication and joint planning to accomplish the ultimate goal of assessment and accountability is vital to the process and progress of implementation.

For inclusive assessment and accountability systems to evolve, we believe that several factors, at minimum, need to be in place (see Box 10.2). We start from the premise that all kids count and must be accounted for. We begin the road of responsibility with the leaders at the state and school district levels and with professional organizations. Until recently, the idea of inclusive assessment and accountability has not been at the forefront of administrators' agendas. Their focus has been on curriculum, instruction, leadership, testing programs, budget and resource allocation, among many others. However, until recently, district and state testing programs have not necessarily pushed administrators to be equipped with a

---

BOX 10.2

Necessary Components for Inclusive Accountability Systems

A belief, mission, or vision statement about the learning and assessment of all students.

The development of an accountability and assessment policy that includes the following:

- Participation of all students, including students with disabilities, in the assessment program
- Accommodation of diverse learner needs in instruction and assessment
- Accounting for all test takers, including those who participate in an alternate assessment
- A plan for the implementation and use of assessment results
- Reporting of the results of the test to parents, teachers, and the community at large
- Observable and measurable benchmarks to mark progress toward inclusive accountability and assessment
- A plan for staff development, technical assistance, information, dissemination, and exchange

---

working knowledge of the broader issues of inclusive assessment and accountability in today's diverse learning society.

The Superintendent

As leader of the school district, in conjunction with the board of education, the superintendent of schools is responsible for broaching policy-level discussion about assessment and accountability. Discussions should be about mission and belief statements and the necessary components needed to foster information gathering and discussion at both the building and district levels. The role of the superintendent is to set a tone that communicates the importance of inclusive accountability—what it looks like for all students, teachers, parents, and the community and how this translates into shifts in beliefs and current practice at the district, school, and classroom levels.

Discussions about policy and guidelines for assessment practices are imperative. If you are in a state with strong local control, you may have more latitude to set these. However, for those of you in states where policy travels from the top down, it is important to converse with your state's assessment department to find out exactly what the statewide policy is for including students with disabilities in assessment. And, we know these change regularly.

Most states that have state assessment programs have written guidelines about their policies, but many of these guidelines are vague, in turn leading to wide and varied interpretation and implementation. In fact, such leeway in interpretation has resulted in some districts and school buildings finding ways to leave students with disabilities out of the assessment or reporting cycle to "look good" or rank high among other buildings and districts. This, however, makes equitable comparisons between school sites or states very difficult (even if the same test is used). If some states, districts, and schools follow the guidelines as suggested and others take latitude in implementation, the result usually is a competitive edge for those who find the loopholes to leave students with disabilities out of assessment reports, creating the opportunity for dissonance among administrators, teachers, parents, and others.

We must begin to examine the practice of "looking good" versus being accountable for all students learning. Superintendents are in the position to streamline what state-level policy means across school districts and how it needs to be implemented (for guidelines, see Chapters 2 and 3). But superintendents too want to "look good" among peers. In fact, superintendents' salary increases and contracts are more and more being tied to the results of test scores in their districts. The temptation to put pressure on teaching staff and assessment personnel in a district to "make it happen" is prevalent at the district administrative level as well. However, if it isn't student focused, then we have concern!

Although most districts and schools have mission statements and visions about learning, they lack the same for assessment. Mission statements for learning need to be grounded in the evaluation of student learning. Only then can we know whether all students are being provided the opportunity to learn as reflected in the school vision. A public mission statement about learning and assessment will help defer some of the temptation to test the best and baby-sit the rest. Public commitment holds us all accountable for our behavior. To heighten the discussion of these issues, superintendents' professional organizations, both regional and national, must make inclusive assessment and accountability central themes of conferences and publications so as to develop ways to address leveling the playing field for all superintendents, districts, and schools.

Boards of Education

Working in tandem with the superintendent of schools, the board of education (BOE) is in the position to approve, support, and operationalize policy into practice in the district. It is important that the BOE has a working understanding of the purpose and responsibility of an inclusive accountability system for all students residing in the state as well as the district's attendance area. For example, include in the information packet that goes to the BOE national and state trends and practices in assessment, including participation, accommodation, and reporting of results. Help create a knowledge base of what leaders in the field of assessment are saying. Provide a balanced view of current practices.

The issue of inclusive accountability should be discussed not as a budgetary item but, rather, as one of ethics and responsibility. The role of the BOE is to make sure that decisions and discussions about inclusive assessment and accountability are proactive and aligned with the published mission/vision statement of the district. If the belief is that all students can learn to even higher levels than before, all students, especially those with disabilities, must be included in the discussion and in decisions about inclusive assessment.

Encourage BOE members to talk to state and national boards. Find out what is going on and how changes are being made. The BOE can create the policies that promote change for the betterment of all students. But until "all" does mean "all" for instruction, assessment, and accountability, vision and mission statements are nothing but words on paper.

District Assessment Coordinators

District assessment coordinators or administrators are critical to policy implementation. While we understand that many districts may not have a person in this position, or the job duties are assumed under another title (e.g., Assistant Superintendent for Curriculum and Instruction), involvement of personnel in charge of implementing the district assessment is key. However, it is important to find out what they know and understand about inclusive assessment and accountability. For example, even though most departments of education at the state level have assessment coordinators or directors of assessment, their work and efforts do not always reflect the inclusion of students with special needs. It is not uncommon for there to be little or no communication between state directors of special education and state directors of assessment. Hence, some policies and practices are created without knowledge or input from very closely related departments. This same scenario may be carried out at the local district as well. That is, policy and practices are implemented that do not reflect special populations.

Most often, the test scores of special needs students have been (and continue to be) excluded because it is argued that any accommodation to the assessment provides an unfair advantage or skews the test results. Some argue that the provision of any accommodation that was not used during the standardization of the test invalidates the results. Counterarguments also raise issues: "How valid are the test results of a student with a disability who is *not* granted a needed accommodation?" "How will you validly assess these students?" "How will you account for those students using nonstandard accommodations?" The answers to these questions have become the focus of recent legal cases (see Chapter 12).

For years it has been too easy to justify the exclusion of special needs students from assessments. We now know too much about assessment, instruction, and how to account for learning for all students to allow this discriminatory practice to continue. One of the roles of the district assessment coordinator is to make sure that "all" means "all."

It is important that assessment coordinators take part in assessment discussions held by the BOE and superintendent. Coordinators need to disseminate information about state and national inclusive assessment practices. It is the role of the assessment coordinator to embrace the concept of an alternate assessment for those students who are unable to meaningfully participate in the general assessment. Assessment coordinators need to be clear and reinforce the fact that an inclusive accountability system means that all students count and are accounted for. This means that all, including the small percentage of students who take an alternate assessment, must be counted and accounted for.

It is the role of the assessment coordinator to meet building administration and other personnel such as curriculum coordinators and department chairpersons to disseminate and exchange information about inclusive assessment. This is no small task. There is often a strong reaction from teachers and administrators when the practice of inclusive assessment and accountability is introduced. We know that most teachers and administrators are put at ease when the "how to" about actual implementation of this requirement is explained. Start with small groups and be prepared to answer or defer until more information about an issue can be explored. The bottom line for all this is alignment to the district and building vision/mission statement about learning and assessment. Backing up what was written—do you really believe that all students can learn?

District Curriculum Coordinators

District Curriculum Coordinators (or Assistant Superintendents), in essence, hold the roadmap of learning that leads to successful achievement on district and state assessments. In many districts they are responsible for coordinating the staff development that supports the standards adopted by the board of education. These folks often lead the charge (and a big one it is) for adopting curricula, programs, and textbooks to support these standards. Must we say more to emphasis how critical curriculum coordinators are to the effort to create strong instructional programs that are assessed and publicly reported?

It is critical for assessment coordinators and curriculum coordinators to work together for a number of reasons, including to: (1) evaluate whether the curriculum and instruction programs are the best for the school district population, (2) provide teachers and administrators the tools to monitor student learning progress in preparation for district or state assessments, (3) evaluate the impact of staff development on instruction and student achievement, and (4) examine overall assessment results for trends.

Additionally, it is critical for special education coordinators and assessment and curriculum coordinators to work together to be sure that students with disabilities are included in all curriculum and instruction programs and staff development efforts. The achievement data of students with disabilities should be disaggregated and shared with teachers and district and school site administrators. In Long Beach Unified School District, for example, the research department created a report that disaggregated the district and state results of students with disabilities served in resource programs and self-contained programs. In addition, reports were generated looking at how many students used assessment accommodations and the types of accommodations they used. Of these students who needed accommodation, those using accommodations considered to be nonstandard for the state test, thereby kicking those assessment results out the of state accountability performance report, were counted. Without this information, inaccurate perceptions grow (e.g., "those students with disabilities will bring down my building test scores"), and decisions are made that have little foundation in reality (e.g., encouraging the use of nonstandard accommodations so students' test scores are excluded from building and district reports). Looking at data has shown some districts that their students with disabilities are making greater gains in scores than other students, and that removing the scores of students with disabilities makes no difference in overall school or district performance.

Building Administrators

Building administrators are responsible for the integrity of the implementation of the assessment program in their school sites. That is, they are responsible for making sure that assessment decisions for students with special needs are informed decisions and that faculty and staff understand the meaning of inclusive assessment and accountability and what it looks like. It is important to avoid portraying the notion that this is a top-down decision, or one that makes no sense for students. It is not uncommon for ideas or policies that go against our own personal belief systems to be announced as "another idea from above" (and sometimes a few colorful adjectives are added). This portrays to faculty and staff that another bandwagon is coming through town. Be very clear and understand that this is not a bandwagon approach. Change for many comes slowly and with great trepidation. As instructional leaders, building administrators have as their charge to lead their staff into changes and implementation of inclusive accountability and assessment for the betterment of all students.

Be sure to examine how and what you think about it before you present it to the staff. Remember, you are a role model for instruction and curriculum and assessment and responsible for student learning and the instruction delivered to them (see the section on Organizing Staff Development, and the Resources section that supports staff development efforts).

As a building administrator, you need to work with the team(s) of personnel that makes the decisions about participation in and accommodation of needs for classroom and district assessments. Most often, this is the Child Success Team (also known by other names such as Instructional Support Team and Teacher Assistance Team) or in some cases the IEP team. The Child Success Team (CST) usually has the charge of providing student-centered interventions, both academic and behavioral, in the classroom. The CST also makes direct recommendations about whether students need and/or qualify for additional services and remedial or special education. These recommendations are usually carried to the IEP team that makes the final decision and approves an Individualized Educational Program for the student.

The place to start is with the IEP team and other personnel who are making the decisions about assessment. Regardless of when or where the IEP teams meet, the members of this team must be equipped with information to allow them to make informed decisions about participation and accommodations for classroom, district and state assessments. These personnel are those who decide what instructional accommodations are needed for a student (e.g., reduced assignments, extended time for projects, and outlines of lecture notes). Instructional and assessment accommodations should be linked and flow naturally from one testing situation to another.

If few instructional accommodations are being delivered in the classroom, a problem may be at hand. Accommodations should not be unveiled on the day of a test, but should be familiar to the student through their use in the classroom. If a teacher does not make this provision during classroom instruction, then two things may occur: There may not be any flow in accommodations, natural or not, from instruction to assessment; and teachers may be reluctant to grant or see the need for an accommodation on an assessment because it is provided during the instructional process.

Even though the best-case scenario is for the district to adopt an IEP form for all IEP teams to use, you do not need to wait for one to be developed. We offer a possible format for documenting assessment accommodation needs that you can use and adapt for the IEPs in your district or building IEP (see Box 10.3). In this example are three sections for both instructional and assessment accommodations that prompt people to think about and identify, up front, what instructional, classroom, and district assessment accommodations are needed. Keep in mind that if a student is to participate in the district assessment with accommodations, these accommodations are determined in light of the purpose of the test using a combination of two considerations: the needs of the student and what is written on the IEP (see Chapters 3 and 4 for a discussion).

As the building administrator, it is important to initiate discussions with the person in charge of IEP teams, usually a district special education administrator. The key is providing a vehicle that encourages personnel to think beyond the paperwork factor of the IEP to what the student sincerely needs to be successful in both the instructional and the assessment process.

Special Education Administrator

The role of the special education administrator in inclusive assessment is vast and important. You basically are "on call" to help problem solve, disseminate information, participate in discussions, and resolve implementation issues. However, as with other education innovations, this effort requires teamwork. We recommend the team or jigsaw approach. That is,

Box 10.3

Student Name _____ Last _____ First _____ IEP Date _____ Page 8 of _____

XIV. INSTRUCTIONAL ACCOMMODATIONS
Supplementary aids, services and other support required to access general education curriculum:

Timing of Instruction	Scheduling of Instruction	Presentation of Instruction	Response to Instruction	Setting of Instruction	Other
Subject:					
Subject:					

XV. DISTRICT/STATE ASSESSMENT
Students will participate in the:

☐ SAT-9 ☐ Without Accommodations ☐ With Accommodations (see below)
☐ District Assessments ☐ Without Accommodations ☐ With Accommodations (see below)
☐ Alternate Assessment (must use IEP page-9 Participation Criteria)

SAT 9 Participation

	All Content Areas	Reading (All Grades)	Math (All Grades)	Language (All Grades)	Spelling (Grades 1-8)	History (Grades 9-11)	Science (Grades 9-11)
STANDARD ACCOMMODATIONS							
Flexible Setting	☐	☐	☐	☐	☐	☐	☐
Large Print Test	☐	☐	☐	☐	☐	☐	☐
Out of Level Testing (one grade level only)	☐	☐	☐	☐			
Revised Test Directions	☐	☐	☐	☐	☐	☐	☐
NON-STANDARD ACCOMMODATIONS	All Content Areas	Reading (All Grades)	Math (All Grades)	Language (All Grades)	Spelling (Grades 1-8)	History (Grades 9-11)	Science (Grades 9-11)
Braille Test	☐	☐	☐	☐	☐	☐	☐
Flexible Scheduling	☐	☐	☐	☐	☐	☐	☐
Use of Aids and/or Aides to Interpret Test Items	☐	☐	☐	☐	☐	☐	☐
PARTIAL PARTICIPATION	All Content Areas	Reading (All Grades)	Math (All Grades)	Language (All Grades)	Spelling (Grades 1-8)	History (Grades 9-11)	Science (Grades 9-11)
Partial Participation	☐	☐	☐	☐	☐	☐	☐

OTHER ASSESSMENTS

Test	Timing	Scheduling	Presentation	Response	Setting

there should be an assessment team assembled to work through all the issues listed above. Different personnel will be able to lend different areas of expertise. Your role is to facilitate the meeting or information dissemination to all general and special educators to introduce and explain the concept and practice of inclusive assessment and accountability.

It has been our experience, and the experience of others, that special educators are often the most distressed by this shift. It requires a change in practice and the perception of protection of students. For years, common practice has been to exclude students, often for altruistic reasons, from taking district assessments simply because they have a special education label. This practice is moving into extinction (thank goodness!). Special educators need to know that inclusive assessment and accountability means that, except for a very small number of students, all students with disabilities should be included and participate in the same assessment as their peers without disabilities.

Special educators may be the first ones to tell you how many of their students are unable to take "those" assessments. Listen carefully to those explanations and make note of the reasons. Are they due to access to curriculum? Student skill deficit? The reason given may be the very ones that have kept students excluded based on decisions made by these teachers attending IEP meetings. However, another shift is required. For years, students with disabilities have been taught using parallel or different curriculum and material. If students with disabilities are to be included in the same assessment as their peers without disabilities, they need to learn similar content. For those students unable to take the assessment, the role of the special education administrator, working with both special education and general education personnel, is to be sure students are accounted for in the building and school district accountability reports.

The concept and practice of alternate assessment (for a small percentage of students) must be introduced to special education teachers, especially those who work with students with more significant needs. The temptation may be strong to place more than a small number of students in the alternate assessment for the same reasons they have been, in the past, left out of others. Be very clear that the alternate assessment is for those students who typically have more significant cognitive disabilities and who may not be working toward a high school diploma (see Chapter 5). It should be very clear to special educators and general educators that the majority of students with disabilities will take the regular assessment with accommodations where necessary.

Special education teachers will most likely be called on by others in their buildings to discuss the issues behind the assessment changes and help problem solve building-based issues for special education students. It is important that these teachers have the knowledge and support to do so. Often, special educators feel ostracized already. Therefore, with the talk of inclusive assessment and accountability, these teachers may feel more vulnerable than before. Your leadership, teamwork, support, and staff development opportunities will be even more important than ever before.

Department Chairpersons and Curriculum Coaches

One of the roles of department chairpersons and curriculum coaches is to help clarify and put into practice the policy of inclusive assessment and accountability. Stay informed and know what this means for the personnel with whom you work. The logistics of implementation is the area in which your help will most likely be needed. Stay involved at the district level and volunteer to serve on assessment committees. Provide suggestions for needed staff development for all teachers and those you supervise. Create task forces to problem solve implementation issues or any other areas in need of addressing. Work collaboratively with all teachers in the department, including special education teachers and site administration.

Putting It All Together:
Monitoring the Integrity of Implementation

With so many roles and so many players, it is easy for things to get lost in the mix. Therefore, it is important that there be a way to document the integrity of implementation. When most educators see the word *monitor*, they immediately associate it with compliance monitoring. We are not suggesting this interpretation. Instead, we are suggesting that there be a mechanism in place to supervise the integrity of the implementation of policy. For many reasons, there will be personnel who look for and find loopholes in the system. For example, some may talk to parents of special needs students to gain support for exclusion of their children from assessment. Parents do have the final say, but they must be fully informed of the purpose of the assessment program and accountability for all students.

We suggest the use of some sort of accountability system for the accountability system. It is not uncommon for practice to lag behind the development and implementation of any policy. At the district level, there needs to be a plan of action, including a documentation format for reporting progress toward benchmarks connected to policy implementation. For example, what is or has been done to ready staff, parents, and the immediate community for inclusive assessment and the reporting of the results of all test takers? What is happening at the building level? What is being used to make participation and accommodation decisions (e.g., checklists)? Who is involved in the decisions? How many students with disabilities are enrolled in the building? How many took the general assessment? How many took it without accommodation? How many with accommodation? How many were missed and why? And so on.

It would seem most logical for the building administrator to document this information and then forward it to the district assessment coordinator, who eventually reports it to the superintendent and board of education. An example of an accountability implementation form that might be used is in Box 10.4. The flow of this process will, of course, depend on the organizational structure of your district. District statistics and trend data should be kept on this information and reviewed yearly.

BOX 10.4

Example of a Building Implementation Form

Building Implementation Document

Year/Test Window: Building:

Name/Form of Test: Grade Level:

Total number of students enrolled in building:
Number of students with disabilities enrolled in building:
Number of students taking this grade-level assessment:
Number of students with disabilities taking this grade-level assessment:
Number of students taking this assessment with accommodation:
Types of accommodations provided:

Number of students with disabilities taking the alternate assessment:
Number of students reported as not taking either assessment:
Reasons:

Last Year's Data
Total number of students enrolled in building:
Number of students with disabilities enrolled in building:
Number of students taking this grade-level assessment:
Number of students with disabilities taking this grade-level assessment:
Number of students taking this assessment with accommodation:
Types of accommodations provided:

Number of students with disabilities taking the alternate assessment:
Number of students reported as not taking either assessment:

Submitted by:

Date:

BOX 10.5

Staff Development Needs Survey

Inclusive Assessment and Accountability Survey

We as a district are moving toward an educational system that is more inclusive both in instruction and in accountability. As we continue this process, we believe it is very important to find out what is needed to continue progress and growth. Our mission and belief is that all students can learn to higher levels than before. We believe all students must be included and accounted for in our efforts to educate all children. With this is mind, please complete the following survey:

Please indicate your position:

_____ General Education Teacher   _____ Special Education Teacher

_____ Administrator   _____ Related Service Professional

_____ Parent/Community Member   _____ Other _____

In the space next to each item, write one or more letters from A to E to indicate your anticipated need for staff development.

A. Need for **TRAINING** (in-service workshop, seminar)
B. Need for **MATERIALS** (literature, resources)
C. Need for **CONSULTATION**
D. Need for **IN-CLASS ASSISTANCE**
E. **OTHER** (please specify)

_____ 1. Overview of the "whys" of inclusive assessment and accountability
_____ 2. Recent laws and mandates that affect all students
_____ 3. Purpose and uses of the district/state assessment
_____ 4. Connection between instruction and assessment, especially as it relates to accommodations
_____ 5. Address the issue of how all students can participate in the district/state assessment program
_____ 6. Session on what kinds of assessment accommodations are allowed, who is eligible for them, and how these decisions are made
_____ 7. Hands-on session on how to decide and provide instructional accommodations to students who need them

(Continued)

BOX 10.5

Staff Development Needs Survey (Continued)

Inclusive Assessment and Accountability Survey

____ 8. How to provide accommodations for both classroom tests and district assesments

____ 9. Roles and responsibilities of teachers, administrators, and other staff in district assessment

___10. Other (please specify)_____

Please write the numbers of your top three priorities on the lines below:

1st _____   2nd _____   3rd _____

Other questions, comments, or concerns:

Organizing Staff Development

Sustained and planned staff development and training is a key component to improving instruction, achievement, and accountability. It is clear that much of what is evolving from school reform (e.g., standards, aligned assessment) needs to be addressed through staff development. Administration, faculty, and staff need to have input on what will make a difference in facilitating the needed shifts in practice and implementation. Unfortunately, all too often educational innovations are expected to be implemented immediately. Little or no training or staff development is provided for educators and administrators. Staff development, information exchange, and dissemination creates a more open minded and accepting environment for change.

We offer in Box 10.5 a staff development survey that can be used districtwide or by building to find out and prioritize what personnel need and want to facilitate growth and development of the new practices. Concerns about the effect of change on current practices and the consequences attached to it result in educators approaching change with extreme caution and even misgiving. The purpose of the survey checklist is to obtain staff input on what they believe they need to meaningfully participate in the change process.

There are many ways to deliver and disseminate information about innovations, policy, and changes in practice. One way is through a series of faculty or staff meetings. It is common for the building administrator to both schedule and conduct them, but others may do so too. In this section, we provide you with an outline to use as a guide when planning a meeting on inclusive assessment and accountability (also see Resources: Staff Development for the most important points that need to be made in each component and some specific activities in which people can engage).

BOX 10.6

Goals of Staff Development

- Disseminate information to teachers and staff about district/statewide assessment requirements and inclusive accountability programs
- Provide decision makers (IEP teams, teachers, parents, etc.) with information they need to make thoughtful, thorough individualized decisions about student participation and accommodations on district/state assessments and classroom use
- Provide an opportunity to evaluate current assessment practices of building(s) and the district: the good, the bad, and the ugly
- Facilitate decisions about "next" steps needed to better align vision of learning, assessment, and accountability for all students
- Provide resources (e.g., where more information and training can be sought, articles of interest, web sites)

The outline we provide will help you formulate information dissemination and awareness of the what, why, how and what-ifs of assessment programs and accommodation decisions. It is important that you be familiar with the requirements and practices of your districtwide assessment program as well as your state assessment system.

This outline or information gathered from it can be used to provide inservice to boards of education, central office and building administrative personnel, building faculty and staff, and community members. The extensiveness of discussions will depend on the role and responsibility of the intended audience.

Goals of Staff Development

The staff development components that we have identified are designed to meet a set of goals. These are presented in Box 10.6. If your goals are different from these, the components of your staff development and the specific activities that you use should be altered to match your goals.

Components of Staff Development

The information on staff development provided here has nine components (see Box 10.7). The coverage of each component can vary. You may want to present the information over two or more sessions. The content within each component is meant to afford you an overall understanding of the issues to help you when preparing for the meeting you will hold.

For each component, it is suggested that you investigate and prepare for how the information relates to the landscape of your school district and

BOX 10.7

Components of Staff Training

Component 1: **New Laws that Promote Educational Reform**
Purpose: To briefly explain the provision of the new laws (Elementary and Secondary Education Act, IDEA), with an emphasis on assessment and accountability

Component 2: **General Overview of Definition of Assessment, Its Purposes, and the Meaning of Inclusive Accountability**
Purpose: To provide an overview of the purposes of assessment
To define and discuss what accountability is and its connection to assessment

Component 3: **Why Assess?**
Purpose: To provide an explanation for the variety of student and school purposes for assessment and the ways in which assessment results might be used

Component 4: **Formats of Assessment**
Purpose: To describe the variety of formats of assessments that are required at the district or state (and classroom levels)

Component 5: **Who's In, Who's Out?**
Purpose: To provide information, based on inclusive accountability, about who participates in the district assessment program and how they participate
To provide reasons and documentation of past exclusionary assessment practices

Component 6: **Who Makes the Decisions?**
Purpose: To deliver information on who makes participation decisions and how they are made

Component 7: **What Are Assessment Accommodations?**
Purpose: To describe what assessment accommodations are, their purpose, and an understanding of what they might look like
To create a link between instruction and assessment accommodations, as well as understanding the range of accommodations that can be delivered for both
To provide an understanding of who may need accommodations

Component 8: **Reporting of Results**
Purpose: To provide an overview of how the results are reported
To provide an overview of how the results are used

Component 9: **Next Steps**
Purpose: To generate discussion on where to go from here
To identify what needs to be done to move forward (or share with personnel the direction in which the district is moving and the benchmarks that are in place to guide that movement)

BOX 10.8

Myth or Truth Answers

MYTH   Most schools and districts have a mission statement for both learning and assessment.
Explanation: Most schools have a vision or mission statement about student learning, but not assessment. [See page 184]

TRUTH   Staff development is provided to prepare staff for inclusive assessment, its purpose, and how to implement it with diverse student learners.
Explanation: Nationally, a plan is lacking for states and districts to provide sustained staff development for creating a system that is both accountable and inclusive. [See page 193]

MYTH   Most administrators have a working knowledge of testing, assessment, and accountability and can distinguish among them within the broader context of inclusive accountability.
Explanation: The nature of assessment program has not necessarily required administrators or assessment coordinators to develop a working knowledge of tests or assessment. Inclusive accountability, until lately, has never really been at the top of the list of issues for administrators. [See page 184]

MYTH   There is uniform implementation of participation, accommodations, and reporting for students with disabilities from building to building and department to department within a school district.
Explanation: Due to the lack of or vagueness of guidelines about participation and accommodation, school personnel are left to interpret and implement them in their own way. [See pages 185-186]

TRUTH   There are many loopholes in assessment practices allow students with disabilities to be left out of accountability reports.
Explanation: Many state assessments have limited allowable accommodations that can be used. In most places the use of nonstandard accommodations results in a test score being considered invalid and thereby left out of reports on student performance. [See page 186]

---

state. This affords participants a grounded view of what is going on in their backyard as opposed to someone else's. The Resources section provides a brief overview of what should be explored and presented to participants. For more specific information, you can refer back to sections in the book. Following each component's overview are suggested activities, handouts, and overheads to help you get started planning your staff meetings. These materials are not meant to be exhaustive. Rather, they provide a springboard from which you can tailor your own sessions.

Summary

In this chapter, we highlighted several of the roles that need to be played by administrators as you move toward inclusive accountability systems. Of utmost importance are communication, stakeholder buy-in, joint planning, and staff development. Administrators are key in moving this forward. There necessarily must be a thoughtful process of planning and implementation with a cross-representative group of stakeholders. Much effort is required in the area of information dissemination and exchange. We also provided you with a plan for training and staff development that we encourage you to review and modify to meet the needs of your situation.

Now check your knowledge about the myth/truth statements presented at the beginning of this chapter (see Box 10.8 for answers). Be sure to give an explanation for why each statement is correctly identified either as a myth or as the truth.

Resources for Further Information

Allington, R., & McGill-Franzen, A. (1992). Unintended effects of reform in New York. *Educational Policy, 6*(4), 397-414.

Elliott, J.L., & Thurlow, M.L. (2000). *Improving test performance of students with disabilities on district and state assessments.* Thousand Oaks, CA: Corwin Press.

ILIAD (2001). *Implementing IDEA: A guide for principals.* Alexandria, VA: Council for Exceptional Children.

Striking a balance between multiple choice and performance assessment. (1996, December). In *The School Administrator, 53*(11), 24-26.

Zlatos, B. (1994). Don't test, don't tell: Is "academic red-shirting" skewing the way we rank our schools? *American School Board Journal, 181*(11), 24-28.

Involving Parents in Testing Decisions

In this chapter, you will . . .

- – learn how to better inform parent/guardians and other participants in the decision-making processes for participation and accommodation in assessment.
- – find out what can be done to support the assessment process at home.
- – learn where to obtain resources for parents/guardians in answering tough questions about assessing children with disabilities in both local and state assessments.

Parents and guardians must be active participants in making assessment and accountability decisions. They are powerful players in their child's education. After all, it is the parent or guardian who has the final word in the implementation of a plan. Therefore, it is vital that parents/guardians be involved in and understand the discussions about assessment participation and accommodations.

The focus of this chapter is on informing parents/guardians and those who work with them about assessment and accountability and how testing might affect their son or daughter. While we recognize that students today are often from complex family backgrounds, for simplicity we use the term "parent" throughout the rest of this chapter. We intend it to include those who are guardians for students as well as students' natural parents.

The information presented here also can be used to guide parent education programs in which topics of assessment and accountability are addressed. While we understand the likelihood of a parent reading this entire book is slim, we encourage you to read this chapter and in turn share its information with parents.

We have found that most parents of students with disabilities think of testing as a process conducted to decide whether a child is eligible for services or renewal of services. There is little thought about the need for group assessments used for accountability, which is a systematic method for checking the educational system and letting the public know whether schools are producing desired results. We are referring to tests or assessments that not only measure achievement gains but also provide an accountability system for the school building, the district, and the state. It is important that these differences are made clear from the start of our discussion.

Historically, accountability for the education of students with disabilities has been solely based on child count and compliance monitoring. Schools and school districts receive dollars based on the number of students with disabilities. Some states use a weighted-pupil funding. That is, different amounts of money are awarded to districts based on the students' severity of disabilities (e.g., mental retardation, autism, learning disability). Compliance monitoring is done by personnel from federal education agencies who visit states to see whether they are in compliance with federal laws and rules. Personnel from state education agencies, in turn, visit districts to audit compliance with state laws, rules, regulations, and guidelines.

These accountability mechanisms are no longer seen as adequate. Parents, community members, policymakers, and educators need and want to know how all students in America's schools, including students with disabilities, are learning and the extent to which education is working. It is no longer enough to base our investment in special education solely on the number of IEPs that have been completed on time, the description of services, or class size. Today, it is necessary to account for student performance and progress.

While there are many resources and networks for parents of students with disabilities, few deal with inclusive accountability systems. A system is accountable for all students when it makes sure that all of them count in the evaluation program of the educational system. This means that all students' learning and progress are accounted for and included when reports about the education system are published.

For parents of students with disabilities, one of the central issues over the years has been gaining access to the general education system, with the result being the inclusive schooling movement or full implementation of education in the least restrictive environment. So, when asked about assessment decisions, many parents are thrilled with the programs their children are receiving and stop there. In our conversations about district or state assessment programs with parents of students with disabilities, common responses have been these:

BOX 11.1

Myth or Truth? Do You Know?

Read each statement below and decide whether it is a myth or the truth about current practice.

- Parents can be powerful players in the decision-making process regarding participation in assessments and the provision of accommodations both for instruction and assessment.
- Most parents understand the concepts of accountability and assessment and the purpose(s) of district and state testing programs.
- Many parents have fought long and hard to gain access to general education curriculum and programs for their students; hence, inclusion in the district/state assessment program is not necessarily a priority.
- Parents of students with disabilities assume that their child's district assessment results are included in the overall report of test results.
- Parents understand the consequences of "Parental Exemption" from a state or district test.

- "Why should my child take that assessment? She is not in that curriculum and is not learning what is on that test."
- "My child attends a different school for his program. Why would he take that test?"
- "She could never take that test, it would be too hard."
- "Why would we put him through that test if he can get out of it?"

Using these questions as our guide, we discuss the issues, information, and resources that both IEP teams and parents need to know to make thoughtful decisions for individual students with disabilities.

When you finish this chapter, you will be able to identify which of the statements in Box 11.1 are myths and which are the truth.

Assessing Students With Disabilities: Should We or Shouldn't We?

"Why should my child take that assessment? She is not in that curriculum and is not learning what is on that test." This question, typically posed by parents, alone encompasses many of the current issues and beliefs about assessing students with disabilities in state and district assessment systems. We must probe further to find out why the student is in a different curriculum and learning information that is not on the test. What are the standards or learning goals of the district? Are they aligned with the test given? If not, why not? What is the nature of the student's disability and how does the severity of the disability preclude this student from being included in the general assessment with accommodations where necessary? And finally, if the student does not participate in this assessment, how are learning and progress assessed?

For those students who receive special education services in schools and classrooms outside their districts of residence, we hear parents comment, "My child attends a different school for his program. Why would he take that test?" We know that if that student does not take the test associated with his home district, he most likely will not take any assessment. No one is accountable for this student. Too often, when students are sent to other programs, the responsibility for their learning is shifted to the receiving school, but no accountability is required. In many cases, each educational institution has different rules and regulations it follows. A private or state-run facility may have different regulations from the sending district. For example, a residential facility may only be concerned with being in compliance with its regulations and less concerned with student accountability systems per se. The school may be responsible for specific IEP goals that the district has sent forward or jointly developed, but it is not ultimately responsible for the student—the sending district is.

Conversely, the sending district often feels relieved of its responsibility for any student in an out-of-district placement. The sending district will re-enroll the student when it has been deemed appropriate, but until then, the student's education is delivered by the outside placement. The question remains—who *is* responsible for the student?

In states like Kentucky, the home school is assigned responsibility for out-of-district students. All students must take the test and the score is assigned back to the school the students would attend if in-district. If these students do not participate in the assessment, they are assigned the lowest score possible. If the school believes that it can educate students to achieve better than the lowest score possible, the incentive is to have students educated in their home school.

Regardless of one's role (parent, teacher, administrator, etc.), it is important to find out who is responsible for monitoring and measuring a child's learning. Some of the facts that parents need to know about participation are presented in Box 11.2. Questions that parents and teachers might want to ask about their student's participation in assessments are included in Box 11.3.

Inform and Include

Often, we have heard parents say, "She could never take that test, it would be too hard. Besides, her teacher says it would cause too much frustration." It is not uncommon for parents to hear this reason and stop there. No one wants students to be in agony while taking a test. However, the cause for the agony must be teased out. Indeed, tests can be frustrating, especially if one is not prepared for the content or format. Who teaches students to take a test? When are they taught test-taking skills? Are they

---

BOX 11.2

Facts That Parents Need to Know

Fact Sheet: Did You Know????

- 85% of students with disabilities can participate in general education assessments with or without accommodations.
- There are three ways students with disabilities can participate in assessments. They can:

  1. Participate without accommodations
  2. Participate with accommodations
  3. Participate in an alternate assessment

- Federal law requires that all students with disabilities participate in state and district assessments, with accommodations as necessary.
- Students who are unable to participate in general state and district assessments, even with accommodations, should take an alternate assessment.
- Less than 1% to 2% of the total school population should be deemed eligible for an alternate assessment. This equals about 10% of the total number of students with disabilities.
- It is still not uncommon for students with disabilities to participate in the assessment and have their test results shared only with parents or not reported in district or state results.

---

taught any at all? Teaching test-taking skills is one way to prepare students ahead of time for a test they will be taking. To parent exempt a student based on the premise that the test will cause too much frustration does not hold much weight; it is not a reasonable argument. Why will it be frustrating? If it is related to content, why aren't the students receiving the content? If it is due to test-taking skills, be sure these are taught. If it is due to needed assessment accommodations, provide them.

Teachers and IEP teams must realize the importance of having all students, especially those with disabilities, in assessment and accountability systems and find ways to provide students the means to do so. Teachers and parents together must realize the importance of the participation of students with disabilities in both inclusive schooling and accountability. For too long, many students with disabilities have not been provided the opportunity to meet their full potential in the least restrictive environment. And too often, in places where they have participated, their educational results have not been included in reports. Often, test results are shared only with parents rather than being combined and reported with the data for all other students.

BOX 11.3

Look Further . . . Questions to Ask

Basic background questions that parents need to ask to gather information needed to make decisions about the participation of their child in assessment:

- What are the goals of instruction for my child?
- What are the standards that all students are working to achieve?
- Are these same standards reflected in my child's IEP? If not, why not?
- What is the written district/state policy about the participation of students in the general assessment?
- Does my child participate in the general education assessment? If not, why not?
- Can my child participate in part of the assessment (with or without accommodations)?
- If my child needs accommodations, how will they be provided?
- How will my child's test scores count with the use of accommodations?
- What, if any, are the consequences for allowing my child to use accommodations on the test?
- How will the learning of my child with significant disabilities be assessed? What is this alternate assessment?
- How are results of alternate assessments reported? Do my child's alternate assessment results count? If not, why not? If so, how?

There is a strong parallel between the creation of an inclusive accountability system and the creation of the inclusive schooling movement. Initial reaction to inclusive schooling for many was disbelief or denial, but eventually acceptance of the benefits for students with and without disabilities occurs. A similar phenomenon is occurring in the area of assessment.

Relevant facts that parents need to know about accommodations are presented in Box 11.4. Questions that parents may want to ask are listed in Box 11.5.

Past Practice: Needed Revisions, Needed Change

Finally, we know there are parents who refer their children for special education evaluation not only to find out what, if any, services they may be eligible for but also to secure testing accommodations for entrance exams such as the SAT and the ACT. In some states, assessment accommodations for classroom tests can be granted to any student by the building administrator. In this case, no evaluation is needed to secure testing accommodations

---

BOX 11.4

Facts That Parents Need to Know

Fact Sheet: Did You Know????

- Less than 1% to 2% of the entire school population may need an alternate assessment.
- There is little research that indicates that using assessment accommodations invalidates test results. There is currently much research under way.
- The 1997 reauthorization of IDEA indicates that all students with disabilities are to be assessed and reported as a part of the general education assessment system. When needed, an alternate form of assessment must be provided to ensure that all students are included in the accountability system.
- The National Center on Educational Outcomes (NCEO) and most states/districts have a working list of assessment accommodations to consider for students with disabilities.
- Some states provide assessment accommodations for all students.

---

for day-to-day testing. However, we have heard parents comment, "Why would we put him through that test if he can get out of it?"

We question the motivation for wanting to leave out any child from an accountability system that evaluates the effectiveness and impact of instruction. We believe that if there is a complete understanding of what an inclusive accountability system is and its purpose, the question might be changed to "How can any state or district get away with leaving *any* student out of assessment and accountability reports?" "On what grounds are they allowed to do this? Who is ultimately responsible for this practice?"

In the past, it was students with disabilities who were excluded from assessment. In some states, students with disabilities could be excluded from testing and still receive credit or a high school diploma. In these states, students needed to meet their IEP goals to receive a high school diploma. Skyrocketing referrals to special education have often resulted in this situation. The motivation behind these referrals has been to not only secure services, but also to guarantee the procurement of a diploma regardless of assessment results.

The purpose of assessment again must be made clear. Is it high or low stakes for students? For schools? What is driving the motivation to leave students out of the assessment results? Do parents and teachers really understand the purpose of assessment and the importance of having all students included in the accountability system? For the small percentage of students (no greater than 1% to 2% of the total school population)

BOX 11.5

Look Further . . . Questions to Ask

Questions that parents need to ask about the facts leading to the decision to have their child participate in the general assessment:

- Will my child participate in the general assessment program? (Be sure your state has a state assessment. If it does not, find out what is used to monitor students' learning in your district.)
- If the facts and discussion lead to exclusion from the assessment, be sure to find out exactly why. These reasons for exclusion are important and should be grounded in valid beliefs. Remember, the ultimate accommodation is exclusion from the assessment itself. If the reason is this:

Different curriculum

- − Find out why your child is in a different curriculum.
- − Find out how this different curriculum aligns with the state assessment.
- − District standards or common core of learning? Is there a direct correlation or link between the curriculum your child is in and the identified learning goals for all children?
- − Find out how the school plans to evaluate your child's learning and progress. What alternate assessment is in place?

Test is too hard

- − Find out why the test is "too hard" for your child (is it due to content, test-taking skills, time constraints, setting, and so on?)
- − Find out what assessment accommodation would provide your child the opportunity to participate in the assessment.
- − Find out what additional teaching (e.g., test and study skills) is needed to allow your child to participate in the assessment.
- − Find out how this assessment differs from the classroom tests your child takes. What are the similarities? How can the gap be closed?

The accommodations your child needs are either not permissible or would invalidate the assessment results.

- − Find out the basis for this. Remind school personnel that there are minimal research data that support this. Note that it is illegal to deny needed accommodations.
- − Regardless, insist that your child be provided needed accommodations to allow complete or partial participation in the assessment.
- − Find out what instructional accommodations are used in classroom instruction and on class tests. Is there a natural flow of instructional accommodations to assessment accommodations?

(Continued)

BOX 11.5

Look Further . . . Questions to Ask (Continued)

We have never done this before—provided accommodations and had students with disabilities use them during the assessment.

- Go for it! Educate and refer folks to IDEA 1997. All kids count and must be accounted for.
- Align service delivery and classroom instruction with assessment practices. Examine all the possibilities of providing your child the opportunity to participate in general education classes.

Attitudinal—"It is not fair to provide accommodations to some but not others."

- Be sure to educate those who say or think these statements that "fair" means all students getting the services or provision they need to be successful—and that this looks different for different students.
- Be sure they understand that accommodations are for need, not advantage.

---

unable to meaningfully participate in the assessment, how will the alternate assessment be counted and reported?

Relevant facts for parents to know are presented in Box 11.6. Questions for parents to ask are listed in Box 11.7.

Parents should be informed partners and participants in the decision-making process about their child's participation in district and state assessments as well as in the reporting of results. Are parents and IEP team members aware of the need for an alternate assessment for a small percentage of students with disabilities? Do they know what it looks like? The answer is usually no. We have reviewed some of the questions to ask and information to gather. In sum, be absolutely sure that parents know about the purpose of the assessment, the need for accountability assessments, the nature of the assessment, the goals of the student's instruction, and test preparation options.

Purpose of Assessment

What is the assessment used for: eligibility or reevaluation decisions for service delivery, classroom instruction decisions, or accountability? If the assessment is for the purpose of accountability, find out whether it is for system or student accountability. That is, does the assessment hope to gain information about how all students in a system or district are doing (system accountability) or how well an individual student is doing (student accountability)? The consequences attached to either one of these may be very different. For example, an assessment that evaluates system accountability could potentially result in the awarding of rewards or sanctions to the school. For student accountability, results on an assessment may mean certifying students for grade promotion or a high school diploma.

BOX 11.6

Facts That Parents Need to Know

Fact Sheet: Did You Know????

- Your child may eligible for testing accommodations without needing to be classified as a special education student. Talk to your building administrator, director of special education, and/or state department of special education services.
- If you parentally exempt your child from the standard assessment, there will be no alternate means in place to assess your child's learning and growth. This means that your child may not be included in the broader accountability system for your school, district, or state.
- In some cases, the high-stakes nature of an assessment provides schools with incentives to find ways to leave out as many students as possible who are anticipated not to do well. In doing so, schools can look good when compared with others because the overall school building score represents students who are thought to achieve better than students with disabilities.

Need for Accountability Assessments

Be sure that all decision makers, including parents, are aware of the importance of knowing how all students are performing in school, not just whether they are in school. If needed, discuss the point that students who do not participate in the assessment tend to be left out of the educational reforms and changes in instruction that accompany assessment used for accountability.

Nature of the Assessment

Be sure that all parties know the following information about each assessment (district and state):

- Name of the test
- Content areas covered by the test
- Grades tested
- How the test is administered (over how many days, how long the testing sessions are)
- Nature of the items (multiple-choice, short answer, writing samples, performance-based)
- What is done with the students' scores

The decision-making process goes more smoothly when more people know what they are discussing.

BOX 11.7

Look Further . . . Questions to Ask

Before parentally exempting your child from the district or state assessment, parents need to consider the following:

- What is the purpose of the assessment?
- What are the stakes involved (student, building, program)?
- How will my child benefit from participating in the assessment?
- How will the accountability system benefit from my child participating?
- How can my child participate? What, if any, accommodations are needed?
- What are other districts of states doing in this area?
- What are the consequences, if any, of not having my child participate in the assessment?

Goals of Student's Instruction

Regardless of prior planning meetings and discussions, be sure that everyone understands and can verbalize the purpose of each student's instruction and educational experiences. Parents need to understand whether their child is pursuing the same instructional goals as other students. If so, he or she should be in the same general assessment system, with accommodations where necessary, as the rest of the students. The question is *how* they will participate, not whether they will participate.

Preparation Options for Assessment

How are students being prepared for the assessment experience? What skills and content need to be taught? Who is teaching and reviewing test-taking skills for the test? Do students know what to do if, say, they don't understand directions? What is being done?

Parents have their own history of experiences with assessments. Often, it can be beneficial to discuss these experiences with their child.

Guidelines and Policies for Assessment

It is important to share with parents the policies, if any, that guide your district or state assessment. If needed, encourage parents to contact your state's assessment office in the department of education or web site to obtain information on, for example, how scores of students who receive accommodations are reported. Are they included in the overall report or left out? Having guidelines and policies available for parents will help them in their role as participants in their child's education program.

We share with you the story of Beth (see Box 11.8) to make a point. The abilities of too many students with and without disabilities have been

(Text continued on page 214)

BOX 11.8

A True Story About Beth

Beth was an extremely bright seventh grader who had gone on a ski trip with her best friend and her family. As the result of a ski accident, Beth sustained traumatic brain injuries so severe that she almost died. After spending months in a rehabilitative hospital and several brain surgeries, Beth returned home, not at all like she was when she left. Beth spent the next year learning to walk, talk, and make her needs known. Educational evaluations were performed, and learning levels and prognoses were discussed. In the summer before her freshman year in high school, a meeting was held with Beth's parents, her neuropsychologist, the school counselor, the school psychologist, and the building administrator. Information was exchanged and reports of progress distributed. As a result of this meeting, new directions for Beth's education as a high schooler began to be outlined. An IEP team meeting was convened and an IEP was written that incorporated all the reports and information about Beth's current condition. A reevaluation date was set for three months. This was due to the fact that the conditions of persons with traumatic head injury can change rapidly and require immediate modification.

Beth had lost her short- and long-term memory capacity as well as her ability to process auditory information, although some of these were making slow and minimal recovery. Therefore, information presented in class had to be modified to include visual presentation. All homework, reports, and other assignments had to be modified and accommodations provided to Beth so that she could participate in the educational process. Cosmetically, Beth looked no different from before. She looked like the average high schooler with no visible indication of her situation. She had learned to mask her gait, one result of the ski accident, and had learned to be resourceful in finding out information about what she needed to do. However, Beth would lose her way from class to class if not escorted by a friend.

Beth's IEP had to be modified tremendously for both class lectures, assignments, and tests, and day-to-day functioning. Beth lived in a state where students were required to take a minimal competency test to gain credit and graduate with a high school diploma. Where once Beth aspired to become a highly educated and skilled professional, she was now faced with the challenge of earning a high school diploma.

The then current IEP form did not have much room to record needed changes in her learning goals and modifications in her education program and had no place for the IEP team to note needed accommodations on class assignments, much less classroom tests and the mandated state competency exams. An addendum listing needed changes was attached to the IEP form. The state did provide a published list of accommodations that it allowed for

(Continued)

BOX 11.8

A True Story About Beth (Continued)

classroom instruction and testing; however, there was no specific reference made to the statewide testing program. The IEP team was faced with figuring out how Beth would meaningfully participate in her general education curriculum and what accommodations were absolutely necessary.

After looking into existing policies and guidelines, they found that the only policy that existed for students with disabilities and the state testing program was that accommodations had to be noted on the IEP at least one year prior to the required exam. With this information as its guide, the IEP team tailored Beth's IEP with her best interests, both emotionally and educationally, in mind. Remember, Beth is a student for whom a general education program would not have been an option if it hadn't been for her parents (and their attorney). Beth maintained her classification of Traumatic Brain Injured while being educated in the least restrictive environment for her.

It clearly would have been easier to have put her in a special education program. However, with strong work from the IEP team, Beth's program was made into one that was predominantly visual. Instead of reading books, she would watch videos; instead of writing assignments, she would dictate to a scribe or tape recorder. For book reports, Beth would make collages. Classroom tests were reformatted to be given orally with visual cues or use predominantly multiple-choice questions. This required the least amount or writing, which was needed as Beth had lost her capacity to spell or formulate written passages. For the minimal complete test, Beth was granted extended time. She took an average of eight hours to complete the test and scored 100 on every exam she took.

In the end, Beth met every requirement for a high school diploma except for one content area. This was because she physically was unable to take a full class load. Beth made the conscious decision to not pursue this final requirement because she did not have it in her to do so. It seemed too much to endure another year or two of the content course and then sit for the respective minimum competency exam. Instead, she graduated with an IEP diploma and went on to attend a private college where she audited art classes.

This true story illustrates in a very abbreviated form what is possible for students with disabilities even as severe and difficult as Beth's. She was capable of earning 100% on the competency exams, given accommodations she needed to participate (e.g., extended and frequent breaks, food ingestion, and a scribe). Beth was provided the opportunity to (a) make a choice as to the path her high school education would go and (b) participate in the accountability system and given the means (accommodations) to show what she knew. This is possible for almost all students who have disabilities.

BOX 11.9

Support From the Home Environment

Ways in Which the Home Environment Can Facilitate Successful Assessment Experiences

- Review an old version of the assessment.
- Seek out review books or other materials.
- Quiz each other on the content of the assessment.
- Inventory your child's testwiseness—how to take a test. Find out what test-related problem-solving skills your child has or lacks. For example, what does your child do if he or she becomes "stuck" or confused on the test? Know how to calculate the amount of time to spend on each section of a timed test (if applicable).
- Show your child how to mentally prepare for the assessment by verbally of cognitively coaching oneself (e.g., "You know you can do this—you have worked hard" or "I know I can pass this test because I have worked hard preparing for it").
- Discuss the importance of getting plenty of sleep and proper nutrition the day before and morning of the assessment.
- Discuss any concerns your child may have over the test.
- Make sure your child is aware of any accommodations allowed for the test and is prepared to advocate for them the day of the assessment, if needed.

---

underestimated. Most students with disabilities are fully capable of participating in general education classes and assessment programs when accommodations and modifications to material have been provided. Don't be afraid to be a trailblazer. Beth's parents persevered and advocated strongly for her. Thinking and service delivery was pushed to greater breadth and depth. In working collaboratively with administration and the IEP team, many things are possible. *However, we know* that in some cases personnel need to be educated about what is possible and legally the right of the student. It is extremely important that parents be informed participants in their child's education program. Refer back to Chapter 8 for IEP forms and checklists that can be used in IEP team meetings.

Role and Responsibility of the Home in the Assessment Process

After the terms for participation in the accountability assessment system have been determined, there are many ways in which parents can support student performance (see Box 11.9). This support can range from having parents ensure their children get the proper amount of rest to making sure they are mentally prepared for the task of assessment. It is important for students to have an anticipatory set for the assessment. That is, do they

---

BOX 11.10

Myth or Truth Answers

TRUTH   Parents can be powerful players in the decision-making process regarding participation in assessments and the provision of accommodations, both for instruction and assessment.
Explanation: Parents have the final say as to what can occur in their child's education program. [See page 201]

MYTH   Most parents understand the concepts of accountability and assessment and the purpose(s) of district and state testing programs.
Explanation: Most parents of students with disabilities are aware of assessment for eligibility purposes and the IEP team but not accountability or specific assessment programs. [See page 202]

TRUTH   Many parents have fought long and hard to gain access to general education curriculum and programs for their students; hence, inclusion in the district/state assessment program is not necessarily a priority.
Explanation: Besides working for inclusion in the general education setting, many parents do not understand the concept of accountability or the importance of having their child participate in the district or state assessment. [See pages 202-203]

TRUTH   Parents or students with disabilities assume that their child's district assessment results are included in the overall report of test results.
Explanation: For those students with disabilities who do participate in district assessments with peers, why would the parents think otherwise? Their child is taking the same test as his or her peers. [See page 204]

MYTH   Parents understand the consequences of "Parental Exemption" from a state or district test.
Explanation: Typically, parents make these decisions for altruistic reasons (e.g., test is too hard, not useful). They are not always aware of the consequences or strings that may be attached to such decisions. [See page 210]

---

know the purpose of the test? Content covered? Format of the test (e.g., multiple-choice, short answer)? Length of the test, and so on. If possible, obtain an old version of the test and have parents walk through it with their child. Hopefully teachers will have already done this, but even so, familiarity can decrease the level of concern.

Summary

As your can see, the process of assessment is one that demands informed decisions and considerations of a student's needs, educational goals and experiences, and abilities. Parents are vital to the process. In this chapter, we provided you with a variety of questions to ask and information to share with parents for them to become informed participants in the assessment system of their child's school. Before decisions about participation and accommodations can be made, it is imperative that both parents and all members of the decision-making committee fully understand the following:

- Information about the assessment
- Its purpose
- The need for an inclusive accountability system
- Nature of the assessment
- The goals of student instruction
- The need for test preparation

Too often, it is easy to rationalize the exclusion of a student from an assessment and thus the accountability system. Although the reasons seem logical (e.g., test is too difficult, never provided these needed accommodations before), all students should be assessed and accounted for in the overall accountability system.

Now check your knowledge about the myth/truth statements presented at the beginning of this chapter (see Box 11.10 for answers). Try to give an explanation for why each statement is correctly identified either as a myth or as the truth.

Resources for Further Information

Council of Chief State School Officers. (1998). *Questions and answers about assessment accommodations and students with disabilities: A guide for parents and teachers*, Washington. DC: Author.

Elliott, J. L., & Thurlow, M. L. (1997). *Opening the door to educational reform: Understanding assessment and accountability*. Berkeley, MA: National Center on Educational Outcomes, Parents Engaged in Educational Reform.

Elliott, J. L., & Thurlow, M. L. (1997). *Opening the door to educational reform: Understanding standards*. Berkeley, MA: National Center on Educational Outcomes, Parents Engaged in Educational Reform.

Elliott, J. L., & Thurlow, M. L. (2000). *Improving test performance of students with disabilities on district and state assessments*. Thousand Oaks, CA: Corwin.

Landau, J. K., Vohs, J. R., & Romano, C. A. (1998). *All kids count: Including students with disabilities in statewide assessment programs*. Boston: Federation for Children With Special Needs.

McGahee, M., Mason, C., Wallace, T., & Jones, B. (2001). Student-led IEPs: A guide for student involvement. Arlington, VA: Council for Exceptional Children.

Implementation:
The Good, The Bad, and The Ugly

Topics

- □ From Corruption to Court Cases
- □ Test Company Contributions to the Chaos
- □ Moving Forward

In this chapter, you will . . .

- find out about unintended outcomes of high-stakes accountability assessments.
- review recent cases of corruption in school-based assessment programs.
- learn about landmark court cases and rulings in the areas of providing accommodations, making modifications, and issues of "otherwise qualified."

In this book, we have discussed the issues surrounding inclusive assessment and accountability. The common theme throughout has been how students with disabilities have been underrepresented and left out of reforms, assessment, and reports on the progress of learning. Historically, educators have underestimated the potential of students with disabilities and their ability to participate both in the mainstream of the education process and in the assessment of that process. In this chapter, we provide a brief discussion of the realities and legalities of restructuring accountability systems that include all students and reflect today's educational reforms. Once again, by the time you finish this chapter, you will be able to identify which of the statements in Box 12.1 are myths and which are the truth.

BOX 12.1

Myth or Truth? Do You Know?

Read each statement below and decide whether it is a myth or the truth about current practice.

- Inclusion and inclusive accountability are aligned and in tandem with each other.
- The education malpractice of tempering with test protocols has become a real issue in the world of high-stakes testing.
- There are court cases that rule in favor of the district not having to modify tests for students with disabilities who are otherwise not qualified to take them.
- Inclusive assessment and accountability is potentially a very litigious area for education.

From Corruption to Court Cases

Historically, standardized tests have been the "straw men" of education. Unfortunately, they have put pressures on schools and educators that have resulted, in some cases, in corruption. Some schools have been pressured to the point of doing whatever is necessary to improve scores or obtain higher scores. The most recent and notable manifestations of these pressures have involved tampering with test protocols. Some of these pressures stem from the following:

- States are implementing high-stakes tests for students and schools.
- Rewards and sanctions are being placed on schools as well as superintendents of school districts.
- Students must pass a test or benchmark to be promoted to the next grade or graduate.
- Schools must show improvement to a preset level or risk sanctions and/or school takeovers.
- Teachers can be removed, administrators let go, and a state-based crisis team sent in to temporarily run the building.

Tempering and Tampering With Testing

There is one ever-present outcome of standards-based inclusive assessment. As the stakes and pressure to perform have risen, so have the critics. These critics range from parents and teachers to students. This is evident across the nation. Within the past two years there have been a number of protests and gatherings at state capitols. In Colorado, more than a thousand parents, teachers, and students surrounded the state capitol and demanded that the governor take the graduation test. The same demand was made of the governor of Massachusetts when 25 students took 800 letters of protest to the capitol. Parents in Louisiana, Indiana, and California have filed lawsuits alleging that the state tests violate civil rights. In Michigan, parents exempted or withheld students from testing, while in Illinois, 200 students claimed to have failed the test on purpose.

As the stakes of assessments continue to increase, so too has the focus on curriculum and instruction. In a national study of teachers (Quality Control, 2001) 70% of those surveyed said that instruction stresses state tests "far" or "somewhat" too much. Sixty-six percent said that state tests were forcing teachers to focus too much on what is tested to the detriment of other important topics. In North Carolina, 75% of teachers in one elementary school left over the summer because their school has been designated as "low performing" (Jones, Jones, Hardin, Chapman, Yarbrough, & Davis, 1999).

Clearly the visibility and voices of opponents have begun to make their dissent known. However, it does not appear that state assessments will disappear anytime soon. In fact, it has recently become mandated that all states test in all grades 3-8 and high school. This mandate is a part of the new No Child Left Behind Act, the reauthorized Elementary and Secondary Education Act.

Consequences of testing can be divided into those that are intended and those that are unintended. Intended consequences are usually those that allow decisions to be made involving either students or schools; in some cases, results are used in teacher and administrative evaluations. Unintended consequences span a wide range of effects, including school climate, morale, and teaching style. The fact that, in general, state tests do not translate well to local school decision making in fact may have led to inappropriate use of test results by localities. When the stakes for students taking tests and their schools are high, consequences can be summed up as what gets tested gets taught . . . unless test tampering occurs.

Test Tampering and Corruption

One of the earliest discoveries of tampering and other loopholes in state assessments was reported by Zlatos (1994), a freelance education writer. He uncovered great discrepancies between school districts' test-taking policies and aggregate test scoring reports. Zlatos found that school districts artificially inflated their test scores by excluding students with disabilities and English Language Learners from the test or from the reports published for the public. Referrals to special education and grade retention kept many eligible students from participating in the district assessment programs. However, in one case where Zlatos factored in all the students who had intentionally been excluded, the passing rate of one school dropped from 96% to 78%.

Recently an elementary teacher in Naples Florida had to surrender her teaching license after pleading no contest to charges that she illegally attempted to photocopy questions from the Florida Comprehensive Assessment Test (Education Week, 2002). If convicted, the teacher could spend up to 60 days in jail.

In April 1999, the Austin Texas school district and one of its top administrators were indicted under charges that officials adjusted student data to raise scores on the state's exam. Sixteen separate indictments charging the school district with altering government records marked the country's first criminal prosecution against a school district. An investigation found that student identification numbers for low-scoring students at three schools were intentionally altered. As a result, the altered information invalidated the student scores, which, in turn, raised the state's ratings of those schools.

Another Texas investigation in the Houston Independent School District resulted in a request for the resignations of a principal and three teachers after finding alleged tampering with state tests. At the time of this investigation, 11 other Texas school districts spanning 33 campuses were submitting information to explain the high number of erasures on the state's tests over the past three years. As a part of that review, a handful of teachers and principals were suspended or asked to resign.

In December 1999, 52 New York City teachers and administrators were named in a report that charged that they had helped students improve their test scores by "a variety of means." In March 1999, Rhode Island officials cancelled five English and mathematics exams after discovering that teachers in 21 districts had kept copies of the previous year's exam and used them to prepare students for the current year's assessment. In May 2001, 71 Michigan elementary and middle schools were under investigation that they allegedly cheated on state tests. However, what was criticized was the handling of evidence that led to the accusation of cheating. Problems were found in the written answers students composed to questions. Numerous answers did not appear to be independent work because they matched too closely. It was unclear whether the cause of the similarities was teacher help, communication among students, or simply rote preparation for the short written essays. Students from the same classes appeared to have handwritten answers that were virtually identical. What appeared to have occurred was that the teachers guessed the state test would have a question on the North Atlantic Treaty Organization (NATO). Using the state's coaching materials, teachers taught the students the definition that included key phrases such as "alliance of country" and "prevent the spread of communism." It was the use of these phrases that were flagged by the graders of the tests. Those administrators and teachers accused of cheating argued, "it's not the case of cheating, rather it's a case of teaching and learning."

Tampering and cheating on tests has probably occurred for as long as tests have been given. But the increased importance of tests may be but one factor leading to the rise of cheating. It has been predicted by many that the increase of state and district policies that reward teachers based on student test scores or deny students high school diplomas for failing a test will no doubt sustain the occurrences of tempering and tampering of tests.

Test Companies Contribute to the Chaos

Perhaps one of the most compelling reasons to consider the big picture of high-stakes testing and inherent corruption is the inevitable test-development errors. All major reputable test development companies advise against the use of a single test for high stakes decisions. The American Educational Research Association, the nation's largest educational research group, specifically warns educators against making high stakes decisions based on a single test. One of the reasons is the inevitability of test errors.

In September 1999 a major testing company informed officials in Indiana, North Carolina, South Carolina, Wisconsin, and New York City that tests in their states had been scored incorrectly. The ramifications for the mistake were strongly felt in New York City where 8,600 students were placed in summer school as a result of "low" test scores. Many of the students involved in this snafu lost scholarships, summer jobs, and senior trips, not to mention the disappointment, embarrassment, and shattered dreams of graduation.

In Arizona, a flawed answer sheet on the 2000 testing cycle incorrectly lowered scores for 12,000 students. In Washington State, 204,000 essays had to be re-scored due to a testing company error.

In 1997 in Kentucky, $2 million in achievement awards were denied to deserving schools because of a test company error. In Minnesota in May 2000, 47,000 students, including those just ready to graduate, were given lower scores than they earned. In 1998, 700 California schools got inaccurate test results and more than 750,000 students were not included in statewide analysis of results. In one case, two tons of test materials deposited after hours at a district office got soaked in the rain. Again in California (1999), the same test company entered demographic data incorrectly, giving the false impression that limited English proficient students performed better than they did on the English test. This rendered unfounded political credence to justifying the elimination of bilingual education voted away by California voters the year before.

All together, testing errors connected with standardized proficiency tests in the past three years has plagued 20 states! However, though the test industry leaders publicly warn against using a single exam for any high stakes decisions it becomes a matter of money and motive when dealing with the political agenda of state education agency or board.

Court Cases

A number of court cases have been judged over the past several years to be directly related to assessment accommodations and the high-stakes nature of tests (for a detailed discussion of the legal implications of both, see Phillips, 1993, 1995, 1996). The new frontier of inclusive assessment and accountability presents itself as a potentially litigious one in many ways.

In 1984, the landmark case *Debra P. v. Turlington* held that a diploma is a property right protected by the Fourteenth Amendment. *Debra P.* found that procedural due process required adequate notice of the testing requirement to pass the state test to earn a diploma for graduation. Although this case did not specifically address the rights of students with disabilities, it has generated at least two major questions: First, can diplomas be denied to students with disabilities who complete their IEPs but are unable to pass a required graduation test? Second, if students require an accommodation to take the test the school or state disallows, and such action results in failure on the test and consequent denial of a diploma, what criteria should be used for making testing accommodation decisions?

Another notable court case, *Brookhart* (1983), involved a minimum competency test mandated by a local school district. Students who failed the test were granted school completion certificates instead of regular diplomas. Students with IEPs who did not pass the graduation test challenged the requirement. These students had varying physical and cognitive disabilities. The court ruled that all students, including those with disabilities, could be required to pass such a test; however, both parents and educators would need sufficient time to determine whether the skills tested should become part of the student's IEP. Finally, the court ruled that assessment administrators must provide accommodations for students with disabilities as long as their use does not "substantially modify" the test.

In *Southeastern Community College v. Davis,* a 1979 case, the Supreme Court ruled that the college was not required to modify its nursing program to exempt a profoundly hearing-impaired applicant from the clinical training. The Court's ruling indicated that an educational institution is not required to lower or substantially modify its standards to accommodate a disabled student and is not required to disregard the disability when determining an applicant's eligibility or fit for a program. In this case, the Court agreed with the college that the student was not "otherwise qualified" for the clinical program because her hearing impairment would introduce communication problems with patients and physicians, especially in a surgical environment where facial masks preclude lip reading.

The 1991 *Anderson v. Banks* case involved a mentally retarded student who was denied a diploma based on a graduation test. The court looked at the issue of "otherwise qualified" and ruled that if a person's disability is extraneous to the skills needed for the test, that person is otherwise qualified, but if that disability prevents that person from demonstrating the required skills, the person is not otherwise qualified. Therefore, the court held that the school district should not be prevented from establishing academic standards for a diploma. The fact that these standards have an adverse impact on students with disabilities does not make the test unlawful.

Board of Education v. Rowley reviewed the intent of the Education for All Handicapped Act (EHA), enacted in 1975 and renamed in 1991 the Individuals with Disabilities Education Act. The court ruled that the Act mandated specialized and individualized education but did not guarantee any specific educational outcome. In fact, the court stated that "the intent of the Act was more to open the field of public education to handicapped children on appropriate terms than to guarantee any particular level of education once inside." Therefore, the denial of diplomas to students with disabilities who are unable to pass a minimum competency test, given proper notification and instruction, did not constitute the denial of a "free and appropriate public education."

One of the first of the recent court cases in the country occurred in Indiana. The Indiana lawsuit was brought on behalf of students who were viewed as not having enough time to prepare for the exams and for "failing to adequately accommodate students' special needs in administering the tests" (Olson, 2000). This suit was decided in the state's favor on the basis of the adequate time concern, with the rationale for the decision being that four years is enough time for any student to prepare for a high school exam.

Most recently, a case in Oregon has brought a lot of attention to the field of assessment, especially as it relates to students with disabilities and their need for accommodations. In February 1999 a class action lawsuit was filed on behalf of students with learning disabilities who attend Oregon public schools (*Advocates for Special Kids v. Oregon State Board of Education, Federal District Court, Portland, Oregon*). The lawsuit challenged Oregon's new statewide assessment system for being illegal and unfair to students with learning disabilities for multiple reasons. In this case, both the plaintiffs and defendants worked together under the direction of the Federal Judge to resolve the suit by appointing a Blue Ribbon Panel to mediate the issues. The charge of the Panel was to review the Oregon Statewide Assessment System (OSAS) to determine the extent to which its provisions and implementation ensure that students with learning disabilities have equal opportunity to participate in and attain all the benefits of the statewide assessment system. Among the many allegations, the one that clearly stood out was that of allowable and not allowable accommodations.

Oregon used a list of accommodations and modifications allowed versus not allowed accommodations for the OSAS. The list of allowable accommodations, however, was found to be too narrow. In the same manner, the modifications were based on extant research and not on studies conducted on the OSAS itself. Therefore, the panel found that accommodations should be allowable, valid, and scored if they are consistent with the instructional and classroom accommodations used and written in a student's IEP—unless research invalidates the construct and purpose of the OSAS. In other words, instead of considering all accommodations first invalid until proven valid, the Blue Ribbon Panel reported that all accommodations should be considered valid unless and until research provides evidence that an accommodation alters the construct or level that the OSAS is measuring. Therefore, any list of approved accommodations published by the Oregon Department of Education was found to be a guide for school districts and should not be deemed as exclusive.

One of the important distinctions in this case is that the OSAS is a criterion-referenced, standards-based assessment that is said to be closely aligned with state standards. It is not a norm-referenced test that is published and standardized by a test company (e.g. SAT9, CTBS). In this way, accommodations are more likely to be friendlier and more widely used because of the fact that the test is not standardized. For a copy of the Blue Ribbon Report and further discussion, see *Do No Harm* at www.dralegal.org/publications.

In May 2001, the same law firm, Disability Rights Advocates (DRA) filed a class action lawsuit *(Juleus Chapman, et al. v. California Department of Education)* against the state of California challenging the state's high school exit exam (see Box 12.2). At this time, the allegations in this case are still being worked through. Issues raised in this suit are (1) that the state of California failed to implement effective standards and procedures for ensuring that students with disabilities obtain reasonable accommodations they need on the exam, (2) the failure to align the subject matter tested with what students with disabilities are actually taught, and (3) the lack of an alternate assessment, as required by law, for students with disabilities who cannot demonstrate their skills on the high school exit exam, even with accommodations. In spring of 2002, the first administration of the California High School Exit Exam (CAHSEE) took place. While all accommodation and modifications for students with IEPs and 504 plans were allowed, much more activity around this lawsuit is forthcoming. Stay tuned!

These are but a few of the most recent and applicable court cases dealing with accommodations for and high-stakes assessment of students with disabilities. As inclusive assessment and accountability become more than the norm and the recognized right of all students, including those with disabilities, we will likely see even more court cases. We have learned from these and other such cases that (a) assessment accommodations cannot be denied, (b) assessment coordinators or administrators must process each request for an accommodation carefully and individually, (c) accommodations that are said to change or modify the skill to be measured should be granted unless data show otherwise, (d) research-based accommodations that invalidate the test constructs or construe a score that misrepresents the student's actual ability may not be granted, and if granted, the reporting of the score needs to indicate the use of such accommodation, and (e) the high school diploma is a protected property under the Fourteenth Amendment, thus students and parents must have adequate notice of the requirement to pass the test to graduate with a diploma.

Inclusive Schooling Is Not Necessarily Inclusive Accountability

Today, a nationwide initiative of inclusive schooling has raised awareness levels about the potential, capabilities, and means of educating students with disabilities. More and more students with disabilities are being educated in general education settings with their peers without disabilities. Students who once would have been educated in a self-contained classroom for special education students are now being integrated and given access to the general education curriculum. Likewise, students with more significant cognitive disabilities are integrated into the general education process with their IEPs driving the instruction they receive. More students with disabilities

Box 12.2

NOTICE TO ALL PARENTS AND GUARDIANS OF CHILDREN WITH AN INDIVIDUALIZED EDUCATION PROGRAM (IEP) OR A SECTION 504 PLAN

The case *Juleus Chapman, et al. v. California Department of Education, et al.*, No. C01-1780 CRB is currently pending in the United States District Court for the Northern District of California. Plaintiffs in the case, a group of learning disabled students, claim that the California High School Exit Exam (CAHSEE), to be given to tenth graders on March 5, 6, and 7, 2002, violates rights guaranteed to learning disabled students under federal law. The court has issued an Order that requires the March CAHSEE to be administered in accordance with the following procedures:

(1) Students shall be permitted to take the CAHSEE with any accommodation or modifications[1] their IEP or Section 504 plan specifically provides for the CAHSEE. If a student's IEP or Section 504 plan does not address the CAHSEE specifically, the student shall be permitted to take the CAHSEE with any accommodation or modifications their IEP or Section 504 plan provides for standardized testing. If a student's IEP or Section 504 plan does not address either the CAHSEE specially or standardized testing generally, the student shall be permitted to take the CAHSEE with any accommodation or modifications their IEP or Section 504 plan provides for general classroom testing.

(2) Some of the accommodations and modifications to which the student's are entitled under this Order, pursuant to (1) above, have already been approved by the State. With regard to others, the State has determined that they will "invalidate" the test score and a waiver will be required before a diploma is granted. While this Order requires that students be permitted to take the CAHSEE with any accommodation or modifications defined in (1) above, the Court has not yet decided how taking the CAHSEE with a modification not approved by the State will affect the receipt of a diploma. A student may choose to forego any accommodation or modification to which he or she is entitled under this Order.

(3) If a student's IEP or Section 504 plan specially provides for an alternate assessment in lieu of the CAHSEE, an alternate assessment shall be provided. If a student's IEP or Section 504 plan does not specifically address the CAHSEE but provides for an alternate assessment in lieu of generalized standardized testing, an alternate assessment to the CAHSEE shall be provided. If a student's IEP or Section 504 plan

(Continued)

Box 12.2

NOTICE TO ALL PARENTS AND GUARDIANS OF CHILDREN WITH AN INDIVIDUALIZED (Continued)

---

does not specifically address the CAHSEE or standardized testing but provides for an alternate assessment in lieu of general classroom testing, an alternate assessment to the CAHSEE shall be provided. Students entitled to an alternate assessment shall not be required to take the CAHSEE, but may do so if they chose.

(4) While this Order requires that an alternate assessment be provided to certain students, the Court has not yet decided how an alternate assessment will affect the receipt of a diploma.

(5) In order for a student covered by this Order to avail himself of any rights under this Order, no additional IEP or Section 504 plan meeting shall be necessary.

[1] California has defined an "accommodation" as a change in the CAHSEE (in format, student response, timing, or other attribute) that does not invalidate the score achieved. California has defined "modification" as a change in the CAHSEE that invalidates the test score because it fundamentally alters what the test measures.

---

are receiving their education in schools and classes they would attend if they had no disability. We know that implementation of the inclusive schooling model is all over the map, just like inclusive assessment.

However, when you stop to think about it, the inclusive schooling movement does not align or match the current accountability system. That is, although more students with disabilities are being educated in the least restrictive environment or an inclusive education setting, these same students are not necessarily accounted for in the larger system of student accountability. On one hand, people have advocated, to varying degrees, and achieved integration and inclusion of students with disabilities in the general education setting; on the other hand, these same students are not being accounted for even when they are there.

Let us be unequivocally direct. You do not necessarily have accountability when you have inclusive schooling, just as you do not necessarily have inclusive schooling when you have accountability. That is, including students in assessment does not mean that inclusive schooling is taking place. Conversely, to tout inclusive schooling as a model of educating students with disabilities without accounting for their learning is equally unacceptable.

Moving Forward

Over the past 10 years, major educational changes have been afoot (see Box 12.3). We know more about the business of educating students,

Box 12.3

Perspective Shift: The Changing Paradigm

Policy

From an emphasis on	**To an emphasis on**
Viewing special education exclusively	Viewing special education inclusively
Segregation	Integration
Labeling	Standards-based

Administration

From an emphasis on	**To an emphasis on**
Centralization	Decentralization
Add-on programs and resources	Child centeredness
	Reallocation of resources

Assessment

From an emphasis on	**To an emphasis on**
Medical model	Educational-needs model
Norm-referenced assessment tools	Criterion-referenced assessmenttools
Failure model	Proactive assessment, prevention, and intervention
	Standards-based assessment

Clientele

From an emphasis on	**To an emphasis on**
Unilingualism	Multilingualism
The dominant culture	Diverse cultures
Predictable and limited needs	Needs over the life span
Homogeneity	Diversity of clients
Student centered	Parent involvement .

Curriculum and Instruction

From an emphasis on	**To an emphasis on**
Central design control	Local design control
Teacher directedness	Child centeredness
Conformity in learning	System accountability
Excellence for a few	Student accountability
One curriculum for all	Individualized curriculum
Access to facilities	Access to general curriculum
Individual teachers taking responsibility	Collaborative teams taking responsibility for all
Academic learning	Research-based practices

(Continued)

Box 12.3

Perspective Shift: The Changing Paradigm (Continued)

Support Services

From an emphasis on
Minimal use of technology
Individually delivered resources

To an emphasis on
Maximum use of technology
Trainer-focused resources
Classroom based/Integrated

including those with disabilities, than we ever did before. We have more tools and technology for assessing learning and progress than ever before. We have rules, regulations, mandates, and court cases to show for these efforts. So where do we go from here?

The reality of standards-based reform is here to stay, as is assessment and accountability. A perspective shift in many arenas has resulted in more, not less, money being allocated for research and development in instruction, assessment, and efforts to create broad-based accountability systems at the local, state, and national levels. We must work hard to make this shifting system one that benefits and includes all students, first in accountability and then in life.

Summary

We must continue our effort of standards-based reform and be sure it reflects all students. We must provide the means to help all students meet higher goals and standards. We must provide sustained staff development and training to educators and parents and fortify the collaboration between home and school in the name of student school success. We must do a better job of communicating and involving a wide selection of stakeholders in school-based decision making and other reforms affecting school change. We must take a serious look at reallocating resources to do a better job of providing needed support in delivering services to students. We must never lose sight of the importance of all students achieving their best and thus must take into consideration individual needs. We must create a school culture that recognizes and celebrates diversity. And we must always put children first!

One last time, check your knowledge about the myth/truth statements presented at the beginning of this chapter and attempt an explanation for each answer that you gave. Correct answers and possible explanations are given in Box 12.4.

BOX 12.4

Myth or Truth Answers

MYTH   Inclusion and inclusive accountability are aligned and in tandem with each other.
<u>Explanation</u>: Perhaps the only thing aligning inclusive schooling and inclusive accountability is the fact that both have met with tremendous resistance.[See pages 224-226]

TRUTH   The education malpractice of tampering with test protocols has become a real issue in the world of high-stakes testing.
<u>Explanation</u>: The pressures of standardized tests and incentives to look good have caused corruption in some testing programs. [See page 218]

TRUTH   There are court cases that rule in favor of the district not having to modify tests for students with disabilities who are otherwise not qualified to take them.
<u>Explanation</u>: Courts have ruled that students who, because of their disability, do not have the skills needed to take and pass a test for graduation do not have the right to demand that a district or state modify its academic standards. [See page 222]

TRUTH   Inclusive assessment and accountability is potentially a very litigious area for education.
<u>Explanation</u>: Many recent court cases are the signs of things to come as states raise standards and stakes of assessment. [See page 224]

Resources for Further Information

Education Week. (2002). Florida teacher loses license for alleged breach of test, xxi(32).

Jones, B. M., Jones, B. D., Hardin, D., Chapman, L., Yarbrough, R., & Davis, M. (1999). The impact of high stakes testing on teachers and students in North Carolina. *Phi Delta Kappan, 81*(3), 199-203.

Lindsay, P. (1996, October 2). Whodunit? Someone cheated on standardized tests at a Connecticut school. And it wasn't the students. *Education Week,* 16(5), 25-29.

Olson, L. (2000, May 31). "Indiana case focuses on special ed." *Education Week, 19*(38), 1, 14-15.

Phillips, S. E. (1993). *Legal implications of high-stakes assessment: What states should know.* Oakbrook, IL: North Central Regional Educational Laboratory.

Phillips, S. E. (1995). *All students, same test, same standards: What the new Title I legislation will mean for the educational assessment of special education students.* Oakbrook, IL: North Central Regional Educational Laboratory.

Phillips, S. E. (1996). Legal defensibility of standards: Issues and policy perspectives. *Educational Measurement: Issues and Practice, 15*(2), 5-19.

Quality counts '99: Rewarding results, punishing failures. (1999). *Education Week, 17*(17).

Zlatos, B. (1994). Don't test, don't tell: Is "academic red-shirting" skewing the way we rank our schools? *American School Board Journal, 181*(11), 24-28.

Resources:
Reproducible Forms

A. Participation Decision-Making Form

B. Alternate Assessment Case Study

C. Checklist of Criteria for Making Decisions About Participation and Needed Accommodations for Classroom, District, and State Assessments

D. Checklist for Deciding Assessment Type

E. IEP Form for Identifying Accommodations

F. IEP Form for Identifying Accommodations, With Examples

G. Accommodations Case Study

H. Test Accommodation Planning Chart

I. Instructional and Assessment Accommodations Worksheet

J. District/State Assessment Accommodations Worksheet

K. Study/Test Skills Checklist

L. Logistics and Strategic Plan for Providing Assessment Accommodations

M. Final Arrangements for Assessment Accommodations

N. Suggestions for Alternate Assessments

O. Student Feedback/Interview Form

P. Building Implementation Document

Q. Inclusive Assessment and Accountability Survey

Participation Decision-Making Form

1. Is the student working on the same instructional goals as
    other students in the classroom?   [ ] YES   [ ] NO

    (If answer to 1 is YES, student should participate in the regular assessment)

2. If NO, is the student working on modified instructional goals
    (many are the same, but some are modified slightly)?   [ ] YES   [ ] NO

    (If answer to 2 is YES, student should participate in the regular assessment)

3. If NO, is the student working on alternate instructional goals   [ ] YES   [ ] NO

    (If answer to 3 is YES, student should participate in an alternate assessment)

4. If the student is working on alternate instructional goals, are
    there any areas of unique skills that could be assessed
    through the regular assessment?   [ ] YES   [ ] NO

    (If answer to 4 is YES, student should participate in both the regular and an alternate
    assessment)

Copyright © 2003 by Corwin Press, Inc. All rights reserved. Reprinted from *Testing Students With Disabilities, Second edition*, by Martha L. Thurlow, Judy L. Elliott, and James E. Ysseldyke. Thousand Oaks, CA: Corwin Press, www.corwinpress.com. Reproduction authorized only for the local school site that has purchased this book.

Alternate Assessment Case Study

BACKGROUND INFORMATION:

Paulita is an intellectually impaired 10th grader. Her verbal IQ is 50; performance IQ is 72; full scale is 61, math grade equivalent is 5.3; reading grade equivalent is 3.7; and written language is 3.0. Paulita exhibits expressive speech and language difficulties. Paulita attends a regular school in a special education class. She is integrated for art and wood technology.

INSTRUCTIONAL INFORMATION:

Paulita requires extra processing time (extra wait time). Directions must be presented multiple times and in stages. Paulita has a short attention span but works well in a small group. She is working on her own individualized goals and objectives according to her IEP and is not expected to graduate with a regular high school diploma.

Based on the information above, suggest some instructional accommodations for Paulita.

How will you assess Paulita's learning and progress? Suggest alternate ways to assess her learning and achievement of her goals and objectives. Consider the following categories:

Observation: Interviews/Checklists:

Testing: Record Review:

Copyright © 2003 by Corwin Press, Inc. All rights reserved. Reprinted from *Testing Students With Disabilities, Second edition*, by Martha L. Thurlow, Judy L. Elliott, and James E. Ysseldyke. Thousand Oaks, CA: Corwin Press, www.corwinpress.com. Reproduction authorized only for the local school site that has purchased this book.

Checklist of Criteria for Making Decisions About Participation and Needed Accommodations for Classroom, District, and State Assessments

Student Name: *Grade:*
School/Program: *Date of Meeting:*

The following accommodation decisions were made by person(s) who know _____'s learning needs and skills. These decisions were based on _____'s current level of functioning and learning characteristics as follows:

Yes   No

SETTING

____ ____   1.   Can work independently

____ ____   1a.   Can complete tasks with assistance or with the following accommodation(s):
                     ___ One-to-one assistance to complete written tasks
                     ___ On-task reminders
                     ___ Directions repeated and/or clarified
                     ___ Other _____

____ ____   2.   Can complete tasks within a large group but quiet setting

____ ____   2a.   Can complete tasks if provided the following accommodation(s):
                     ___ Test administered in a separate location with minimal distractions
                     ___ Test administered in a small group, study carrel, or individually (circle one)
                     ___ Special lighting
                     ___ Adaptive furniture—specify _____
                     ___ Noise buffer (e.g., earplugs, earphones, other _____)
                     ___ Other _____

TIMING

____ ____   1.   Can work continuously for 20- to 30-minute periods; if not, specify the average length of time student is able to work continuously.

____ ____   1a.   Can work in a group without distracting other test takers

Copyright © 2003 by Corwin Press, Inc. All rights reserved. Reprinted from *Testing Students With Disabilities, Second edition,* by Martha L. Thurlow, Judy L. Elliott, and James E. Ysseldyke. Thousand Oaks, CA: Corwin Press, www.corwinpress.com. Reproduction authorized only for the local school site that has purchased this book.

Yes   No

SCHEDULING

____ ____   1.   Can complete tasks if provided periodic breaks or other timing consideration(s)/accommodation(s):

____ Test administered over several sessions, time per session not to exceed _____ minutes

____ Allowed to take breaks as needed, not to exceed ____ breaks per 20- to 30-minute period

____ Test administered over several days, each session not to exceed _____ minutes in duration

____ Test administered in the morning, early afternoon, late afternoon (circle one)

____ Extended time to complete the test in one session

____ Other _____

PRESENTATION

____ ____   1.   Can listen to and follow oral directions given by an adult or on audiotape

____ ____   1a.   Can listen to and follow oral directions with assistance or the following accommodation(s):

____ Visual cues or printed material to facilitate understanding of orally give directions

____ Directions repeated, clarified, or simplified

____ Directions read individually

____ Visual magnification device

____ Auditory amplification device

____ Other _____

____ ____   2.   Can read and comprehend written directions

____ ____   2a.   Can comprehend written directions with assistance or the following accommodation:

____ Written directions read

____ Directions repeated, clarified, or simplified

____ Key words or phrases in written directions highlighted

____ Visual prompts (e.g., stop signs, arrows) that show directions to start, stop and continue working

____ Written directions presented in larger and/or bold print

____ Written directions presented with one complete sentence per line of text

____ Visual magnification device

____ Auditory amplification device

____ Other _____

Yes   No

_____ ____ 3. Can read, understand, and answer questions in multiple-choice format

_____ ____ 3a. Can understand and answer questions in multiple-choice format with assistance or the following accommodation(s):
____ Reader to read the test*
____ Pencil grip
____ Access to prerecorded reading
____ Test signed
____ Test presented in Braille or large print
____ Visual magnification device
____ Auditory amplification device
____ Increased spacing between items and/or limited items presented per page
____ Templates or masks to reduce visible print
____ Papers secured to desk (e.g., magnets, tape)
____ Other _____

RESPONSE

____ ____ 1. Can use paper and pen/pencil to write short answer or paragraph-length responses to open-ended questions

____ ____ 1a. Can respond to open-ended questions when provided assistance or the following accommodation(s):
____ Pencil grip
____ Word processor
____ Scribe (someone to record verbatim oral responses to questions)
____ Brailler
____ Copy assistance between drafts of writing
____ Write an outline to a question and, using a tape recorder, dictate the body of the response, per the written outline
____ Dictate answer into a tape recorder
____ Visual magnification devices
____ Touch Talker or other communication device
____ Calculator*
____ Abacus
____ Arithmetic tables*
____ Spell checker or spelling dictionary*
____ Other _____

____ ____ 2. Can use pencil to fill in bubble answer sheets

____ ____ 2a. Can use pencil to fill in bubble answer sheets with assistance or the following accommodation(s):
____ Pencil grip
____ Bubbles enlarged
____ Bubbles presented on the test itself next to each question

Yes   No

           ____ Bubbles enlarged and presented on the test itself next to each question
           ____ Scribe
           ____ Calculator*
           ____ Abacus
           ____ Arithmetic tables*
           ____ Spell checker or spelling dictionary*
           ____ Other _____

Use the following section to guide decisions about participation in assessments.

LEVEL OF PARTICIPATION

____ ____   1.   ____ 's current level of skill and noted accommodations allow him/her to meaningfully participate in all/part (circle one) of the following assessments:
           ____ Classroom
           ____ District—specify which one(s)
           ____ State/national—specify which one(s)

If partial participation is considered more appropriate, specify which part of the assessment. The decision for partial participation on the assessment is based on the following:

____ ____   2.   ____ is incapable of meaningfully participating in the ___ assessment, regardless of accommodation. This decision is based on the following:

____ ____   3.   Consideration has been given to how ___'s learning will be assessed. An alternate assessment of learning will be conducted as follows:

____ ____   4.   The consequences of alternate assessment participation and/or use of accommodations (if applicable) have been discussed with ____'s parent/guardian.

____ ____   5.   Proactive planning is under way to provide _____ the opportunity to meaningfully participate in the assessment cycle (either entire or partial) next year as follows (specify who is involved in the planning process):

____ ____   6.   ____ 's parent/guardian is fully aware of these participation and accommodation decisions and has been a part of the process. Explain, if necessary.

Your signature on this form indicates that you were a part of the participation and accommodation decision-making process for _____. You are in agreement with the decisions.

_____   _____   _____
IEP Team Chair   Building Administrator   Student

_____   _____   _____
Parent/Guardian   Student's Teacher(s)   Others

Date of Meeting: _____

* Careful consideration must be given to the purpose of the test for which these accommodations are provided.

Form D

Checklist for Deciding Assessment Type

Name: School Year:

School: Special Education Teacher:

Grade: Date:

The purpose of this checklist is to facilitate and justify what district or state assessment program _____ will be a part of. Three options are being considered: general (or the name of the district/state assessment), alternate, or both (general/alternate) assessments. The final decision must be justified and validated by several parties including, but not limited to _____ (student, if deemed appropriate), parent/guardian, special and general education teachers, and involved related personnel.

On _____ (date), the IEP team, after much discussion and consideration, has decided that _____ is a candidate for:

____ ____ 1. General assessment (or the name of the district/state assessment)
               ___ a. Without accommodation
               ___ b. With the following accommodation(s):
____ ____ 2. Alternate assessment (student is not working toward diploma)*
____ ____ 3. General/Alternate.* List the content areas_____
               _____

*This decision is based on the following (list any and all factors that led to the above decision—be specific):

While this decision was made based on the above factors, we recognize that the decision is not a permanent one and may change, if warranted and appropriate, at another scheduled IEP meeting.

Parent/Guardian _____   Other _____

Administrator   _____   IEP Chair _____

Special Educator _____   General Educator _____

Related Service Providers: _____

                            _____

                            _____

Copyright © 2003 by Corwin Press, Inc. All rights reserved. Reprinted from *Testing Students With Disabilities, Second edition*, by Martha L. Thurlow, Judy L. Elliott, and James E. Ysseldyke. Thousand Oaks, CA: Corwin Press, www.corwinpress.com. Reproduction authorized only for the local school site that has purchased this book.

IEP Form for Identifying Accommodations

Student: *Grade:*   *School/Teacher:*

Date:

Instructional Accommodations:

General accommodations needed for instruction.

Specific instructional accommodations needed for applicable content areas:

Copyright © 2003 by Corwin Press, Inc. All rights reserved. Reprinted from *Testing Students With Disabilities, Second edition*, by Martha L. Thurlow, Judy L. Elliott, and James E. Ysseldyke. Thousand Oaks, CA: Corwin Press, www.corwinpress.com. Reproduction authorized only for the local school site that has purchased this book.

Form F

IEP Form for Identifying Accommodations, With Examples

Name: *Grade:*   *Date:*

Use the following checklist to guide decisions about what instructional accommodations are needed by this student.

INSTRUCTIONAL ACCOMMODATION CHECKLIST:

SETTING

_____ Distraction-free space within classroom (e.g., doorway, windows, other students, front of class, back of class)
_____ One-to-one assistance to complete written tasks
_____ On-task reminders
_____ Several verbal prompts to initiate a task
_____ Verbal encouragement, praise, or recognition to continue a task
_____ Directions repeated and/or clarified
_____ Small group or partner instruction, especially when learning or practicing new facts, concepts, and strategies
_____ Adaptive furniture
_____ Other_____

TIMING

_____ Periodic breaks during work sessions (specify)
_____ Other_____

SCHEDULING

_____ Extended time to complete class/homework assignments
_____ Length of assignments shortened to complete as overnight homework assignments
_____ A daily assignment sheet
_____ A weekly quick strategic assignment meeting
_____ A weekly or monthly assignment calendar
_____ A weekly or monthly assignment calendar with check-in and due dates posted

PRESENTATION

_____ Visual cues or printed material to facilitate understanding of orally given directions
_____ Directions repeated, clarified, or simplified
_____ Directions read individually
_____ Visual magnification device

Copyright © 2003 by Corwin Press, Inc. All rights reserved. Reprinted from *Testing Students With Disabilities, Second edition*, by Martha L. Thurlow, Judy L. Elliott, and James E. Ysseldyke. Thousand Oaks, CA: Corwin Press, www.corwinpress.com. Reproduction authorized only for the local school site that has purchased this book.

_____   Auditory amplification device
_____   Written directions read
_____   Key words or phrases in written directions highlighted
_____   Visual prompts (e.g., stop signs, arrows) that show directions to start, stop, and
          continue working
_____   Written directions presented in larger and/or bold print
_____   Written directions presented with one complete sentence per line of text
_____   Reader to read the text
_____   Pencil grip
_____   Access to a prerecorded reading
_____   Test presented in sign language
_____   Written information presented in Braille or large print
_____   Increased spacing between items and/or limited items presented per page
_____   Templates or masks to reduce visible print
_____   Papers secured to desk (e.g., magnets, tape)
_____   Calculator*
_____   Abacus
_____   Arithmetic tables*
_____   Spell checker or spelling dictionary*
_____   Manipulatives
_____   Other_____

RESPONSE

_____   Text-talker converter
_____   Speech synthesizer
_____   Pencil grip
_____   Word processor
_____   Scribe (someone to record verbatim oral responses to questions)
_____   Brailler
_____   Copying assistance between drafts of writing
_____   Option to write an outline to a question and, using a tape recorder, dictate the
          body of the response, per the written outline
_____   Option to dictate answer into a tape recorder
_____   Visual magnification device
_____   Touch Talker or other communication device
_____   Calculator*
_____   Abacus
_____   Arithmetic tables*
_____   Spell checker or spelling dictionary*
_____   Other_____

*Based on the purpose of the assignment and what and how the skill(s) will be assessed.
Additional Instructional Accommodations Needed for Specific Content Areas: List content area
and any additional instructional accommodations needed.

Accommodations Case Study

STUDENT: Yu Kanduit

Yu Kanduit is an eighth grader who was retained in first grade. Yu has been identified as a student with a learning disability in the area of written communication/basic reading skills. Yu attends school regularly. Yu has an integrated special/general instruction schedule. He receives resource room services and in-class support for mathematics. Science and social studies are taken in the general education classroom.

Yu reads on a third-grade level. His writing is hampered by his inability to spell. He has wonderful ideas and communicates them well. With the use of a tape recorder, Yu is able to record his ideas. His writing skills are improving with his reading skills. Yu shows excellent auditory comprehension, and his attention to task is above average. He actively participates in class activities and discussions.

Yu exhibits low self-esteem toward school. However, he will ask for and accept help from teachers. Yu is well accepted by his peers and is "looked up to" within the school context.

INSTRUCTIONAL ACCOMMODATIONS

Using the above information, suggest instructional accommodations for Yu.

ASSESSMENT ACCOMMODATIONS

Now that you have identified possible instructional accommodations, suggest accommodations that would be needed for assessment.

Setting: Presentation:

Timing: Response:

Scheduling: Other (specify):

Copyright © 2003 by Corwin Press, Inc. All rights reserved. Reprinted from *Testing Students With Disabilities, Second edition*, by Martha L. Thurlow, Judy L. Elliott, and James E. Ysseldyke. Thousand Oaks, CA: Corwin Press, www.corwinpress.com. Reproduction authorized only for the local school site that has purchased this book.

Form H

Test Accommodation Planning Chart

Test Accommodation Planning Chart					
Student Name	Class/ Teacher	Test Format	Needed Accommodation or Modification	Test Date	Actions

Copyright © 2003 by Corwin Press, Inc. All rights reserved. Reprinted from *Testing Students With Disabilities, Second edition*, by Martha L. Thurlow, Judy L. Elliott, and James E. Ysseldyke. Thousand Oaks, CA: Corwin Press, www.corwinpress.com. Reproduction authorized only for the local school site that has purchased this book.

Instructional and Assessment Accommodations Worksheet

Student: _____ *Grade:* _____ *Date:* _____

Teacher/Class: _____ *Class/Content Area:* _____

Service Provider:

Student's Content-Related Strengths   *Student's Content-Related Needs*

Based on student need, list below the instructional accommodations that will be provided. Then list which of these naturally flow to classroom tests. Mark (**) those test accommodations that apply to the district/state assessment.

Instructional Accommodation(s)   *Classroom Test Accommodation(s)*

Copyright © 2003 by Corwin Press, Inc. All rights reserved. Reprinted from *Testing Students With Disabilities, Second edition,* by Martha L. Thurlow, Judy L. Elliott, and James E. Ysseldyke. Thousand Oaks, CA: Corwin Press, www.corwinpress.com. Reproduction authorized only for the local school site that has purchased this book.

Form J

District/State Assessment
Accommodations Worksheet

Use this worksheet to identify the skills measured on specific tests. Based on this information, identify reasonable accommodations that need to be provided. Keep in mind that these accommodations should be taken/recommended from those being currently provided during instruction.

Student: _____ *Grade:* _____ *Date:* _____

Test: _____

Skill(s) Measured   *Needed Accommodation**

Comments/Further Action Needed:

*Indicate potential for compromising the construct assessed.

Completed by:

Copyright © 2003 by Corwin Press, Inc. All rights reserved. Reprinted from *Testing Students With Disabilities, Second edition,* by Martha L. Thurlow, Judy L. Elliott, and James E. Ysseldyke. Thousand Oaks, CA: Corwin Press, www.corwinpress.com. Reproduction authorized only for the local school site that has purchased this book.

Form K

Study/Test Skills Checklist

Student: _____ Grade: _____ Date: _____

Teacher:

Test: _____

Test Skills Needed	Date Taught (Initials)	Date Acquired (As evidenced by)

Comments:

Completed by:

Copyright © 2003 by Corwin Press, Inc. All rights reserved. Reprinted from *Testing Students With Disabilities, Second edition*, by Martha L. Thurlow, Judy L. Elliott, and James E. Ysseldyke. Thousand Oaks, CA: Corwin Press, www.corwinpress.com. Reproduction authorized only for the local school site that has purchased this book.

Logistics and Strategic Plan for Providing Assessment Accommodations

Name: *School Year:*

Assessment: *Special Education Teacher:*

Day/Time of Test: *Case Coordinator:*

Building Administrator:

Assessment accommodations student needs for this assessment and date arranged:

1.

2.

3.

4.

Comments:

Person responsible for arranging accommodations and due date:

1.

2.

3.

4.

Comments:

Room Assignment for Assessment:

Planners for This Process (Signatures/Dates)

Copyright © 2003 by Corwin Press, Inc. All rights reserved. Reprinted from *Testing Students With Disabilities, Second edition,* by Martha L. Thurlow, Judy L. Elliott, and James E. Ysseldyke. Thousand Oaks, CA: Corwin Press, www.corwinpress.com. Reproduction authorized only for the local school site that has purchased this book.

Final Arrangements for
Assessment Accommodations

Name: *School Year:*

Case Coordinator: *Assessment:*

Special Education Teacher: *Date/Time of Test:*

Building Administrator: *Room Assignment:*

The following assessment accommodations have been arranged (initial and date):

Setting:

Timing:

Scheduling:

Presentation:

Response:

Other:

Copyright © 2003 by Corwin Press, Inc. All rights reserved. Reprinted from *Testing Students With Disabilities, Second edition,* by Martha L. Thurlow, Judy L. Elliott, and James E. Ysseldyke. Thousand Oaks, CA: Corwin Press, www.corwinpress.com. Reproduction authorized only for the local school site that has purchased this book.

Form N

Suggestions for Alternate Assessments

Below is a list of possible data sources for developing or providing supporting documentation for an alternate assessment.

Checklists for:

_____ Daily living skills
_____ Community mobility skills
_____ Social skills
_____ Self-help skills
_____ Adaptive behavior skills

Interviews:

_____ Service providers
_____ Parents/guardian
_____ Peers
_____ Employers

Observation:

_____ Note the frequency, intensity, and/or duration for target skill
_____ Informal observation of student in a variety of settings
_____ Formal or systematic observation using checklists, criteria, rubrics
_____ Videotaping of performance
_____ Application of skill(s) in varied settings (natural or staged)
_____ Demonstrate community mobility skills in real setting
_____ Use of technology (specify)

Tests:

_____ Portfolios
_____ Performance based
_____ Quantitative or qualitative

Record Review:

_____ School cumulative records
_____ Student products
_____ Anecdotal records (IEP objectives and general progress)

Copyright © 2003 by Corwin Press, Inc. All rights reserved. Reprinted from *Testing Students With Disabilities, Second edition*, by Martha L. Thurlow, Judy L. Elliott, and James E. Ysseldyke. Thousand Oaks, CA: Corwin Press, www.corwinpress.com. Reproduction authorized only for the local school site that has purchased this book.

Student Feedback/Interview Form

Student: *Grade:*

Assessment: *Case Coordinator:*

Date of Assessment: *Special Education Teacher:*

Date of Interview: *Interviewer:*

1. How did you think the test went? What was easy? What was hard?

2. How prepared were you for the

    Test format:

    Test content:

    Timing of the test:

    Any surprises?

    Other:

3. What (if any) testing accommodations did you use?

    a. Were they helpful?

    b. If so, how? If not, why?

    c. What, if any, other accommodations did you feel you needed?

4. Was there any information that was "new" to you? Specify.

5. Did this test allow you to show what you know? Was it a good demonstration of what you know and can do?

    a. If yes, why and how?

    b. If no, why? What kind of test or method would allow you to better show what you know?

6. Anything else you would like to share about your testing experience?

Copyright © 2003 by Corwin Press, Inc. All rights reserved. Reprinted from *Testing Students With Disabilities, Second edition*, by Martha L. Thurlow, Judy L. Elliott, and James E. Ysseldyke. Thousand Oaks, CA: Corwin Press, www.corwinpress.com. Reproduction authorized only for the local school site that has purchased this book.

Form P

Building Implementation Document

Year/Test Window: *Building:*

Name/Form of Test: *Grade Level:*

Total number of students enrolled in building:

Number of students with disabilities enrolled in building:

Number of students taking this grade-level assessment:

Number of students with disabilities taking this grade-level assessment:

Number of students taking this assessment with accommodation:

Types of accommodation provided:

Number of students with disabilities taking the alternate assessment:

Number of students reported as not taking either assessment:

Reasons:

Last Year's Data

Total number of students enrolled in building:

Number of students with disabilities enrolled in building:

Number of students taking this grade-level assessment:

Number of students with disabilities taking this grade-level assessment:

Number of students taking this assessment with accommodation:

Types of accommodations provided:

Number of students with disabilities taking the alternate assessment:

Number of students reported as not taking either assessment:

Submitted by:
Date:

Copyright © 2003 by Corwin Press, Inc. All rights reserved. Reprinted from *Testing Students With Disabilities, Second edition,* by Martha L. Thurlow, Judy L. Elliott, and James E. Ysseldyke. Thousand Oaks, CA: Corwin Press, www.corwinpress.com. Reproduction authorized only for the local school site that has purchased this book.

Form Q

Inclusive Assessment and Accountability Survey

We as a district are moving toward an educational system that is more inclusive both in instruction and in accountability. As we continue this process, we believe it is very important to find out what is needed to continue progress and growth. Our mission and belief is that all students can learn to higher levels than before. We believe all students must be included and accounted for in our efforts to educate all children. With this in mind, please complete the following survey:

Please indicate your position:

_____ General Education Teacher   _____ Special Education Teacher
_____ Administrator   _____ Related Service Professional
_____ Parent/Community   _____ Other _____
Member

In the space next to each item, write one or more letters from A to E to indicate your anticipated need for staff development.

A. Need for *TRAINING* (in-service workshop, seminar)
B. Need for *MATERIALS* (literature, resources)
C. Need for *CONSULTATION*
D. Need for *IN-CLASS ASSISTANCE*
E. *OTHER* (please specify)

_____   1. Overview of the "whys" of inclusive assessment and accountability
_____   2. Recent laws and mandates that affect all students
_____   3. Purpose and uses of the district/state assessment
_____   4. Connection between instruction and assessment, especially as it relates to accommodations
_____   5. Address the issue of how all students can participate in the district/state assessment program
_____   6. Session on what kinds of assessment accommodations are allowed, who is eligible for them, and how these decisions are made
_____   7. Hands-on session on how to decide and provide instructional accommodations to students who need them
_____   8. How to provide accommodations for both classroom tests and district assessments
_____   9. Roles and responsibilities of teachers, administrators, and other staff in district assessment
_____ 10. Other (please specify) _____

Copyright © 2003 by Corwin Press, Inc. All rights reserved. Reprinted from *Testing Students With Disabilities, Second edition*, by Martha L. Thurlow, Judy L. Elliott, and James E. Ysseldyke. Thousand Oaks, CA: Corwin Press, www.corwinpress.com. Reproduction authorized only for the local school site that has purchased this book.

Please write the numbers of your top three priorities on the lines below:

1st _____   2nd _____ 3rd _____

Other questions, comments, or concerns:

Resources: Staff Development

Conducting Staff Development

Staff development and training are key components of today's educational reform agenda. This is true for all kinds of reform, not just those associated with standards and assessments. But the need for staff development and training is particularly critical when it comes to topics that have not been addressed before, such as the participation of students with disabilities in district and state assessments.

This section is designed to help you deliver and disseminate information about the what, why, how, and what-ifs of assessment programs and accommodations decisions for students with disabilities. It includes information on some of the most important points that need to be made in each of nine components and on some specific activities in which people can engage. Reproducible handouts and overheads are provided as well.

The information included here can be used to provide in-service to boards of education, central office and building administrative personnel, building faculty and staff, and community members. The components can be altered to meet the needs of different groups, as can the materials and activities within components.

Overview

There are nine components to this informational session on inclusive assessment and accountability. The coverage of each one can vary, and/or you may want to present the information over two sessions. The content within each component is meant to provide you with an overall understanding of the issues to help you as you prepare for the meeting you will hold. For each component, we suggest that you gather relevant information on how the issues under discussion have had an impact on your school district and/or state. This provides participants with relevant information to which they can relate.

Component 1:   New Laws That Promote Educational Reform (page 259)
Component 2:   General Overview of Definition of Assessment, Its Purposes, and the Meaning of Inclusive Accountability (page 264)
Component 3:   Why Assess? (page 269)
Component 4:   Formats of Assessment (page 274)
Component 5:   Who's In? Who's Out? (page 279)
Component 6:   Who Makes the Decisions? (page 287)

Component 7:   What Are Assessment Accommodations? (page 291)
Component 8:   Reporting of Results (page 298)
Component 9:   Next Steps (page 304)

Considering Staff Development Stages

Before starting the process of staff development on inclusive assessment and accountability, it is wise to consider the levels of awareness of development about the topics or activities you are about to present. The Concerns-Based Adoption Model (CBAM) by Hall, Wallace, and Dossett (1973) provides you with the opportunity to get a feel for an individual or group and help guide staff development for a particular topic.

The CBAM proposes that people differ tremendously in their readiness to accept major changes, such as inclusive accountability. As staff members become ready, they move through various stages. We have adapted CBAM to identify various stages of staff development activities for promoting inclusive accountability and assessment, no matter what stage of readiness individuals may be at. The following are the adapted stages:

Awareness—Very low level of involvement. These are staff members who act as though they have not even heard of accountability or inclusive assessment.

Informational—General awareness and interest but still relatively uninvolved. These are staff members who realize that something to do with inclusive accountability and assessment is going on in the building or district but do not believe it will affect them.

Personal—Staff members begin to consider the impact of the innovation on themselves. They worry that they may be asked to include students with disabilities in their classroom, provide needed accommodations for both instruction and classroom assessment, and be involved in decisions concerning participation in the district assessment.

Management—Concern focuses on efficient and effective methodologies. These are staff members who have been informed about the policy and practice changes about assessment and accountability and now are extremely concerned to find out what to do and how to do it.

Consequence—Here, attention is on student outcomes and accountability. These are staff members who, after learning more about inclusive assessment (participation, accommodation, and reporting of results), begin to raise questions about outcomes about learning results, fairness, progress, evaluation, and/or resources to make it happen.

Collaboration—Here, the focus is on working with others and becoming involved with change. These are staff members who recognize that colleagues, especially those with inclusive schooling and assessment experience, may be able to help.

Refocusing—Interest here is in refinement, improvement, and innovation. These are staff members who, with some successful experience behind them, are ready to make the situation even better for all students.

For each stage, we offer some suggestions to consider if you have staff members who may need additional information on inclusive assessment and accountability according to their stage of CBAM development.

Stage	*Activity*
Awareness	<ul><li>Overview or brief workshop</li><li>Awareness-level information explaining the whys and whats about inclusive assessment and accountability</li><li>Easy-reading professional or newspaper articles on the state of assessment and inclusive accountability systems</li><li>Ongoing staff meetings</li></ul>
Informational	<ul><li>Full-day workshops based on needs assessment</li><li>Presentations from other districts' personnel on what they are doing in the area of assessment, accommodation, participation, and reporting of all student learning</li><li>Easy-reading professional or newspaper articles on the state of assessment and inclusive accountability systems</li></ul>
Personal	<ul><li>Topical sessions that provide for group discussions on areas of concern or interest</li><li>Presentations and question-and-answer sessions by personnel most familiar with what it takes to create and facilitate the development of inclusive assessment and accountability systems</li></ul>
Management	<ul><li>Practical strategies for approaching "how to's"</li><li>Problem-solving sessions with a group or consultant</li><li>Networking with other districts and/or states working on similar efforts and initiatives</li><li>Visits to other districts and various personnel in charge of district assessment program and inclusive accountability system</li></ul>
Consequence	<ul><li>Professional and information-based articles depicting the consequences of exclusion or selective accountability system</li><li>Articles and information showing past practice and the unanticipated outcomes or results</li><li>Aligning efforts with intended outcomes and mapping action steps to get there</li><li>Study groups and support groups</li></ul>
Collaboration	<ul><li>Research projects and grants within the district</li><li>Staff meeting updates on progress and efforts</li><li>Assessment and accommodation committees</li><li>Peer support groups that focus on improvement</li></ul>

Refocusing
- Reading alert club—highlight and distribute key articles that lend valuable information to the process
- Conferences
- Revisiting where you began, where you currently are, and where you are going next
- Creation of independent study or progress plans to promote better practice for meeting both instruction and assessment needs of all students

You may want to consider making a CBAM needs assessment that covers each stage of the model. First, you would provide a brief explanation of the model and the stages (as shown above). Then you could develop questions depicting current situations or directions your district is planning on taking and ask your staff to rate each item from 1 to 7, where 1 is awareness and 7 is refocusing. For example,

1 2 3 4 5 6 7   I am aware of the reporting procedures of our district assessment. That is, I know who is included and reported in the results.

SOURCE: Hall, G., Wallace. R., & Dossett, W. (1973). *A developmental conceptualization of the adoption process within educational institutions.* Austin: University of Texas, Austin Research and Development Center for Teacher Education.

Component 1:
New Laws That Promote
Educational Reform

Purpose

- To briefly explain the provisions of the new laws (No Child Left Behind Act-Title I, IDEA), with an emphasis on assessment and accountability

Background Information

The information in this section covers the key points to be made for this component of staff development. The facilitator of staff development sessions must decide how much of the information is needed by the targeted audience. It is important to relate the background information to the local situation in which the facilitator is working.

What Is Educational Reform All About?

Reform usually means "change for the better." Today, our education system is undergoing major changes in response to concerns about its adequacy. Why are we concerned?

- International comparisons suggest that in some areas, U.S. students do not perform as well as students in many other countries.
- Colleges and universities are having to give remedial work to more and more students before they are ready for college-level classes.
- U.S. businesses have complained that high school graduates in our country do not have the skills needed to be good workers in today's global economy.

While some may disagree about whether these statements are true, most people do agree that we should support out educational system and, at the same time, push for it to improve. Thus, we are always interested in changing education for the better. In many states and across the nation, policymakers, educators, and parents alike are pushing harder than usual for reforms in education.

Educational reform has implications for students with disabilities, especially now when the focus is on producing workers who can help the United States compete in a global economy. Too often, students with disabilities are not thought about in discussions of educational reform. Yet we want all individuals to be contributing members of our society, including those with disabilities. We want our educational system to be *accountable* for all children.

What Are Some Common Educational Reforms?

There are many reforms in the news today. Most of them are said to be "systemic"—occurring throughout the system. Systemic reform can occur in local schools, school districts, or states. You may have heard about site-based management, cooperative learning, teaming, collaboration, and other reform strategies.

Although many reforms are being promoted, different people push different reforms because there is disagreement about which are the best approaches. Yet there remains a strong push for schools to help students learn at a high level—that is, to challenging standards. Schools must show that their students meet these challenging standards through assessments that now are more varied and real-world based and that result in better information about student learning. These reform themes are reflected in several federal education laws and in the education laws of many states. They are themes that have significant implications for students with disabilities.

What Laws Promote Educational Reform?

Two federal education laws are important steps toward helping states in their reform efforts: the Individuals with Disabilities Education Act (IDEA), and the No Child Left Behind (NCLB) Act.

Individuals With Disabilities Education Act (IDEA, Public Law 105-117)

The reauthorized IDEA (June 1997) continues to provide federal funds to assist states and school districts in making a free, appropriate public education available to students who have been identified as having a disability. Some of the changes in the law address IEPs and state/district assessments. IEPs must now document how a student's disability affects involvement and progress in the general curriculum; individual modifications needed for students to participate in state and district assessments; and, if the student is unable to participate in the general assessment, why and how learning will be assessed. Public reporting requirements are also included in the reauthorization of IDEA: (a) the number of students with disabilities assessed (by July, 1998), (b) the performance of students in the general education assessment (by July, 1998), and (c) the performance of students with disabilities in an alternate assessment (by July 2000).

No Child Left Behind Act (NCLB, Public Law 107-110)

The latest reauthorization of the Elementary and Secondary Education Act (ESEA) was signed into law by President Bush on January 8, 2002. Known as the *No Child Left Behind (NCLB) Act*, it replaced the *Improving America's Schools Act (IASA)* of 1994. *NCLB* brought with it several sweeping changes in plans for educational reform, particularly in its Title I program. Among the most notable of the provisions in this law is a requirement for much stronger accountability provisions than ever before—accountability based on student results. To meet the requirements of the law, states must:

- have strong academic standards for reading, math, and science
- administer tests in each grade from grade 3-8, and during high school
- produce annual state and district reports that show results for each designated student group
- monitor the extent to which students in each group are making adequate yearly progress toward proficiency
- assign real consequences to districts and schools that fail to make progress

Students with disabilities comprise one of the designated subgroups in *NCLB*. This means that they, like all other students, must be included in state and district assessments, have access to the educational programs aligned to high standards, and receive the benefits and resources available to other students.

Activity

Use the Myth or Truth Worksheet on the next page to warm up people in the training session. Most people are willing to guess at the extent to which each statement is the truth or a myth. Answers to the statements are as follows:

1) M	4) M	7) M	10) M	13) T
2) T	5) M	8) M	11) T	14) M
3) M	6) M	9) M	12) T	15) M

Handouts and Overheads

Use the handouts and overheads presented on the pages following the Myth or Truth Worksheet to convey information on educational reform. Add others that are relevant to your situation.

Myth or Truth Worksheet

Assessment and Accountability:
Where Are Students With Disabilities?

The statements below represent current myths or truths about educational reform and students with disabilities. Read each and write M (myth) if you think the sentence describes an inaccurate statement about current practice and T (truth) if you think the statement describes an accurate statement.

_____ 1. A well-established accountability system is one where all students take the same tests.

_____ 2. Providing accommodations to students with disabilities is an attempt to "level the playing field."

_____ 3. The majority of students with disabilities participate in district and state assessments.

_____ 4. There is agreement about the purpose of assessment accommodations.

_____ 5. There is a common set of assessment accommodations allowed by states.

_____ 6. The scores of students with disabilities typically are included in reports of district and state scores.

_____ 7. Parents are fully informed about their child's participation in all assessments.

_____ 8. Administrators are aware of the importance of an accountability system for all students, including those with disabilities.

_____ 9. Teachers are aware of the importance of an accountability system for all students, including those with disabilities.

_____ 10. State and local directors of assessment and special education, in general, inform each other about what is occurring in their departments.

_____ 11. Criteria exist for developing policy about participation, accommodation, and reporting of assessment results so that students with disabilities are included.

_____ 12. The IEP is one of the critical links in providing students with disabilities the opportunity to participate in assessments.

_____ 13. Parents are key players in putting into play the participation and accommodation pieces in assessment.

_____ 14. There is a significant amount of research indicating that when students with disabilities are allowed to participate in assessment, with or without accommodation, the results are skewed.

_____ 15. Educators and administrators have little impact on establishing guidelines or criteria for standards and assessment that reflect "all" students.

Educational Reform: What Is It? Why Do We Need It?

What: Educational reform

✓ "Change for the better"

✓ "Mechanism to bring about change"

Why: Dissatisfaction with the quality of high school graduates

✓ Need for remedial work in post-secondary school settings

✓ U.S. business concern over lack of skills to compete in a global economy

✓ Poor performance in international comparisons

Copyright © 2003 by Corwin Press, Inc. All rights reserved. Reprinted from *Testing Students With Disabilities, Second edition*, by Martha L. Thurlow, Judy L. Elliott, and James E. Ysseldyke. Thousand Oaks, CA: Corwin Press, www.corwinpress.com. Reproduction authorized only for the local school site that has purchased this book.

Component 2:
General Overview of Definition of Assessment, Its Purposes, and the Meaning of Inclusive Accountability

Purpose

- To provide an overview of the purposes of assessment
- To define and discuss what accountability is and its connection to assessment

Background Information

The information in this section covers the key points to be made for this component of staff development. The facilitator of staff development sessions must decide how much of the information is needed by the targeted audience. Remember to relate the background information to the local situation.

Assessment

What is assessment? Assessment is the process of measuring learning against a set of standards. Assessment and the notion of using new forms of assessment are integral parts of new legislation such as the No Child Left Behind (NCLB) Act. One of the characteristics most apparent in current school reforms is a shift from documenting the process of educating students to measuring the results of the educational process.

There are many purposes to assessment. To develop a coordinated assessment system, the purposes for which assessment information are needed and at what level(s) such information is needed must be determined. The primary functions of state and district assessment programs include the following:

- Accountability (describing the educational status)
- Instructional improvement (making decisions on what and how to teach)
- Program evaluation (effectiveness of programs and curricula)
- Student diagnosis (eligibility for service/programs)
- High school graduation (certification of mastery or accomplishment)

Accountability

What is accountability? Accountability is typically defined as a systematic means of assuring those inside and outside the educational system that schools are moving in desired directions. *Accountability* is a more encompassing term than *assessment*. It can include more than the collection of data via test, record review, and other performance assessments. Rather, a system is accountable for all students when it makes sure all students count or participate in the evaluation program of the educational system.

Accountability has a number of layers. These layers include the classroom, building, district, and state.

- *Classroom accountability* can focus on the individual student as well as on the group as a whole. Individual student accountability examines the degree to which a student is learning what she or he is supposed to be learning and the extent to which the student is moving through the curriculum at the expected rate of progress. Classroom accountability looks at the degree to which students as a group are learning and progressing through the curriculum. Both individual student and classroom accountability provide teachers and administrators with information they can use to make teaching decisions for individual students and groups of students.
- *School building accountability* provides information to both building and central office administrations about the overall picture of student learning. It must include all students in the building. Every student enrolled in the school building must be accounted for. Only then can there truly be an inclusive accountability system for the school. Using this information, administrators and policymakers can make programmatic decisions about curriculum and instruction. Support for adoption of new materials or programs, as well as staff development, typically is gleaned from information rendered from assessment and accountability reports.
- *School district accountability* allows the state to examine how it is doing in providing an education to those enrolled in schools throughout the state. It provides a crude comparison of districts across the states. The estimate is crude because many variables (e.g., the number of students enrolled, socioeconomic status, the number of children excluded from assessments) create an uneven level with which to accurately measure how states compare with each other.
- *State-level accountability* allows for national comparisons. That is, one state may be compared with another in terms of test scores, number of school-age students, and percentages of English-as-a-second-language learners and special education students, to mention a few.

Relationships Between Assessment and Accountability

Assessment and accountability are closely related. Whereas assessment provides information about student and system growth and progress toward a set of standards, accountability provides those inside and outside the education system information about how students in America's schools are learning.

Assessment and accountability results tell us how students are doing against a set of learning goals or standards. Accountability systems tell you how students in the classroom, school building, and state are achieving. The important thing is that all students are included in the accountability system so that accurate information about all students is reported. Inclusive accountability systems are those that account for all students in the district or state, regardless of what kind of test they take (general assessment or alternate assessment).

Activities

Use either or both of the following activities to promote the involvement of participants in this component's content.

Activity 1

This activity can be done by individuals or in small groups. Or the entire activity can be completed first individually and then processed in small and then large groups.

Take a minute to brainstorm the purposes of testing, assessment, and accountability. Then identify similarities or differences among the three. Mark items similar to testing with a **T**, those similar to assessment with an **A**, and those similar to accountability with **AC**.

Activity 2

In small groups, have participants discuss the following statement: *Educational accountability has a number of layers.* Identify and discuss the layers of accountability in education.

Handouts and Overheads

Use the handout/overhead on the following page to convey information on assessment and accountability. Add others that are relevant to your situation.

Accountability

What Is It?

A means to show those both inside and outside the education system how students in America's schools are learning.

Why Do Accountability Systems Exist?

Accountability systems are meant to provide student-based information about curriculum, instruction, and learning. They are a means of providing information about return on the public's investment (tax dollars).

Copyright © 2003 by Corwin Press, Inc. All rights reserved. Reprinted from *Testing Students With Disabilities, Second edition*, by Martha L. Thurlow, Judy L. Elliott, and James E. Ysseldyke. Thousand Oaks, CA: Corwin Press, www.corwinpress.com. Reproduction authorized only for the local school site that has purchased this book.

How Do They Work?

There are at least four layers of accountability, each of which may organize information in different ways:

- *Classroom:*   by individual or group
- *Building:*   by classroom and grade level
- *District:*   by school building, curriculum, and instruction
- *State:*   by school district

What if We Do Not Have Inclusive Accountability Systems?

All students enrolled or residing in each layer of the accountability system must be accounted for. No student may be left out or not reported. If so, an incomplete picture of performance and learning is portrayed and decisions are made that do not have the best interest of all students in mind.

Copyright © 2003 by Corwin Press, Inc. All rights reserved. Reprinted from *Testing Students With Disabilities*, *Second edition*, by Martha L. Thurlow, Judy L. Elliott, and James E. Ysseldyke. Thousand Oaks, CA: Corwin Press, www.corwinpress.com. Reproduction authorized only for the local school site that has purchased this book.

Component 3:
Why Assess?

Purpose

- To provide an explanation for the variety of student and school purposes for assessment and the ways in which assessment results might be used

Background Information

We have identified some of the key points for this component; however, the facilitator of staff development should decide how much of the information is needed by the targeted audience. Relate the background information to the local situation.

Purposes of Assessment

Educational assessments are conducted for a variety of reasons. In schools, assessments commonly are used for screening purposes, for determining eligibility for programs/services, for evaluation of programs and service delivery, and for program planning. Another useful distinction is the one between two broad types of assessment: individual and large-scale. For our purposes, we will focus on large-scale assessment, including performance-based tests. Important points to know about large-scale assessments include the following:

- Large-scale assessment is a form of testing in which large groups of students are tested across a broad domain in a relatively short period of time.

  ✓ Typically, it is administered under uniform conditions so that results can be compared across groups of students within districts, states, and the nation.

  ✓ Its main purpose is to document how students are performing (and thus may be used to push for instructional change), but generally it is not useful for individualized decisions about instruction or diagnosis.

- Performance-based large-scale assessment is considered by many to be a new form of assessment.

    ✓ It is a multifaceted approach to measuring knowledge and competencies in ways that tap higher-order thinking skills as well as content knowledge.

    ✓ It takes a variety of forms, ranging from essays, open-ended problems, hands-on science, the production of artwork, and portfolios of student work to computer simulations.

Assessment programs can provide a plethora of information about individual students and systems at a variety of levels. The kinds of information range from monitoring to allocation of resources. Below is a list of the types of information that can be gathered using assessment systems.

Monitoring

- *Individual student level:* Provide periodic measurements of student progress in order to determine the education "growth" of a student from year to year.
- *System performance:* Provide a periodic measure of the perfromance of groups of students to track performance over time.

Information and Accountability

- *Parents and students:* Inform parents and students about performance so as to encourage students or teachers to improve performance.
- *Public:* Provide the public with information about the performance of groups of students so as to encourage schools to improve the system.

Improving Student Performance

- *Individual student level:* Provide data to teachers and students to encourage effective instruction geared to the needs of individual students to help them achieve at high levels.
- *System level:* Provide information to educators on groups of students, such as at the school level, that can be used to review current instructional strategies and materials at one or more grade levels and to make improvements.

Allocation of Resources

- *Human:* Use information to determine where additional staff are needed.
- *Financial:* Determine where financial resources should be used.

Selection/Placement of Students

- *Selection:* Help determine the eligibility of students for various education programs or services.
- *Placement:* Determine the program or service most appropriate for the instructional level of the student.

Certification

- *Individual student level:* Provide a means to determine the competence level of individual students (e.g., basic skills, grade promotion, graduation).
- *System level:* Provide data to certify the acceptability of an education system, such as in accreditation programs.

Program Evaluation

- Provide the information needed to determine the effectiveness of an education program or intervention.

Activity

Use the following Think-Pair-Share activity. The procedures for this activity are provided in Steps 1 through 5. Use these steps for either or both of the two information stems provided below and/or come up with your own stems.

1. Have participants individually THINK about one of the information stems (see below). When in the THINK step, there should be no eye contact or talking. Encourage participants to write things down if they choose.

2. After a period of about 3 to 5 minutes, have participants PAIR up and tell each other about what is on their lists.

3. After about 4 minutes, have pairs get together with other pairs (to form groups of 4) to SHARE their collective information.

4. Have each group select a spokesperson who will summarize the group's findings or highlights for the entire group.

5. Be sure to record the overall themes of the group. You can then return to them anytime during the session, as needed or relevant.

Information Stems

✓ Brainstorm as many types of tests as you know. Then identify their respective purposes.
✓ Identify the types of information that can be gathered using assessments.

Handouts and Overheads

Use the handouts and overheads on the next two pages to convey information on educational reform. Add others that are relevant to your situation.

Why Assess?

- New emphasis on higher educational standards

- Two general types of assessment
    - ✓ Individual
    - ✓ Large-scale

- Large-scale assessment
    - ✓ Not necessarily useful for making individualized decisions about instruction

- Performance-based
    - ✓ Multifaceted approach to measuring knowledge
    - ✓ A variety of forms

Copyright © 2003 by Corwin Press, Inc. All rights reserved. Reprinted from *Testing Students With Disabilities*, *Second edition*, by Martha L. Thurlow, Judy L. Elliott, and James E. Ysseldyke. Thousand Oaks, CA: Corwin Press, www.corwinpress.com. Reproduction authorized only for the local school site that has purchased this book.

Purposes of Assessment

Monitoring

- ✓ Student level
- ✓ System performance

Information and Accountability

- ✓ Parents and students
- ✓ Public

Improving Student Performance

- ✓ Student level
- ✓ System level

Allocation of Resources

- ✓ Human
- ✓ Financial

Selection/Placement of Students

- ✓ Selection
- ✓ Placement

Certification

- ✓ Student level
- ✓ System level

Program Evaluation

- ✓ **Provide information needed to determine the effectiveness of an education program or intervention**

Copyright © 2003 by Corwin Press, Inc. All rights reserved. Reprinted from *Testing Students With Disabilities, Second edition*, by Martha L. Thurlow, Judy L. Elliott, and James E. Ysseldyke. Thousand Oaks, CA: Corwin Press, www.corwinpress.com. Reproduction authorized only for the local school site that has purchased this book.

Component 4:
Formats of Assessment

Purpose

- To describe the variety of formats of assessments that might be used at the district or state and classroom levels.

Background Information

The information in this section covers the key points to be made for this component of staff development. The facilitator of staff development sessions must decide how much of the information is needed by the targeted audience. It is important to relate the background information to the local situation in which the facilitator is working.

Assessment Formats

The format of an assessment can refer to either the type of items used within an assessment (e.g., multiple-choice, essay) or the type of test overall (e.g., norm referenced, criterion referenced). Another distinction has been whether assessments are on-demand (requiring performance immediately, during a defined time frame) or are extended-time assessments. Until recently, most large-scale assessments were multiple-choice tests, with essays used on occasion. Similarly, most large-scale assessments were norm referenced, and most were on-demand assessments.

Because the nature of the skills that educators consider important is changing, the manner in which these skills are assessed is also changing. For example, to see whether students are capable of defining an issue, determining what information is needed to respond to the issue, and providing a rationale for their response to the issue, students need to be assessed in a way that allows them to set up the problem, select the information needed, and then provide their unique and extended responses to it. Different kinds of assessment formats are needed.

Some alternative formats that might be used are extended-response formats (including essays), the use of an interview, hands-on-performance exercises, group performance exercises, and the like. Different types of formats are categorized and described in different ways. Some of the types of assessments that might be used within the two broad categories of on-demand and extended-time are summarized here.

On-Demand Assessments

- *Selected response exercises:* Here students select one or more answers from a list of suggested responses. These exercises have the advantage of speed, which may make them well suited for assessment of a broad set of content goals. The disadvantage is that it is difficult to develop selected-response exercises that tap student thinking.
- *Short answer, open ended:* In these exercises, students write in an answer to a question. The response is usually a phrase, sentence, or quick drawing or sketch. Less guessing is involved here, but these exercises do not tap much student thinking.
- *Extended response, open ended:* Students are required to compose a response that may be several pages in length. Much thought is required on the part of the student. Remember, this is only first-draft student work and thus may not represent what students could do given additional time and encouragement in which to compose a final draft.
- *Individually administered interview:* The assessment is given to each student on a one-on-one basis. This may be because the exercise requires special equipment, such as science equipment, or requires the individual student to perform or the observation of the student in the process of responding to the question. This format permits the interviewer to ask each student questions about the topic being assessed. It has the advantage of tapping important skills often desired of students. However, keep in mind that this process is both time-consuming and expensive to administer and score.
- *Individually administered performance events:* These are exercises that are completed by individual students within a class period and involve some type of performance on the part of the student. Tasks may range from hands-on exercises in a content area to playing a musical instrument, completing a drawing in visual arts, or writing an essay in a writing assessment.
- *Group-administered performance events:* These are exercises to which groups of students respond. These may be existing groups or those made up just for assessment purposes. For example, students in a band or orchestra are considered an existing group, while a group of five students assessed for teamwork skills is not. Here, students typically perform as a group, and the group interaction and/or performance is scored as a whole.

Extended-Time Assessments

- *Individual performance tasks:* Here students may work for several days, weeks, or months to produce an individual student response. For example, a science experiment may include designing and planting a garden and making observations of it over time.
- *Group performance tasks:* These exercises are ones on which groups of students may work for several days, weeks, or months to produce a group and/or an individual student response. An example could be a health education task where students are to design a school lunch menu for a month that is nutritious, affordable, and that would be appealing to students.

- *Portfolio assessment:* These assessments include an assembly of a collection of the best work of individual students. Portfolios provide the opportunity to document students' improvement over time and their ability to achieve important learning outcomes designated by state or national goals.
- *Observations:* Structured observations are those that are prearranged in perhaps a classroom setting and provide students the opportunity to choose from several activities in which to participate. Unstructured observations are the events that occur in the day-to-day classroom that teachers choose to record for the future. For example, a teacher may observe a student struggling with the writing process during instruction and therefore not picking up on the knowledge needed to take the assessment.
- *Anecdotal records:* There are other sources of information about students, such as notes from teachers, parents, and other people involved in the student's education.

Activity

On an overhead or chart paper, draw a box and divide it into quadrants. Below the box write the following statement stem: "Learning about types of assessment is like (a)_____ because. . . ."

Learning about types of assessment is like
(a) _____ because . . .

Cover up the statement stem and solicit four nouns—any words—from the participants. One word for each quadrant. The words can be about anything. The more fun the words, the more fun the activity.

After you have written a word in each quadrant, instruct the participants to get into groups of 4 to 5 and complete the sentence stem. They should choose a recorder and have four sentences, one for each word, at the end of the activity.

You can use any statement stem you would like. The sky is the limit. Try to keep the sentence stem closely related to the upcoming discussion. This activity helps you get a read on the participants' knowledge and attitudes as well as engaging them in a fun-related activity.

Handouts and Overheads

Use the handouts and overheads on the following pages for this component on the formats of assessment.

Formats of Assessment

On-Demand Assessments

✓ Selected response exercises

✓ Short answer, open ended

✓ Extended response, open ended

✓ Individually administered interview

✓ Individually administered performance events

✓ Group-administered performance events

Extended-Time Assessments

✓ Individual performance tasks

✓ Group performance tasks

✓ Portfolio assessment

✓ Observations

✓ Anecdotal records

Copyright © 2003 by Corwin Press, Inc. All rights reserved. Reprinted from *Testing Students With Disabilities*, *Second edition*, by Martha L. Thurlow, Judy L. Elliott, and James E. Ysseldyke. Thousand Oaks, CA: Corwin Press, www.corwinpress.com. Reproduction authorized only for the local school site that has purchased this book.

Free Association:
Let It Flow!

Learning about types of assessment is like
(a)_____ because . . .

Copyright © 2003 by Corwin Press, Inc. All rights reserved. Reprinted from *Testing Students With Disabilities*, *Second edition*, by Martha L. Thurlow, Judy L. Elliott, and James E. Ysseldyke. Thousand Oaks, CA: Corwin Press, www.corwinpress.com. Reproduction authorized only for the local school site that has purchased this book.

Component 5:
Who's In? Who's Out?

Purpose

- To provide information on who participates in the district assessment program and how they participate
- To provide information on typical reasons for exclusion and documentation of past exclusionary assessment practices

Background Information

This section covers the key points for this component. The staff development facilitator decides how much of the information needs to be presented and relates it to the local situation.

Participation in Assessments

Educators and policymakers have decided that it is important to assess the extent to which students have accomplished the goals of education. Schools are being held accountable for all students attaining those skills. Key questions to ask are these: How do we assess the accomplishment of desired skills? How will schools be held accountable for attainment of those skills? How will diverse learners, including students with disabilities, be assessed?

What do we know about current practice in the assessment of what we want students to know and be able to do when they leave school and at various points along their educational careers? There are several key things that we know:

- First, it has been the diverse learners, particularly students with disabilities, who have been left out of assessment activities. If one of the purposes of assessment is to describe the status of students in the educational system, why would any child be excluded?
- One implication of exclusion from assessment is that students who are left out of assessments tend not to be considered during reform efforts. Educators, parents, policymakers, and the general public want and need to know the extent to which all students, including those with disabilities, are profiting from their educational programs and schooling experiences.

- Despite improvement over the past few years in the knowledge that states have about the participation of students with disabilities in state assessments, relatively few states are able to report the number of students with disabilities included in their statewide assessments.

Why should we be concerned about the participation of students with disabilities in assessment? Because out of sight is out of mind. Those individuals excluded from assessments are not likely to be considered in policy decisions that affect all students. Students with disabilities must be considered and included in the process of assessing what they know and can do.

Past Practice: Reasons for Excluding Students With Disabilities

Students with disabilities have been excluded from assessment for a variety of reasons. Among those most frequently identified are the following:

- ✓ *Lack* of written policy *guidelines*
- ✓ *Vagueness* of wording in guidelines, which leads to different interpretation and implementation
- ✓ *Lack* of successful *monitoring* of the extent to which the guidelines are followed
- ✓ Test administration that *does not include students who are in separate schools or who are not in graded programs* (e.g., residential placements, juvenile homes, hospitalized or homebound students)
- ✓ *Lack* of available *accommodations* in the actual tests themselves as well as the procedures
- ✓ *Incentives* created by the desire to have a school or state look good in comparison with others in the state or nation
- ✓ *Altruistic motivation*, such as lessening the emotional distress to the student who is either not expected to do well or does not perform well under test conditions (e.g., anxiety ridden)

For there to be an inclusive accountability system, an assessment system must be in place that accounts for and assesses all students. This does not mean that all students must take the same test but that all students must be accounted for. A small number of students will require an alternate way to assess what they know and can do. The bottom line is that all students residing in a school district and attending a school will be assessed and results accounted for.

Activities

Use one or more of the following activities to promote the involvement of participants in this component.

Activity 1

Have participants turn to their neighbor to brainstorm all the reasons they think students are excluded from district and state assessments.

Activity 2

In small groups, have participants discuss and decide how decisions should be made about who participates in or is excluded from district and state assessments.

Activity 3

Use either one or both of the worksheets on the following pages for participants to reflect on their feelings about exclusion and the current status of assessment in their own school or district.

Handouts and Overheads

Use the handouts and overheads on the pages following the worksheets to present the information for Component 5.

Exclusion Worksheet

Too often in today's society, people are included in or excluded from different events and life experiences for a variety of reasons. Take a minute to jot down how it feels to be included in an activity or society at large.

Now take a minute to think how it would feel to be excluded from the same activity or social situation.

How does it feel to be INCLUDED?   How does it feel to be EXCLUDED?

How would these feelings make you act?

What changes would make a difference in your feelings and behavior?

Copyright © 2003 by Corwin Press, Inc. All rights reserved. Reprinted from *Testing Students With Disabilities*, *Second edition*, by Martha L. Thurlow, Judy L. Elliott, and James E. Ysseldyke. Thousand Oaks, CA: Corwin Press, www.corwinpress.com. Reproduction authorized only for the local school site that has purchased this book.

Educational Accountability and Reform Survey

Use this survey to briefly inventory the current status of your school or situation related to educational accountability. Please take a minute to respond to the following items.

One of the greatest challenges related to educational reform for students in my school is . . .

One of the greatest challenges related to educational reform and students with disabilities in my school is . . .

Some immediate needs I see in my school for students with disabilities related to standards and assessment are . . .

One thing I can contribute to the process of all students and issues of standards and assessment is . . .

Copyright © 2003 by Corwin Press, Inc. All rights reserved. Reprinted from *Testing Students With Disabilities, Second edition*, by Martha L. Thurlow, Judy L. Elliott, and James E. Ysseldyke. Thousand Oaks, CA: Corwin Press, www.corwinpress.com. Reproduction authorized only for the local school site that has purchased this book.

Systemic Reform and Special-Needs Students

✓ How can special-needs students, specifically students with disabilities, be included in general education reforms while still preserving what is "special" in special education?

✓ How can we focus more on the results of education and still protect compliance and procedural safeguards?

✓ How can education be individualized to the needs of students and still be oriented toward the achievement of high standards?

✓ How can we develop assessments that can measure the progress of students with disabilities in the same way that they measure the progress of students without disabilities?

Copyright © 2003 by Corwin Press, Inc. All rights reserved. Reprinted from *Testing Students With Disabilities*, *Second edition*, by Martha L. Thurlow, Judy L. Elliott, and James E. Ysseldyke. Thousand Oaks, CA: Corwin Press, www.corwinpress.com. Reproduction authorized only for the local school site that has purchased this book.

Assessment Issues

✓ # WHO PARTICIPATES? (PARTICIPATION)

✓ ## How do they participate? (Accommodation)

✓ ## How are they counted? (Reporting)

Copyright © 2003 by Corwin Press, Inc. All rights reserved. Reprinted from *Testing Students With Disabilities, Second edition*, by Martha L. Thurlow, Judy L. Elliott, and James E. Ysseldyke. Thousand Oaks, CA: Corwin Press, www.corwinpress.com. Reproduction authorized only for the local school site that has purchased this book.

Reasons for Exclusion

- *Lack* of written policy *guidelines*

- *Vagueness* of *guidelines*

- *Lack* of successful *monitoring*

- *Not including* students who are in *separate schools* or *ungraded programs*

- *Lack* of available *accommodations*

- *Incentives* to look good

- *Altruistic motivation*

Copyright © 2003 by Corwin Press, Inc. All rights reserved. Reprinted from *Testing Students With Disabilities*, *Second edition*, by Martha L. Thurlow, Judy L. Elliott, and James E. Ysseldyke. Thousand Oaks, CA: Corwin Press, www.corwinpress.com. Reproduction authorized only for the local school site that has purchased this book.

Component 6:
Who Makes the Decisions?

- To deliver information on who makes participation decisions and how they are made

Background Information

The information in this section covers the key points for this component. The facilitator should decide how much of the information is needed by the targeted audience and should adapt the information to the local situation.

Decisions About Who Participates and How They Participate

For some students, meaningful participation in assessments requires the use of testing accommodations. What do we know about accommodations in large-scale assessments?

- States and districts vary considerably in the policies they may have, both for making decisions about the participation of students with disabilities in assessment and for deciding the kinds of accommodations and adaptations that are used during assessments.
- Assessment guidelines generally defer decisions to the team that develops the student's IEP. Some state guidelines recommend that participation and accommodation decisions be based on the student's category of disability.

Each of the options just described is problematic. Leaving decisions to the IEP team may be problematic if the team is not trained in the purpose and use of inclusive assessment and accountability systems.

Recommendation

A better indicator than any of the previously identified criteria is the alignment between what the test is intended to measure and the student's instructional goals. The instructional goals, rather than the setting or category of disability, should be the factor that determines the nature of the assessment.

Activity

Using the following scenarios, have participants make participation decisions for each student—should the student participate in assessment? Have participants be specific in their recommendation, designating what assessment the student will take (e.g., regular assessment, regular assessment with accommodations, partial assessment, or alternate assessment).

Scenario 1: Chester

Chester is an eighth-grade student with a learning disability who receives resource room services once a day. His area of learning disability is written expression. Chester is enrolled in general education classes. The state that Chester resides in has mandated a writing test for all eighth graders.

> What test should Chester be required to take?
> What is the basis for your decision?
> What additional information may you need?

Scenario 2: Keri

Keri is a ninth-grade student who has been classified as having mental retardation since kindergarten. In the state where Keri lives, students must pass mandated tests in reading, writing, math, science, and history in order to graduate with a high school diploma. Keri is instructed in a curriculum that focuses on vocational and life skills.

> What test should Keri be required to take?
> What is the basis for your decision?
> What additional information may you need?

Scenario 3: Aaron

Aaron is a fourth grader who has a reading disability and is reading two years below level. In Aaron's district, all fourth graders are required to take a reading test. His Title I reading teacher claims that the required reading test is too hard for Aaron and will cause undue stress on him.

> What test should Aaron be required to take?
> What is the basis for your decision?
> What additional information may you need?

Handouts and Overheads

Use the handouts and overheads on the following pages as you present the information from this component.

Three Ways Students With Disabilities Participate in Assessments

Those who

. . . **are able to participate without accommodations**

. . . **are able to participate with accommodations**

. . . **will need to take an alternate assessment**

Copyright © 2003 by Corwin Press, Inc. All rights reserved. Reprinted from *Testing Students With Disabilities, Second edition*, by Martha L. Thurlow, Judy L. Elliott, and James E. Ysseldyke. Thousand Oaks, CA: Corwin Press, www.corwinpress.com. Reproduction authorized only for the local school site that has purchased this book.

Issues of Participation

- **Who participates?**

- **Who decides?**

- **In what assessment?**

- **Responsibility for results?**

- **Unanticipated consequences?**

Copyright © 2003 by Corwin Press, Inc. All rights reserved. Reprinted from *Testing Students With Disabilities, Second edition*, by Martha L. Thurlow, Judy L. Elliott, and James E. Ysseldyke. Thousand Oaks, CA: Corwin Press, www.corwinpress.com. Reproduction authorized only for the local school site that has purchased this book.

Component 7:
What Are Assessment
Accommodations?

Purpose

- To describe what assessment accommodations are, their purpose, and what they might look like
- To create a link between instruction and assessment and to identify the range of accommodations that can be delivered for both
- To produce understanding of who may need accommodations

Background Information

Key points of this component are covered here. Remember to adapt the information to the audience and local needs.

Purpose of Accommodations

Assessment accommodations provide students the means to show what they know without being impeded by their disability. Accommodations provide equal footing for students (i.e., level the playing field), not an advantage. Most states have made provisions for students with disabilities to use accommodations during statewide tests, probably because both statutory law and constitutional law imply that policies should provide students with disabilities the opportunity to participate in assessments with appropriate accommodations. Providing assessment accommodations should be based on what the student needs, not what the student would benefit from.

Accommodations fall into several categories (e.g., timing, scheduling, setting, presentation, and response). There are a number of accommodations that can be provided within each category.

Eligibility for Accommodations

Depending on state and district policy, any student with a disability is eligible for an assessment accommodation if in fact it is needed to show what the student knows. Some places are beginning to examine accommodations for all students in need, not just students with disabilities.

Decisions About Accommodations

Decisions about who receives what kinds of accommodations are important ones. These decisions are left to the building or district IEP teams. It is imperative that these decision makers understand the purpose of a district's assessment program and the appropriateness of granting accommodations. For example,

- If a reading test is given to evaluate a student's ability to decode, providing a reader for the test (i.e., someone who reads the test to the student) is inappropriate. However, if the same test is given for the purpose of measuring a student's understanding of written text, a reader is appropriate.
- Often, the use of calculators is controversial. If the test purports to measure a student's ability to calculate numbers, providing a calculator is inappropriate. However, if we are interested in evaluating whether a student understands when to use a formula to derive an answer, a calculator is an appropriate accommodation.

Decisions to provide individual students with assessment accommodations and reasons given for their use need to be documented.

Current Practice

There is much activity centered on accommodations policies and the provision of assessment accommodations. The use of assessment accommodations has been one of great controversy for test developers and measurement people.

- Many argue that the introduction of an accommodation contaminates or changes what the test intends to measure. However, most of these statements are made on the basis of opinion, not fact. Those based on data are from assessments unlike those we are discussing.
- Currently, research is under way that examines the impact of assessment accommodations on test integrity for large-scale accountability assessments.
- Until we have a better understanding of the impact of the use of assessment accommodations, to deny their use to students who need them raises legal questions—especially if there are high stakes attached for the student. If there is a question about the provision of an assessment accommodation, it is usually best to provide the accommodation.
- It is important to remember that not all students with disabilities need accommodations during assessment. But for those who do need them, assessment accommodations should not be introduced for the first time during the administration of a test but, rather, should align with those provided during the instructional process.

- Providing accommodations to students who need them increases the number of students with disabilities who can take district and state assessments and thus be included in the accountability system.

Activities

Activity 1

Using the chart below, generate examples of the types of accommodations that could fall under each category.

Activity 2

Using the information presented in the case study in Handouts, suggest instructional and assessment accommodations for Mao.

Handouts and Overheads

Using the handouts and overheads on the following pages as you present the information for this component.

Activity 1

Accommodations:

Timing   Scheduling

Setting   Presentation

Response   Other

Copyright © 2003 by Corwin Press, Inc. All rights reserved. Reprinted from *Testing Students With Disabilities*, *Second edition*, by Martha L. Thurlow, Judy L. Elliott, and James E. Ysseldyke. Thousand Oaks, CA: Corwin Press, www.corwinpress.com. Reproduction authorized only for the local school site that has purchased this book.

Activity 2

Background:

Mao is an eighth grader who has lived in the United States for three years. Her primary language is Hmong. Mao had limited education in her home country. She has been identified as having a learning disability with severe language disabilities. Areas in need include receptive/expressive language, written communication, basic reading, basic math (computation and problem solving), prior knowledge in many areas, and social-emotional skills.

Instructional Needs:

Mao is at the first-grade level for reading, writing, and mathematics. She is able to work independently and in groups of two or three but with the assistance of an adult. She likes to work in workbooks. In general, Mao works well with a buddy and in cooperative learning groups. Mao does not accept school authority or routines well. She requires frequent breaks during instruction. Given specific teacher direction and close proximity, Mao is able to write in her daily journal. Use of a computer and a tape recorder do not improve performance.

Suggest Instructional Accommodations for Mao:

Suggest Assessment Accommodations:

Setting   **Timing**

Scheduling   **Presentation**

Response   **Other**

Copyright © 2003 by Corwin Press, Inc. All rights reserved. Reprinted from *Testing Students With Disabilities, Second edition*, by Martha L. Thurlow, Judy L. Elliott, and James E. Ysseldyke. Thousand Oaks, CA: Corwin Press, www.corwinpress.com. Reproduction authorized only for the local school site that has purchased this book.

Assessment Issues

✓ **Who participates? (Participation)**

✓ **HOW DO THEY PARTICIPATE? (ACCOMMODATION)**

✓ **How are they counted? (Reporting)**

Copyright © 2003 by Corwin Press, Inc. All rights reserved. Reprinted from *Testing Students With Disabilities, Second edition*, by Martha L. Thurlow, Judy L. Elliott, and James E. Ysseldyke. Thousand Oaks, CA: Corwin Press, www.corwinpress.com. Reproduction authorized only for the local school site that has purchased this book.

Issues in Accommodation

- **What is a "reasonable" accommodation?**

- **Available for ALL?**

- **Disability specific?**

- **The "fair" argument**

- **Linkage to instruction**

- **Validity of results**

Copyright © 2003 by Corwin Press, Inc. All rights reserved. Reprinted from *Testing Students With Disabilities, Second edition*, by Martha L. Thurlow, Judy L. Elliott, and James E. Ysseldyke. Thousand Oaks, CA: Corwin Press, www.corwinpress.com. Reproduction authorized only for the local school site that has purchased this book.

Accommodations

Timing

Scheduling

Setting

Presentation

Response

Other

Copyright © 2003 by Corwin Press, Inc. All rights reserved. Reprinted from *Testing Students With Disabilities*, *Second edition*, by Martha L. Thurlow, Judy L. Elliott, and James E. Ysseldyke. Thousand Oaks, CA: Corwin Press, www.corwinpress.com. Reproduction authorized only for the local school site that has purchased this book.

Component 8:
Reporting of Results

Purpose

- To provide an overview of how results are reported
- To provide an overview of how results are used

Background Information

This section covers key points for this component. Actual staff development sessions should reflect the information needs of the targeted audience and the local situation.

Reporting and Use of Results

It is not uncommon for students with disabilities to be excluded when reporting assessment results. In fact, some students with disabilities are allowed to take the assessment, but their test protocols are destroyed or shared only with those students' parents. Test scores of these students are not included in building, district, or state reports. Often, there is no record of any district or state assessment in the student's cumulative file. There are several reasons why this practice is inappropriate.

- What accountability system do students with disabilities belong to if they are not in the one that all students belong to? All students count and need to be accounted for. Student learning, regardless of the test, must be reported in the results of district and statewide accountability systems.
- Students who, for any reason, do not participate in traditional assessment must be accounted for. The manner in which this is done will vary by the types of assessment program (e.g., traditional or alternate forms). Documentation of these decisions, reasons for them, and their results must be done on an individual student basis. However, all student performance must be reported to better decipher program effectiveness and learning trends and to make instructional decisions.
- The issue of reporting has vast impact on school buildings and districts. Many bond issues are won or lost based on how well students

do on the assessments. Districts and states are constantly compared with each other, and the media often shows no mercy in its front-page display of results. Therefore, there are incentives for school buildings, districts, and states to selectively report the results of assessment.

Participation Rates Key to Reporting

The issue of reporting is centered around who is included when the participation rate for the assessment is calculated. It is not uncommon for students with disabilities to be excluded from this calculation, accommodated or not. Others exclude only those students who receive accommodations.

Some states start with the number of students with disabilities who are eligible to participate in the assessment and use this number to reflect all students with disabilities. For example, District A has 500 students with disabilities. After participation decisions are made (usually by the IEP team), only 150 students with disabilities take the assessment. District A then reports that 90% of students with disabilities passed the assessment. Using these results, District A appears not only inclusive in its assessment program, but programmatically meeting the needs of students with disabilities. However, a closer look begs the question "90% of what number?" The reality is that approximately one-third of all students with disabilities in the district actually took the test. What about the 350 students with disabilities who did not take the assessment?

Considerations

Determining an accurate number of students with disabilities who currently are participating in district and state assessments must begin with creating a means to account for them. Many states and districts are collecting this information by adding demographic descriptors to student answer sheets. To do this successfully requires collaboration and coordination between general and special education personnel. Because general educators may not always be aware of which students are receiving special education services, it is essential that these educators verify assessment rosters.

- Policy and procedural guidelines need to be identified to standardize the calculations of participation rates. Because of their inclusiveness, some suggest December 1 child counts of students with disabilities. However, this number does not take into account those students who become eligible for special education services between December 1 and a spring testing cycle or those who discontinue services. The result can be an exaggerated or underestimated rate at which students with disabilities participate in assessment.

- Keep lines of communication open. Much of the current confusion about who the students with disabilities are and how they get reported can be resolved through better and more open communication between departments within both state and school district education agencies.

Failure to include students with disabilities in assessment and accountability systems leads to failure to assume responsibility for all students, for included in "all" are students with disabilities. Policymakers, community members, and parents need and want to know how students in America's schools are learning. Inclusive accountability systems are a means to that end.

Activities

Activity 1

In a small group or dyad, discuss the following:

- What is the purpose of reporting assessment results?
- What gets reported?
- Whose scores are reported in school/district reports?

Activity 2

In a small group or dyad, discuss the following:
- How is the reporting of assessment results useful?
- How could they be more useful?

Activity 3

Think about the pluses, minuses, and interesting (PMI) aspects of including all students in the overall reporting of assessment results. Jot down some of the pluses (positives), minuses (potential negatives), and interesting thoughts (things you may need more information about).

When directed, gather into a small group and collectively share your P's, M's, and I's. Make a list for each category. Then, using consensus, identify the top three P's, M's, and I's that represent your group's ideas about the topic of reporting. Select a spokesperson to report to the entire group (see handout).

Handouts and Overheads

Use the handouts and overheads on the following pages as you present the information on this component.

Assessment Issues

✓ **Who Participates?
(Participation)**

✓ **How do they participate?
(Accommodations)**

✓ **HOW ARE THEY COUNTED?
(REPORTING)**

Copyright © 2003 by Corwin Press, Inc. All rights reserved. Reprinted from *Testing Students With Disabilities*, *Second edition*, by Martha L. Thurlow, Judy L. Elliott, and James E. Ysseldyke. Thousand Oaks, CA: Corwin Press, www.corwinpress.com. Reproduction authorized only for the local school site that has purchased this book.

Issues in Reporting Results

- How are the results used?

- Who sees them?

- Are all test scores included in the accountability report?

- Are results reported together or separate?

- Where are scores assigned?

- What kinds of scores are used?

Copyright © 2003 by Corwin Press, Inc. All rights reserved. Reprinted from *Testing Students With Disabilities, Second edition*, by Martha L. Thurlow, Judy L. Elliott, and James E. Ysseldyke. Thousand Oaks, CA: Corwin Press, www.corwinpress.com. Reproduction authorized only for the local school site that has purchased this book.

PMI

Reporting Assessment Results of All Students

Pluses (What are the pluses? What are the positives?)

Minuses (What are the minuses? What might be negative?)

Interesting (What could be interesting? Something we need more information about is . . .)

Copyright © 2003 by Corwin Press, Inc. All rights reserved. Reprinted from *Testing Students With Disabilities*, *Second edition*, by Martha L. Thurlow, Judy L. Elliott, and James E. Ysseldyke. Thousand Oaks, CA: Corwin Press, www.corwinpress.com. Reproduction authorized only for the local school site that has purchased this book.

Component 9:
Next Steps

- To generate discussion on where we go from here
- To identify what needs to be done to move forward

An Action Plan

In less than a decade, there has been a dramatic increase in the amount of attention that our nation pays to assessments given both in and outside the classroom.

- Assessment and accountability have moved to the forefront of restructuring efforts.
- It is imperative that special-needs students, including those with disabilities, be considered in the process of planning and development as states and school districts strive to rework existing curricular frameworks and corresponding assessments.
- Building a system that is accountable for all students should be a goal of our education system. If we begin our planning and development of assessments with this end in mind, we can proactively address the issues of accountability for all students' learning.

We recognize that many states have local control. That is, the school districts and schools have autonomy in setting selected practices and policies. Furthermore, we recognize that even within a school district, autonomy is granted to school buildings. Despite this, policy is policy. The overall assessment policy should be firm even though the ways in which districts and schools ready themselves for implementation and train their staff may differ.

Without policy and/or guidelines for assessment participation, accommodations, and reporting of results, it will be virtually impossible to level the accountability playing fields of school buildings, districts, and states. We encourage you to set policy at both the state and local district levels so as to provide a framework from which implementation can occur on a relatively consistent basis.

Actions Steps at the School District Level

- Conduct meetings on specific issues or topics that your school, district, and state face. Gather information from a stratified stake-holder group composed of parents, general and special education teachers, administrators, and even students. Be sure that both general and special education personnel are present and participate.
- Hold information-gathering meetings with central office and building administrators.
- Provide training for personnel involved in the assessment decision-making process. These include, but are not limited to, members of the IEP team and building administrators.
- Provide a public forum or hold informational meetings that allow for dissemination and information exchange on assessment issues such as participation, purpose, accommodation, and reporting of results. Parents and community members need to be informed up front about changes in or alterations to the assessment program.
- Develop a vision for learning and assessment for all students. Make sure that they are aligned and include accountability for all learners.
- Develop and/or revise assessment policies and practices to reflect an inclusive assessment and accountability system, including participation, accommodations, and reporting.
- Create a task force or team to train the trainers or answer any questions that may arise from changes in the assessment program.
- Develop a monitoring system to ensure that policy and guidelines are implemented correctly.
- Make connections with state education personnel and include them when needed and appropriate.

Activity

Use the chart on the following page to have participants summarize their learning and to identify next steps or directions. This activity can be done alone or in small or large groups.

Handout and Overhead

Use the handout and overhead on the next page to work through possible action steps.

Using the chart below, record any questions, concerns, or challenges you may have as the result of the assessment session(s). What do you see as immediate and long-term needs for our district in the area of inclusive assessment and accountability? Suggest some action steps that could facilitate meeting those needs.

Concerns, Questions, and Challenges	Needs	Action Steps

Action Steps:
Where Do We Go From Here?

Options and Considerations

- Topical meetings with a stratified group of stakeholders

- Develop criteria or policy guidelines on participation and accommodation of students with disabilities in large-scale assessment

- Training for assessment process decision makers

- Informational and public forum meetings

- Develop a vision and mission statement for learning and assessment

- Task force to plan training and staff development and information dissemination on the assessment, learning, and accountability connection

- Develop a system to oversee implementation

Copyright © 2003 by Corwin Press, Inc. All rights reserved. Reprinted from *Testing Students With Disabilities*, *Second edition*, by Martha L. Thurlow, Judy L. Elliott, and James E. Ysseldyke. Thousand Oaks, CA: Corwin Press, www.corwinpress.com. Reproduction authorized only for the local school site that has purchased this book.

Resources: Technical Assistance and Dissemination Networks

For more information on research and development efforts in the areas of instruction, assessment, and accountability, contact:

Office of Educational Research and Improvement (OERI)
U.S. Department of Education
555 New Jersey Avenue NW
Washington, DC 20208-5500
Fax: 202-219-2135

Office of Special Education and Rehabilitative Services (OSERS)
U.S. Department of Education
330 C Street SW
Mary E. Switzer Building
Washington, DC 20202-2500
Telephone: 202-205-5465
Fax: 202-205-9252

National Center on Educational Outcomes
University of Minnesota
350 Elliott Hall
75 East River Road
Minneapolis, MN 55455
Telephone: 612-626-1530
Fax: 612-624-0879
Web: http://education.umn.edu/nceo

National Center for Research on Evaluation, Standards, and Student Testing
CRESST UCLA
GSE & IS Building
Box 951522
300 Charles E. Young Drive N.
Los Angeles, CA 90095-1522
Telephone: 310-794-9148
Fax: 310-825-3883
Web: http://www.cse.ucla.edu

Education Policy Reform Research Institute
University of Maryland
1308 Benjamin Building
College Park, MD 20742
Telephone: 301-405-6509
Fax: 301-314-9158
email: eprri @ umail.umd.edu
Web: http://www.eprri.org

For a state and local policy perspective, contact:

National Association of State Boards of Education (NASBE)
277 S. Washington Street, Suite 100
Alexandria, VA 22314
Telephone: 703-684-4000
Fax: 703-836-2313
email: boards @nasbe.org
Web: http://www.nasbe.org

Consortium for Policy Research in Education (CPRE)
Graduate School of Education
University of Pennsylvania
3440 Market Street, Suite 560
Philadelphia, PA 19104-3325
Telephone: 215-573-0700
Fax: 215-573-7914

National Association of State Directors of Special Education (NASDSE)
1800 Diagonal Road, Ste. 320
King Street Station I
Alexandria, VA 22314
Telephone: 703-519-3800
Fax: 703-519-3808
Web: http://www.nasdse.org

For state-based regional resource centers, contact:

Federal Resource Center for Special Education (FRC)
Academy for Educational Development
1875 Connecticut Avenue NW, Ste. 900
Washington, DC 20009
Telephone: 202-884-8215; TTY: 802-860-1428
Fax: 202-884-8443
Web: http://www.aed.org/special.ed/frc.html

Region 1: Northeast (Connecticut, Maine, Massachusetts, New Hampshire, New Jersey, New York, Rhode Island, Vermont)

Northeast Regional Resource Center (NERRC)
Learning Innovations at WestEd
20 Winter Sport Lane
Williston, VT 05495
Telephone: 802-951-8226; TTY: 802-951-8213
Fax: 802-951-8222
Web: http://www.wested.org/nerrc
email: nerrc@aol.com or nerrc@wested.org

Region 2: Mid-South (Delaware, District of Columbia, Kentucky, Maryland, North Carolina, South Carolina, Tennessee, Virginia, West Virginia)

Mid-South Regional Resource Center (MSRRC)
Human Development Institute
University of Kentucky
126 Mineral Industries Building
Lexington, KY 40506-0051
Telephone: 859-257-4921: TTY: 859-257-2903
Fax: 859-257-4353
email: msrrc@ihdi.uky.edu
Web: http://www.ihdi.uky.edu/msrrc

Region 3: Southeast (Alabama, Arkansas, Florida, Georgia, Louisiana, Mississippi, Oklahoma, Texas, Puerto Rico, U.S. Virgin Islands)

Southeast Regional Resource Center (SERRC)
Auburn University, Montgomery
School of Education
Montgomery, AL 36124-4023
Telephone: 334-244-3100
Fax: 334-224-3101
email: bbeale@edla.aum.edu
Web: http://edla.aum.edu/serrc

Region 4: Great Lakes (Illinois, Indiana, Iowa, Michigan, Minnesota, Missouri, Ohio, Pennsylvania, Wisconsin)

Great Lakes Area Regional Resource Center (GLARRC)
Center for Special Needs Populations
Ohio State University
700 Ackerman Road, Ste. 440
Columbus, OH 43202-1559
Telephone: 614-447-0844
Fax: 614-447-9043
Web: http://www.glarrc.org

Region 5: Mountain Plains (Arizona, BIA, Colorado, Kansas, Montana, Nebraska, New Mexico, North Dakota, South Dakota, Utah, Wyoming)

Mountain Plains Regional Resource Center (MPRRC)
Utah State University
1780 North Research Parkway, Ste. 112
Logan, UT 84341
Telephone: 801-752-0238 TTY: 801-753-9750
Fax: 801-753-9750
Web: http://www.usu.edu/mprrc

Region 6: Western (Alaska, California, Hawaii, Idaho, Nevada, Oregon, Washington, American Samoa, Federated States of Micronesia, Commonwealth of the Northern Mariana Islands, Guam, Republic of the Marshall Islands, Republic of Palau)

Western Regional Resource Center (WRRC)
University of Oregon
Eugene, OR 97403-1268
Telephone: 541-346-5641; TTY: 541-346-0367
Fax: 541-346-5639
email: dls@oregon.uoregon.edu
Web: http://interact.uoregon.edu/wrrc/wrrc.html

Other technical assistance and dissemination networks to contact:

National Assistive Technical Research Institute
229 Taylor Education Buildings
University of Kentucky
Lexington, KY 40506-0001
Telephone: 859-257-4713; TTY: 859-257-4714
Fax: 859-257-1325
email: natri@coe.uky.edu
Web: http://natri.uky.edu

National Clearinghouse for Professions in Special Education
Council for Exceptional Children
1110 North Glebe Rd, Suite 300
Arlington, VA 22201-5704
Telephone: 800-641-7824; TTY: 866-915-5000
Fax: 703-620-2521
email: ncpse@cec.sped.org

National Information Center for Children and Youth With Disabilities
(NICHCY)
Academy for Educational Development
P.O. Box 1492
Washington, DC 20031-1492
Telephone: 202-884-8200; Voice/TTY: 800-695-0285
Fax: 202-884-8441
email: nichcy@aed.org
Web: http://www.aed.org/nichcy

Council for Exceptional Children
1110 North Glebe Rd, Suite 300
Arlington, VA 22201-5704
Telephone: 703-620-3660
Fax: 703-264-9494
Web: http://www.cec.sped.org/
Email: service@cec.sped.org

Transition:

National Center on Secondary Education and Transition (NCSET)
Institute on Community Integration
University of Minnesota
6 Pattee Hall
150 Pillsbury Drive, SE
Minneapolis, MN 55455
Telephone: 612-624-2097
Fax: 612-624-9344
email: ncset@icimail.coled.umn.edu
Web: http://www.ici.umn.edu/ncset

Parents:

Parents Engaged in Educational Reform (PEER)
Federation for Children With Special Needs
95 Berkeley Street, Ste. 104
Boston, MA 02116
Telephone: 617-482-2915
Fax: 617-695-2939
email: peer@fcsn.org
Web: http://www.fcsn.org/peer/

The Alliance
PACER Center
8161 Normandale Blvd.
Bloomington, MN 55437-1044
Telephone: 952-838-9000; 888-248-0822
Fax: 952-838-0199
email: alliance@taalliance.org
Web: http://www.taalliance.org

Early Childhood:

Early Childhood Technical Assistance System
137 East Franklin Street, Suite 500
Chapel Hill, NC 27514-3628
Telephone: 919-962-2001; TTY: 877-574-3194
Fax: 919-996-7463
email: nectas@unc.edu
Web: http://www.nectas.unc.edu

Other:

ERIC Clearinghouse on Assessment and Evaluation
1131 Shriver Laboratory, Bldg 075
University of Maryland
College Park, MD 20742
Telephone: 301-405-7449; 800-464-3742
Fax: 301-405-8134
email: feedback2@ericae.net
Web: http://ericae.net

Education Commission of the States
700 Broadway, 1200
Denver, CO 80202-3460
Telephone: 303-299-3600
Fax: 303-296-8332
email: ecs@ecs.org
Web: www.ecs.org

U.S. Department of Education
400 Maryland Avenue SW
Washington, DC 20202-0498
Telephone: 800-USA-LEARN
Web: http://www.ed.gov

Selected Web Site:

No Child Left Behind Act of 2001 (NCLB)
http://www.ed.gov/legislation/ESEA/index.html/ (case sensitive)
Presents the law for the act

National Clearinghouse for English Language Acquisition (NC)
http://www.ncbe.gwu.edu
Addresses critical issues dealing with education of linguistically and culturally diverse students in the United States

Other Assessment Resource:

Thomas: U.S. Congress on the Internet
http://thomas.loc.gov/home/thomas.html
Reports on floor activities of the week, status of major legislation, committee reports, and more

Index

CORWIN PRESS

The Corwin Press logo—a raven striding across an open book—represents the happy union of courage and learning. We are a professional-level publisher of books and journals for K-12 educators, and we are committed to creating and providing resources that embody these qualities. Corwin's motto is "Success for All Learners."

5870